W9-ARL-796

PRODUCING ON BROADWAY

PRODUCING ON BROADWAY

A Comprehensive Guide

by

Donald C. Farber

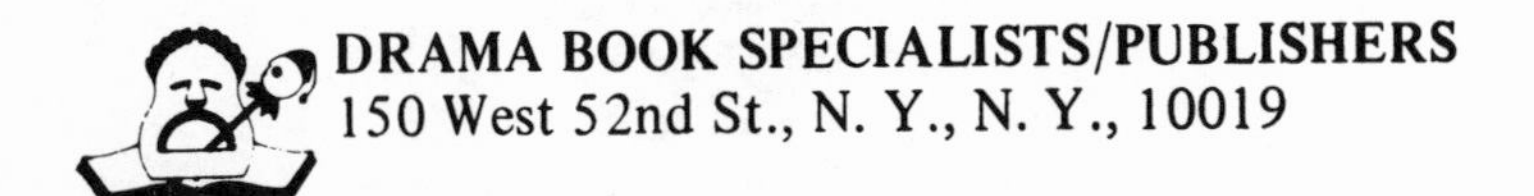
DRAMA BOOK SPECIALISTS/PUBLISHERS
150 West 52nd St., N. Y., N. Y., 10019

Published in the United States of America
DBS PUBLICATIONS, INC.
Library of Congress Catalog Card Number: 69-15669

Second Printing

Printed in U.S.A. by
NOBLE OFFSET PRINTERS, INC.
New York, N.Y. 10003

Encore for Annie, Patty and Seth,
and for the beautiful people who
make my work fun . . .

CONTENTS

Preface xxix

Introduction xxxiii

CHAPTER 1 OBTAINING A PROPERTY **3**

Purchase Original Work 3
Purchase Adaptation or Translation of Copyrighted Work 3
Purchase Adaptation or Translation of Public Domain Work 4
Produce Play in Public Domain 4
Hire Adaptor for a Public Domain Work 5
Purchase Basic Work and Have it Adapted 5
Putting a Musical Together 5
Price of Basic Work 6
Negotiations with Bookwriter, Composer, and Lyricist 7
Bargaining Power Is Decisive 8
Merger of Rights 8
Control of Play 9
Negotiations Are Varied 9
Write or Adapt Play to Produce 9

CHAPTER 2 THE DRAMATISTS GUILD INC., CONTRACTS **11**

Guild Membership 11
Terms Sometimes Above Minimum 12
Guild Approval 13
Contract Parts 13
Some Confusion in Contract 14
Some Unresolved Questions 14
Contract Is a License to Produce Play 15
Dramatic Production Contract 15

Option Cost 15
Length of Option 16
Minimum Basic Royalty Payments 17
Variances from Basic Minimum Royalty Payments 18
reduced royalty for all artistic personnel 19
limitation of royalty during first four weeks out-of-town 21
alternative payment first three weeks in New York 22
alternative royalty from fourth week in New York 23
road company limitation 24
Author's Warranties 24
guarantees of originality 24
no warranty of title 24
Grant of Production Rights 25
Author's Billing and Credits 25
Author's Approval 26
Changes in Script 27
Rights Acquisition Time 27
Additional Production Benefits 28
Interest in Subsidiary Rights 29
basic rights covered 30
percentage interest 30
interest in British subsidiary rights 31
interest outside United States, Canada, and England 31
restrictions on other grants by author 32
English Production 33
English royalty payments 34
alternative interest in English production 34
Right to Reopen Play 35
right to reopen English production 36
Special Concessions 37
other concessions 38
Sale of Motion Picture Rights 38
prior disposition of motion picture rights 39
play revival 40
The Film Negotiator—Duties 41
temporary replacement, alternate, or new negotiator 42
no author conflict of interest permitted 42

aggrieved producer's rights 42
Procedure Followed by Negotiator Varies 43
Plays Produced by Backers Independently of Motion Picture Backing 44
producer, author, and negotiator joint effort 44
procedure if author's terms unacceptable to producer 45
Plays Financed by Motion Picture Producers in Whole or in Part 46
Procedure Where Producer Discloses Motion Picture Backing at Contract Signing 46
offer to motion picture backer 47
proof of motion picture backer's interest 47
Procedure Where Producer Discloses Backing After Signing But Prior to First Day of Rehearsal 49
Procedure Where Producer Makes No Discloser But Cannot Satisfy Negotiator of Independence of Motion Picture Backing 49
Compensation of Negotiator 50
the 3½% fund disposition of proceeds 50
by whom 3½% contributed 51
Producer's Defaults 51
Debts by Author 52
Motion Picture Release Date Conflicts 52
Producer's Participation in Sequels 52
House Seats 53
Stage Manager's Script 53
Author's Reservation of Rights in Foreign Grant 54
Author's Agent 54
author's agent may take share from producer 54
author and producer may not use same attorney or agent and other conflicts 55
Payments 55
Arbitration 56
arbitration obligation 56
arbitration procedure 56
the complaint 56
the answer 57

guild participation 57
selection of arbitrators 57
power of arbitrators 58
immediate arbitration 58
Definitions 59
author 59
commercial uses 59
end of first-class run 59
new york and off-broadway 60
production expenses—weekly operating profits 60
gross weekly box office receipts 61
Defense of Law Suits 62
Assignments of Contract 63
Adaptation 64
Repertory 64
Producer Cannot Offset Claims Against Author 64
Author's Expenses Out-of-Town and Transportation 64
Author's Money Held by Producer in Trust 65
To Whom Checks Payable and to Whom Sent 66
Producer Furnishes Statements 66
Address of Notices 67
Guild Countersignature and Corporate Producer 67
Author Approves Co-Producer 67
Closing 68
Termination of Contract by Author 68
Automatic Termination 68
Contract Interpretation 69
Dramatico-Musical Minimum Basic Production Contract 69
Payment for Option 69
Completed Book 69
Minimum Royalty Payments 70
Variances From Basic Minimum Royalty 70
reduced royalty for all artistic personnel 70
minimum royalty and limitation of first 4 weeks out-of-town 71

alternative royalty payment for first 3 weeks in New York 71
royalty after fourth week 71
road company limitation 72
Royalties in British Isles 72
Author's Approval and Billing 72
Interest in Subsidiary Rights 73
division of receipts 73
cast album 74
Musical Schedule Terms 74
revue numbers 74
producer furnishes score of music 75
producer may get reimbursed up to 50% for score 75
composer and lyricist control publishing 76
musical score available to guild 76
song for movie use 76
no publishing until first performance 77
Waivers on a Musical 77
Other Dramatists Guild Inc. Contracts 78
Revue Production Contract 78
Collaboration Contract 78
Stock Try Out Production Contract 78

CHAPTER 3 MOVIE DEALS 80

Investors Expect to Share in Movie 80
Film Company May Also Own Basic Play Rights 81
Dramatic Rights 81
Film Rights—Option of First Refusal 82
share of sale to other film company 82
film company may want cast album and publishing 82

CHAPTER 4 THE PRODUCING COMPANY 84

Partnership or Corporation 84
Why a Limited Partnership? 84
tax benefits 84
limited liability 85
Corporation May Be a General or Limited Partner 85

Characteristics of Corporation for Tax Purposes 87
Limited Partnership Agreement 88
Basic Provisions 88
Usual Provisions 89
Definitions 90
"the play" 90
"contributions of limited partners" 90
"aggregate limited contributions" 90
"sinking fund" 91
"estimated production requirements" 91
"gross receipts, expenses, production expenses, running expenses, other expenses, and net profits" 92
"author" 92
Miscellaneous 92
Representations and Warranties by the General Partner 93
Formation of Limited Partnership 93
Term of Partnership 94
Death of Limited Partner 94
General Partner May Add General Partners 95
Rights in Play Assigned to Partnership 95
General Partner's Expenditures 95
Use of Funds Invested 95
Investment of Bond or Theatre Guarantee 96
Use of Funds—Smaller Capitalization Finally 97
Overcall 98
Investment Held in Special Bank Account 98
Books of Account 99
General Partner's Services 100
General Partner's Fee and Cash Office Charge 100
Fee and Cash Office Charge If More Than One Company 101
Additional Limited Partners 101
Advances and Loans 101
Additional Services by Producer 102
Share of Profits 102
Limited Partners' Limited Liability 103
Payments in Cash 104
Return of Contributions 104

Distribution of Profits 104
Distribution upon Closing 105
Return of Contributions or Profits to the Company 105
Abandonments 106
Substitute Limited Partner 106
Additional Company to Produce Here or in Great Britain 107
use of company funds 107
general partner's involvement in other company 107
general partner's acquisition of rights after termination of partnership 108
Motion Pictures 109
Execution of Agreement 109
Arbitration 110
Certificate of Limited Partnership 110
Contents of Certificate 111
Publication of Certificate 112

CHAPTER 5 CO-PRODUCERS AND ASSOCIATE PRODUCERS 113

Co-Producer a General Partner 113
Co-Producers Operate As a Joint Venture 114
Joint Venture Agreement 114
basic terms 114
sharing of profits by co-producers 114
who makes decisions 115
who signs checks and agreements—billing credits—arbitration 115
personnel agreed upon 116
termination of joint venture 116
Associate Producers—Money 116
Front Money 117
Amount Needed and Uses 117
Reimburse Producer for Front Money Not Used to Raise Money 117
Agreement Should Set Forth Facts 117
Front Money Arrangements 118

CHAPTER 6 RAISING MONEY—NECESSARY FILINGS—THE SECURITIES AND EXCHANGE COMMISSION AND ATTORNEY GENERAL 119

The Securities and Exchange Commission and Attorney General 119
S.E.C. Exemption from Registration 121
Documents to Be Filed 121
Form 1-A—Notification under Regulation A 121
The Prospectus or Offering Circular 123
front cover 124
the offering 124
the risk to investors 125
subscriptions 125
overcall 125
the producer 126
the play 126
the author 126
the director 126
the cast 126
theatre 127
scenic designer 127
compensation of general partner 127
use of proceeds 127
estimated weekly budget 127
net profits 128
return of contributions—share of profits 128
production and subsidiary rights 128
other financing 128
financial statements 128
production personnel 129
S.E.C. Full Registration Pursuant to Form S-1 129
The Facing Sheet 129
The Prospectus 130
Contents of the Prospectus 131
introductory 131
the producer 132

acquisition of property 132
estimated cost of production and aggregate contributions being offered 133
return of contributions if partnership not formed 134
general nature of offering/plan of offering interests to public 134
subscription to limited partnership 134
restriction on right of limited partner to withdraw from the partnership 135
right of assignee of a limited partner 135
use of proceeds 135
purpose of partnership 136
commencement of partnership 136
contracts and assignments thereof 136
sources of partnership income 136
expenses of conducting business 137
disposition of partnership income; return of contributions; profits and losses 137
net profits 137
effect of federal income taxes 138
additional funds 138
additional companies 138
theatre tickets 138
control by general partner 139
remuneration of general partner 139
reimbursement of general partner 139
interest of general partner in certain transactions 139
abandonment of production 139
the creative elements 140
termination of partnership 140
underwriting 140
miscellaneous 140
other s.e.c. information required 140
The Attorney General 141

CHAPTER 7 THE LEAGUE OF NEW YORK THEATRES 143

Purpose of the League 143

Dues 144
Collective Bargaining Agreements Negotiated 144
agreements for theatre owners or lessees 144
Agreements for Producers 145
agreements for both theatre owners and producers 146
Agreements Made with League 147
Employer and Employee Also Sign Agreement—Term of Employment 147
Terms in Common 147
union sole bargaining agent 147
employee must join union—no strikes or lockout 148
scope and jurisdiction 148
rates—pension and welfare 148
business agent may enter theatre 148
grievance procedure and arbitration 149
pension and welfare chart 149
Contracts with Theatre: CHART 150
Contracts with Producer: CHART 151
Contracts with Theatre and with Producer: CHART 152

CHAPTER 8 CONTRACTS WITH THE THEATRE 153

Hiring Personnel 153
Theatrical Protective Union, Local #1, I.A.T.S.E. 153
Jurisdiction 153
Term of Employment 154
Work Week 154
Wage Rates 154
Key Men 155
Take-In and Take-Out 156
Regular Work Week Hours 156
Minimum Hours and Repertory 156
Extra Performances and Sign Work 157
Vacation and Temporary Closings 157
Fire Proofing and Inspections 157
Discharge for Cause—Severance Pay 157
Rehearsals and Construction Work 158
Dark Houses & Safe Conditions & Photos 158

Treasurers and Ticket Sellers Union, Local #751 158
Jurisdiction 158
Wage Rates 159
Advance Sale and Benefits 160
Refunds 160
Contract for Season 160
Season, Box Office Staff, Subscriptions, and Benefits 161
Minimum Hours 162
Bonding of Treasurers and Assistants 162
Termination of Employment 162
Transfer of Theatres and Closing Notice 162
Discharge for Cause 163
Notice if Theatre Sold 163
Miscellaneous and Riot, Fire, Strikes, etc. 163
Ticket Cannot Be Sold for More Than Stated Price 164
Legitimate Theatre Employees' Union, Local #B-183 164
Jurisdiction 164
Term of Employment 164
Wage Rates 165
Eight Performance Week 165
Back Stage Doormen Week 165
Overtime (Other Than Back Stage Doormen) 165
Program Insertions and Cancelled Performances 166
Time Employees May Leave Theatre 166
Special Uniforms 166
Notice of Discharge 166
Theatre, Amusement and Cultural Building Service Employees, Local #54 167
Jurisdiction 167
Wage Rates 167
Basic Crew 168
Discharge for Cause 168
Seasonal Employment 168
Sunday Performances 168
Hours of Work 169
standard week & overtime 169
cleaning women's standard week and overtime 169

matrons' standard work and overtime 169
Uniforms and Equipment Supplied 170
Local Union #30 of the International Union of Operating Engineers 170
Jurisdiction 170
Work Week 170
Wage Rates 170
Holidays and Vacations 170
Season 171

CHAPTER 9 CONTRACTS WITH THE PRODUCERS 172

Actors' Equity Association 172
Casting 172
Star and Director 172
Three Standard Contracts 173
Contracts Include Agreement with League and Equity Rules 173
Deputies 174
Minimum Salaries 174
Origin Point 175
Cost of Living Increase 175
Rehearsal Payments 175
Certain Extra Payments for Chorus 176
Televising, Recording, and Motion Pictures 176
Show Album 177
Broadcast of Part of a Production 177
Number of Performances 177
Performances Lost 178
Rehearsal Hours and Recesses 179
during rehearsal period and prior to NY or road tour opening 179
final week of rehearsals prior to 1st public performance 179
after opening—recesses 179
after 1st performance but prior to NY opening—maximum hours 180
during pre-Broadway tour—day off every three weeks 180

after NY opening—½ hour call 180
after NY or road tour opening—chorus hourly limit 181
after NY or road tour opening—principals' hourly limit 181
overtime pay for rehearsals 181
overtime pay for travel 181
if no pre-Broadway—hourly limits after NY opening 181
Term of Employment and Notice 182
Guarantees—Minimum and Run of Play Contracts 182
Converting Standard Contract of Principal Actor to Run of the Play 184
increased salary and written notice 184
no probation and five week guarantee for principal actor 184
Chorus Six Month Run of the Play Contract 185
extensions of chorus six month run of play contract 185
Conversion to Chorus Six Month Run of Play Contract 186
Extra Chorus Payment 186
Number of Chorus 186
No Pay For Actors' Fund 186
Paid Previews Before Opening Count Toward Minimum Guarantee 187
Termination Standard Minimum Contracts 187
before or during rehearsals 187
dismissal during probationary period 188
individual termination after opening 188
termination by the company after opening 189
termination by actor after opening 189
payment where actor does not work out notice 189
Termination—Run of the Play Contracts 190
notice of closing 190
exceptions to foregoing closing provisions 190
Closing Notice 192
Hiring "As Cast" and "Understudy As Cast" 192
Juvenile Actors 193
Extras 193
Understudies 194
dramatic plays 194

extra payment for performance–principal actor 194
chorus–extra payment for performance 195
chorus understudying a star 195
understudies present at all performances 195
time of hiring and commencement of performance as understudy 196
Termination of Principal Actor and Replacement 196
Stage Managers and Payment 197
Lay-Offs 197
Death of Star or Illness 198
Part Cut Out of Show 198
Producer May Terminate Contract for Absence by Actor 198
Abandonment of Play 199
Billing 200
Billing If Understudy Plays Part 200
Clothes and Makeup 200
Transportation and Baggage 201
Photographs and Publicity 201
Plays in Supper Club (Las Vegas) 201
Alien Actors 201
individual actor–or less than entire cast 201
unit company 203
special character 203
Theatrical Wardrobe Attendants Union, Local #764 203
Jurisdiction 203
Wardrobe, Stars, Duties, Defined 204
Star's Dressers 204
Changes in the Law–May Reopen Negotiations 204
Rates of Pay–Hours of Work and Overtime 205
Eight Performance–Six Day Week and Overtime 206
Dressers 207
dressers' work time 207
dressers' hours and overtime 207
dresser minimum 207
dressers accompany wardrobe 208
dressers' holidays and vacations 208
Rehearsals 208

Number of Employees and Minimum Hours 208
Closing—Wardrobe Supervisors and Assistants 209
Rest Periods 209
After Midnight 209
Wardrobe Supervisors Packing for TV 209
TV at Theatre 209
Publicity Pictures 210
Working Conditions 210
Equipment Furnished 210
Making a Costume 211
Travel and Transportation 211
Bus Travel 211
Layoffs and Reductions and Dismissal for Cause and Replacement 211
Dismissal for Cause 212
Termination and Renegotiation 212
Society of Stage Directors and Choreographers 212
Directors—Extra Payment for Rewriting 212
Jurisdiction 213
Producer/Director or Producer/Choreographer 214
One Waiver of Royalties Permitted 214
Twenty Year Waiver on Bargaining Certain Issues 214
Renegotiable Items 214
Cost of Living Adjustment 215
Director and Choreographer Terms 215
fees 215
royalties 216
gross box office receipts defined 216
option to direct future companies and payments 217
length of employment 217
strike—lock-out—fire—flood—etc., and suspension rates 218
out-of-town expenses 218
billing credits 218
dismissal for cause 218
after opening supervision 219
Terms Applicable Solely to Choreographer 219
assistant 219

dance captain 219
approval of rehearsal pianist 220
United Scenic Artists, Local #829B 220
Jurisdiction 220
Minimum Scenic Design Fees 220
Minimum Lighting Design Fees 222
Minimum Costume Design Fees 222
Scenic–Lighting–and Costume Provisions in Common 223
dates of fee payments 223
duties and obligations 223
abandonment 225
transportation–out-of-town and other expenses 225
billing credits 225
no design alterations and additional payments 226
time for completion 226
additional pay for tv 226
strikes–fire–acts of God 226
title to designs 227
kick-backs forbidden 227
producer limits authors use of designs 227

CHAPTER 10 CONTRACTS WITH THE PRODUCERS AND THEATRES 228

Association of Theatrical Press Agents and Managers, Union #18032 228
Jurisdiction 228
Wage Rates 229
Doubling Prohibited 229
Work Week 229
Time of Salary Payments 230
Summary Dismissal 230
Production of Radio–Industrial–TV–or Movies from Theatre 230
Closing Run of Less Than Four Weeks 230
Closing Run of Over Four Weeks 231
Fire–Strike–Riot–Etc. 231

Termination of Employment—Notice—Company Manager or Press Agent 231
Midnight and Extra Performances—Pay and Commercial TV 232
Managers—Specific Terms 232
minimum term of employment—company manager 232
minimum term of employment—house manager 232
limited engagement—company manager 233
sunday—extra pay—house and company managers 233
House Staff Employees 233
house staff defined 233
seasonal employment 233
dismissal during first week 234
automatic renewal 234
severance pay 234
ownership change—severance pay 234
theatre owner guarantees house manager and staff 235
Press Agents 235
minimum term of employment 235
part time 235
opening postponed—abandonment 236
after opening closing 236
temporary closing 237
exclusive services 237
Advertising Agency 237
Associated Musicians of Greater New York, Local #802 American Federation of Musicians 238
Hiring of Musicians 238
Jurisdiction 239
Contract Houses and Penalty Houses 239
Minimum Number of Musicians—Musical 239
Minimum Number of Musicians—Dramatic 240
Minimum Number—Ballet—Grand Opera—Vaudeville—Etc. 240
Mechanical Devices 240
Wage Rates 241
in New York City 241
out-of-town, break-in 241

work outside pit 241
week's work defined 241
contractor paid extra 242
assistant conductor paid extra 242
librarians paid extra 242
Rehearsal Rates 242
2½ hours or less up to 6:30 P.M. 242
overtime 242
for 1 hour after night performance 243
for 1 hour before evening performance 243
for 1 hour on 2 performance day or after matinee 243
after midnight 243
during break-in period 243
rehearsal pianists 244
doubling rates 245
Notice of Closing 245
Temporary Lay-off 245
Dressing Rooms 246
Musicians Cannot Invest in Show 246
Pay TV 246
Original Cast Album 246
Schedule Changes 246

CHAPTER 11 OUT-OF-TOWN PRE-BROADWAY 247

Purpose—Audience Response 247
It Depends on the Play 247
Dramatic Differs from Musical 247
How Long on the Road—And Previews 248
Sets And Props Moved By Truck or Train 249
Where to Go Pre-Broadway 249
Desirable Musical Houses 250
Moving a Show—Deck Complicates Move 250
Some Shows Own Two Decks 250
Out-of-Town—Union Requirements 251
Out-of-Town Advertising 251
New York Advertising 251

Out-of-Town—When Fold—When Get Help—Etc. 251
Musicians—On the Road 252
Out-of-Town Advance Man 252
Out-of-Town License Agreement 253

CHAPTER 12 BROADWAY AND OUT-OF-TOWN THEATRE LICENSES 254

Theatre Arrangement 254
Broadway Theatre License Agreement 254
License—Not Lease 254
No Standard License Argeement 254
Date of Occupancy 255
What Theatre Furnishes 255
What Producer Furnishes 255
Star Named and Term of Occupancy 256
Percentage Payment for Theatre 256
Theatre Guarantee 256
License Fee—Percentage of Gross 256
Gross Receipts Defined 257
Charge for Air Conditioning 258
Stop Clause 258
Stop Clause Amount Computation 258
Break Even 259
Stop Clause Termination Procedure 259
Theatre Security Deposit 259
Increase in Stop Clause Sum and Guarantee 260
Sharing Expenses 261
compute each week separately 261
share only amounts actually spent 261
may limit theatre share of items 262
maximum advertising limit 262
newspaper limit 262
outdoor advertising limit 262
preliminary advertising limit 262
theatre tries to spread payments 263
eight performance week 263

joint control of advertising	263
share cost of signs after three weeks	264
producer may urge additional sharing	264
paid previews shared—other extras cost producer	264
ticket cost shared	265
some taxes shared	265
preliminary box office help shared	265
additional box office help shared	265
mail order costs shared	266
contracts differ on box office sharing	266
sharing of musicians	266
retroactive wages—pension and welfare shared	267
theatre shares only amount worked—not amount paid	267
Take In and Take Out—Similar to Sharing	267
Must Vacate Theatre Within Fixed Time	268
Producer Pays Extra For Star's Temporary Absence	268
Producer Pays Extra for Star's Termination or Non-Appearance	269
Theatre May Terminate Agreement If Star Leaves	269
Producer Pays If Opening Delayed	269
Theatre Sometimes Waives Late Opening Payment	270
Theatre May Terminate If Opening Is Delayed	270
Guarantee Doubled for Early Closing	270
Producer's Insurance	271
Concessions are Theatre's	271
No Radio—TV—or Other Theatre Production	271
Producer Responsible for Theatre Alterations—Compliance with Laws—Etc.	271
Theatre May Terminate If Fire—Act of God—Etc.	272
Producer Will Not Interfere with Union Agreements	272
Theatre Controls Box Office	272
Theatre House Seats and Free Seats	273
Press Seat Limitation	273
Theatre May Terminate If Producer Has Not Funds	273
Theatre May Terminate If Producer Breaches or Law Suit Likely	274
Play Must Continue in Theatre	274

Physical Limitations 275
Theatre May Use Injunction 275
Changes and Approvals Must Be in Writing 275
Limitation on Assignment 275
Theatre May File Form 1099 276
Out-of-Town License Agreement 276
Sharing of Gross Receipts 276
Guarantee and Deposit 276
No Stop Clause Usually 277
Sharing of Expenses 277
sharing advertising 277
sharing take in and take out 277
promotion shared 277
sharing on musicians 277
theatre party costs shared 278
Air Conditioning Charge 278
Equipment Must Comply with Laws 278
P.A. System Furnished but Not Operator 278
Souvenir Book Sales 278
Penalty to Producer if Star Out 279
Theatre Furnishes Treasurer and Assistant 279
Theatre Use Before Opening 279
Theatre Designates Newspaper for Advertising—Insurance—Fireproofing Sets—and Miscellaneous 280

CHAPTER 13 PRE-OPENING—DURING RUN—AFTER OPENING 281

Pre-Opening 281
Star and Director—Raising Money 281
Record Company Financing 281
Insurance 282
Bonds Required 283
Independent Booking Office, Out-of-Town Booking 284
Play Doctor 284
payment 284
billing 285

Advertising 285
Advance Sale 285
Ticket Sale Deductions 286
Ticket Brokers 286
Theatre Parties 286
Scene Changes—Automated 287
Computerizing a Box Office 288
During Run 290
Range of Production Costs 290
Potential Weekly Gross and Weekly Net 291
Time Necessary to Recoup 291
After Opening 292
Reviews—What To Do 292
New York Advertising 292
When to Close 292
National Company 293
Producer 293
APPENDIX **295**
DRAMATISTS GUILD, INC., MINIMUM BASIC PRODUCTION CONTRACT TENTH: ADDITIONAL CLAUSES 296
CO-PRODUCTION AGREEMENT 304
ESTIMATED PRODUCTION BUDGET—DRAMATIC SHOW 312
ESTIMATED WEEKLY OPERATING BUDGET—DRAMATIC SHOW 314
S.E.C. OFFERING CIRCULAR UNDER REGULATION A 315
ESTIMATED PRODUCTION BUDGET—MUSICAL 347
ESTIMATED WEEKLY OPERATING COSTS—MUSICAL 349
OFFERING CIRCULAR FOR S.E.C. REGISTRATION 350
MOTION PICTURE RIGHTS AGREEMENT 378
AGREEMENT FOR ACQUISITION OF BASIC RIGHTS 385

PREFACE

Because I was lucky enough to write a book about theatre, I was given the opportunity to do a second one. Having never written a book before, when I finished the first one I was determined that if I ever wrote another one again I would dedicate it to anyone who had ever written a book.

The first book, *From Option to Opening*, published by DBS Publications, Inc., Drama Book Specialists, attempts to explain in non-legal language all of the legal documents and relationships involved in the production of a play off-Broadway. It is intended as a primer for those who may never have had any experience with theatrical producing, as many persons who produce off-Broadway are in fact without any experience.

This book about Broadway producing, on the other hand, is intended as a text for those who have at least a nodding acquaintance with the business. Hopefully, it will be helpful to the experienced producer as well as the initiate. It is written, however, with the thought in mind that the reader will know the meaning of some of the very basic terms which I found necessary to define in detail in the first book. If this seems too advanced, then *From Option to Opening* may serve as a helpful primer to this book.

My editor (God bless him) in discussing this second book, suggested that the book should have all the answers that anyone might ever be faced with in the business. Of course, this is impossible as we all know; there is no such book. There cannot be such a book. No book, course, or study can replace experience. The most experienced producers will be the first to admit that they do not know all the answers.

thank the four unions which did cooperate with me; however, to do so would necessitate, by omission, my naming the others, and though they probably deserve it, I won't do it.

I am deeply appreciative and want to express my thanks to my good friend Leonard Soloway for his various and sundry assistance.

Special thanks must be accorded to my good friend David Le Vine of the Dramatists Guild for his valuable helpfulness.

My secretary Jayne Matthews deserves thanks for her devotion to duty, and my secretary Eleanor Garz for her help.

I must also pay tribute to the marvelous East Hampton sand, and especially the Main Beach. The sun and swim did little to make the writing easier, but it did make it more fun.

And last but not least to my Editor-Publisher, Ralph Pine of DBS Publications, Inc., who has now become my good friend, warm thanks with the cautious observation that I think I may be finished now—at least for a year or two.

This book deals with very complicated legal documents. I know it will be difficult reading. It was difficult writing. (I only wish that everyone who reads this book would first try reading some of the contracts discussed in the book, especially the Dramatists Guild Minimum Basic Production Contract.) I should like to make everything easy, but this is impossible. If I make things understandable, even if not easy, I will have accomplished my purpose.

INTRODUCTION

Of course there is no business like show business. That has to be the case because the song says so. Many people accept this axiom without really fully accepting the fact that it is a "business." Show business is all kinds of things to all kinds of people. It represents excitement, glamour, and thrills for the uninitiated, at the same time representing backbreaking work, nervous anxiety, and emotional exhaustion for many on the inside looking out. The business is an overcrowded, highly competitive business for most of the people who are in it. It's a business of feast or famine and even the stars, with all the glamour and the big money, with a few exceptions, will never know the financial security that the person taking home a regular weekly check enjoys.

The actor, when he's starting, must play for a marginal salary in stock or off-Broadway so that his work may be seen. If he is lucky and makes it big, then he may work, but it may add up to a total of six or eight weeks a year. He may earn big money during this short time which must be spread out so that he can live the entire year. With the tax bite and with the star having to live like a star even when unemployed, there are oftentimes big deficits by the end of the year for the people who enjoy the privilege of having their name above the title.

During the last thirty years the business has indeed grown. During the 1937–38 season the total gross paid for tickets at the box office was approximately $11½ million. During the 1967–68 season, just 30 years later, the total gross box office receipts was almost $59 million. Of course, some of this may be accounted for by the inflation in this country; however, we must not overlook the fact that the business has grown. There is a demand for good theatre tickets. Theatre tickets at the same time cost more money.

The number of plays opening each year during this same period has substantially declined. For an example, during the 1937–38 season there were a total 111 new plays and revivals. During the 1967–68 season there were a total of 74 new plays and revivals. The cost of getting a play on has increased many times and producers have become somewhat more selective.

In addition to growing, the business here is changing. There seems to be a larger incidence of foreign productions being imported. In fact, Actors' Equity has repeatedly made demands for restricting the importation of foreign actors competing with American actors.

Contract agreements with unions expire and are renegotiated—budget requirements change just as theatregoers' preferences change. One cannot be certain that anything one does on this subject, or any subject, is immutable. At the same time we should realize that certain basic concepts are less likely to change, and if those do change, the change will be at a slow pace.

Wherever a contract discussed in this book has a fixed terminable date, the date is noted. Changes which occur will, in most instances, be "non-basic" and will be the kind of facts and details that are easily ascertainable. It is of primary importance that one understand the framework and the basic concept of the various contracts as well as the relationships and obligations of the various contributing parties.

There are 34 Broadway theatres at the present time, 17 of which are owned by the Shuberts. Shortly after this book is published there are sure to be two or three other theatres built on the site that was formerly occupied by the Astor Hotel. Sometimes a producer will purchase a theatre so that there isn't the problem of finding one when he wants to bring his show in. During recent seasons there has been a critical shortage of Broadway theatres during the height of the season; that is, during September, October, November, and December. A critical shortage means that there are more shows waiting to get into theatres than there are theatres available. Perhaps this will be solved in the future with the building of new theatres and with the heightened sensitivity of producers to the kind of plays that stand a chance of being successful.

If one is going into the business one ought to know as much as one can learn about the business. Contracts involved in producing a show are in many instances understood by too few people.

In a recent discussion I had with someone who should know, I was nonchalantly told that there are three or four attorneys who do know and understand the Dramatists Guild Contract. Now isn't that a shocker? Just think about it for a moment. The Dramatists Guild Contract is used (and has been for many years) to option each and every play produced on Broadway by an American author (with but one exception), and I am informed that maybe three or four attorneys in the business know and understand it. I would be much less disturbed if the person who said this were not in a position to really know what he is talking about.

It's no secret that the Dramatists Guild Contract is one of the most confusing, most ambiguous documents ever labeled a contract. The contract obviously just grew like so many other agreements which have been negotiated and renegotiated through the years. I presume that what happened was that whenever a change was made, the parties were careful that some other part of the contract that they had previously agreed upon was not altered. If they attempted to change the language, there would perhaps develop disagreement about the language change. In spite of this, however, the contract, which includes a Basic Contract, the Schedule of Additional

Production Terms, and an Appendix, could be unified into one organized, cohesive document. Since the document is and has been (with the one exception) used to option every play written by an American that is produced on Broadway, whether you like the format or not, it should be understood.

One can, of course, produce a show without knowing anything about the agreements. One can hire a competent attorney, manager, and accountant who between them should know, or act like they know, the terms of most of the agreements. They will deal with the various unions and parties. I think, however, the producer really ought to know as much as he can about his relationship with the people with whom he is working. This relationship, being a contractual relationship, ought to be understood. One should know what one's rights, duties, and obligations are to the people with whom one is working. One need not wave the contract under the other parties' nose, nor need one use it as a threat. One should, however, understand.

The Dramatists Guild Contract, like the other agreements, is discussed with the view toward understanding each contract as a single cohesive unit and, at the same time, understanding it with respect to other contractual obligations to which a producer binds himself in producing a Broadway show.

In many instances there are disputes as to the meaning of certain contract provisions. It will serve no useful function to examine the detailed arguments supporting each point of view. For our purposes at this time it should suffice to know that there are discrepancies and disagreements in certain areas which may someday be resolved.

One should also bear in mind that what happens in reality is sometimes very far removed from the contract terms and provisions. In many instances a contract is entered into on the Union form and the parties signing are little aware of most of the terms.

There are also instances where through custom, certain ways of doing things have developed which are in direct contradiction to the specific contract terms setting forth how this should be done. In such case, the parties (if they even know the contract terms) have just not bothered to comply with the contract because doing what they do is more suitable to accomplish the end. Little would be served by changing procedures to comply with a written document if the changed procedures did not serve some useful purpose.

If one learns the contents of this book, one would then know more than any other single person usually knows about the contractual relationships involved in producing for the Broadway stage. As a practical matter, what usually happens is that some of the contracts discussed in this book are drafted after very careful consideration and negotiation between the attorney for the producer and the other party. However, in other instances, there are contracts entered into by either the company manager or the house manager which the attorney for the producer never even sees. In fact, I would go so far as to say that there are many contracts that the theatre has with unions which affect the producer which many people in the business, including attorneys, know nothing about or have never seen.

This book combines the contracts and agreements that would be within the scope of experience of the attorney for the producer, the house manager, and company manager, as well as the attorney for the theatre.

The producer of a Broadway show together with the theatre owner must deal with an even dozen associations and trade unions. The contracts between the theatre owners and/or producers and each union and association are discussed in detail in this book.

There is a great deal of space devoted to the Dramatists Guild Contract, for this contract, unlike the others, has continuing importance. In every other instance the contract is entered into for a show (or for a season in the case of a theatre) and when the show (or season) is over, the contract ends. It is not so with the Dramatists Guild Contract. If certain things happen, then the Producer may enjoy benefits long after the show is closed. The Dramatists Guild Contract, in a sense, creates a relationship which may continue long after a show is ended. For this reason, among others, the Dramatists Guild Contract has received exceptionally detailed consideration.

It goes without saying that there is a vast amount of information that could never be learned from a book and will only be learned through the difficult but ever rewarding process of acquiring experience through doing.

PRODUCING ON BROADWAY

CHAPTER 1

OBTAINING A PROPERTY

When one decides to produce a Broadway show, there are several ways that one may acquire the rights to produce the Play.

1. Purchase Original Work

Purchase the option to present an original copyrighted creation from the Author (the Author, Composer, and Lyricist if it be a Musical) or the Owner who may have purchased or inherited the rights to the Play. If the Writer is an American, the rights will be acquired by entering into a Dramatists Guild Minimum Basic Production Contract. If the Author is a foreigner, then terms will be negotiated which may be similar to the provisions of the Dramatists Guild Contract in many ways.

2. Purchase Adaptation or Translation of Copyrighted Work

Purchase the option to present an adaptation or translation from the Adaptor or Translator (or Owner) who acquired the rights to do the adaptation or translation from the Owner of the Basic Work that it is based on, which Basic Work is covered by Copyright protection. If the Adaptor or Translator is an American, this would also be accomplished by entering into a Dramatists Guild Minimum Basic Production Contract. Care must be taken that the Adaptor or Translator really owns the rights to do the adaptation or translation that he is selling.

3. Purchase Adaptation or Translation of Public Domain Work

Purchase the option to do an adaptation or translation from the Adaptor or Translator of a work that is in the Public Domain, that is, a work that does not enjoy Copyright protection. This too would be accomplished by entering into a Dramatists Guild Contract if the Adaptor or Translator is an American. The problem here is that if the basic work does not have Copyright protection, then anyone may do an adaptation or translation. A Producer might find that he is in competition with the same show that he is doing when it opens across the street. The adaptation which you purchase will have Copyright protection no doubt, but the basic work may be used so long as the competing Adaptor sticks to the Basic Work plus his own creation and does not borrow from any other Adaptor.

4. Produce Play in Public Domain

Produce a Play in the Public Domain. You need pay nothing for the right to produce. There are no royalties for the production, no negotiations, and no Contract. At the same time, you do not own exclusive rights, so as was earlier pointed out, you may end up in competition with the Play you are producing.

5. Hire Adaptor for a Public Domain Work

Hire someone to do an Adaptation of a Play or other property that is in the Public Domain. To the extent that your Adaptor, Composer, and Lyricist create something original, it may be copyrighted and you will have an exclusive. To the extent that it is the original Public Domain property, anyone may use it or adapt it in a different way. You could have a similar kind of competition with yourself if someone decided to adapt the same Play you adapted. The Adaptor, Composer, and Lyricist would again be covered by a Dramatists Guild Contract.

6. Purchase Basic Work and Have It Adapted

Purchase the rights to do an Adaptation or Translation of a Basic Work with copyright protection and then set about to have it adapted, scored, translated, or whatever. The Basic Work may consist of a Novel (published or to be published), a Moving Picture (made or to be made), a radio or television production, a previously presented Play (a Dramatic Play might be updated, or it might be converted into a Musical), a Comic Strip, a foreign work, or any other story source which enjoys the protection of the Copyright Laws.

If the Basic Work is the work of an American, and the Adaptor is an American, then Dramatists Guild Contracts would be entered into with each.

Putting a Musical Together

It can sometimes become very involved when a Producer goes about trying to put a Musical together. The Producer first acquires the rights from the Author or Owner of the basic work. The negotiations may be difficult if the basic work is a hot new property that other persons are interested in. One must always bear in mind that after paying the Basic Owner, it will be necessary to pay each of the other writers. Since there is some limit to how much one can pay, one should plan carefully even at this point. I am firmly convinced that 90% of nothing is nothing, and 2% of something could be a lot of money, so don't lose a good deal if it means paying to get something worthwhile. There is, however, much risk involved in this business, and with the job of putting a Musical together from scratch, the work is somewhat overwhelming. One ought to negotiate carefully and wisely.

Price of Basic Work

In purchasing the right to do a Musical Adaptation the Producer will have to pay a fixed amount of money as an advance against royalties. The fixed amount may vary betwee $1,000 and $10,000 (and, of course, may be much more or less) for the right to do the Adaptation and to get it presented within a specified time—usually a year to get the Adaptation done and a year to get the Play presented, that is, to open on Broadway. The Owner of the basic work will want a royalty of either 1% or 2% (maybe more, but not likely) and will want a proportionate share of the subsidiary rights of the Play. A proportionate share of the subsidiary rights means that proportionate part of any payment which his royalty bears to the aggregate royalties payable to all of the Author (s), Composer (s), and Lyricist (s) including the payment to the Author or Owner of the basic work. It is not unusual that there be a limit on the aggregate royalties for the purpose of this computation. The limit may be 10%, 12%, or 15%.

Thus if the Owner of the basic work were paid a royalty of 1% and a total of 6% is paid to the Author, Composer, and Lyricist together with the Basic Owner, then the Owner of the basic work would share in the receipts from the subsidiaries by receiving one-sixth of the Author's share of such subsidiaries.

If there is a 10% limitation written into the contract and the Basic Owner receives a royalty of 1%, then he cannot receive less than one-tenth of such interest even if the total royalties payable to all Authors (which would include the Owner of the basic work, the Bookwriter, Composer, and Lyricist) is in an amount greater than 10%. The limitation will be requested by the Bookwriter, Composer, and Lyricist, as well as by the Basic Owner—so be prepared.

If the basic work is a hot property, the Producer must also be prepared to give away a part of the Producer's profits of the Producing Company. The Producer generally gets 50% of the net profits from the Producing Company, payable after the Limited Partners investments have been returned to them, and it is from this 50% that pieces will have to be given away.

Negotiations with Bookwriter, Composer, and Lyricist

Having acquired the basic work, the Producer must then go through the same procedure and negotiations with the Bookwriter, the Lyricist, and the Composer. Each will want a substantial payment as an advance against royalty payments (or perhaps a fee payment which is not an advance), a liberal royalty payment with the subsidiaries interest, a part of the Producer's profits, and lots of artistic leeway. Each negotiation is complicated by the fact that there are conflicting demands being made. For an example: it's impossible to make everyone's name the biggest in the billing. How the parties share in the Original Cast Album is always a hassle. The Composer and Lyricist generally claim that the album consists entirely of their work and they should be entitled to more than simply a proportionate share. The Bookwriter,

Composer, and Lyricist together claim that the Owner of the basic work should get no part of the Album. The deal may already have been made with the Basic Owner giving him part of all subsidiaries, including the Album, and on and on and on.

Bargaining Power Is Decisive

The extent of the demands are related to the parties' reputation and success—I should add "at the moment." The old expression that you are only as good as your last show is worth repeating. In any event, a successful Composer will not permit you to add to any of the music of the show with work of another Composer. You have to buy him on reputation or on faith. He may have done several good works, but you don't have any idea how he will treat your property, so this could be somewhat difficult. He may compose 8 good or even great songs, but you may need 13. If the Contract prevents your using another Composer's work, then you have to settle for his 8 good songs and his 5 not so good ones. The same will be true of the Lyricist. If he is successful, you have to take him, and no one else, for that Show.

Bear in mind that after you have negotiated the Contracts with the Author, Composer, and Lyricist, you will have similar Contracts to negotiate with the Star or Stars and with the Director. Of course they will want, in addition to all else, a percentage of the Gross Receipts and perhaps a share of the Producer's profits.

Merger of Rights

The Contracts entered into will be Dramatists Guild Contracts. The Agreements will provide that unless the Play is presented on or before a certain date, all rights in the basic work will revert to the Basic Owner, and the other parts created will belong to the respective parties. If the Play is presented (sometimes for one, or sometimes for twenty-one performances), then the Agreement will provide that the rights in the basic work merge with the rights in the Play and that the rights in the basic work can only be dealt with together with the rights in the Play.

Control of Play

Control raises another area of some dispute. It usually makes little difference to the Producer who controls the uses of the Play. The Producer does not control the uses of the play, but as the Man-in-the-Middle, he has to work out the details of such use, or make certain that the Bookwriter (s), Composer (s), and Lyricist (s) have between themselves worked them out. Composer and Lyricist generally control and receive the receipts from the music and lyrics (and from the records as distinguished from the Original Cast Album) and the Bookwriter, Composer, and Lyricist each generally have one vote as far as the disposal of the other uses of the Play. The Basic Owner may, but usually does not, have any voice in this matter.

Negotiations Are Varied

A book could be written about the negotiation and contracting for a Musical Adaptation of a property. The above should give some hint of the complexity of the problems and the difficulties encountered. It is a big job. It can be a frustrating job. It might turn out to be a greatly rewarding job, both materially and creatively.

7. Write or Adapt Play to Produce

Since we are enumerating the ways to acquire a Play to produce, we must not overlook the fact that the Producer could, of course, write a Play, or adapt a Play, or compose the music, or write the lyrics, or do any and all of these things. If you do any or all of these things, it is often wise to find someone else to produce. If no one but you wants to produce your work, one might observe that the Producer is less than unbiased toward the Writer's work, and the Producer's objectivity and business judgement should be carefully considered. Perhaps there are people who can write well, compose well, direct well, and then also produce well. There just aren't many. Most people would do well to handle any one of these jobs with a degree of professionalism.

Bear in mind that the Dramatists Guild Contract, hereinafter discussed in detail, will be adapted so that it is applicable to either the Author, Adaptor, Composer, or Lyricist, or such of them to which it is applicable.

CHAPTER 2

THE DRAMATISTS GUILD INC. CONTRACTS

The option to produce a Broadway Show is known as a Dramatists Guild, Inc. Minimum Basic Production Contract, sometimes referred to as the "Dram Guild Contract." There are separate contracts for a dramatic production and for a dramatic musical production. There are also Dramatists Guild, Inc. contracts for a review, for stock tryouts, and for a collaboration. If the Author is not a member of the Guild, and you wish to option his play for a Broadway production, then he will become a member of the Guild.

For many years there was an agreement which Producers signed with the Guild which contained the same provisions that are now contained in the agreement that is entered into by a Producer with a specific Author. In 1961 that agreement lapsed, and only the individual Contract with each Author for each show is signed.

Guild Membership

In order to become a member of the Guild, one must first become an associate member after approval by the membership committee and payment of a $10. annual fee. After a first-class performance, the associate member, again with approval, becomes an active member and the fee is $20. annually. Active members may vote. In adition to the $20. annual fee, the Guild retains 2% of the Author's royalty on a dramatic show if the royalty payable to all Authors on that particular show is $3,000. per week or less, and 3% of the royalty if the author's total royalties exceed $3,000. that week. On a musical the Guild retains 2% of the royalties payable to the Bookwriter, Composer, and Lyricist if the weekly royalties payable to all the Authors (which would mean all Bookwriters, Composers, Lyricists, and Authors of underlying properties' receipts combined) is $4,000. or under, and 3% if the total payable to all Authors is over $4,000. that week. In addition, whether the property is dramatic or musical, the Guild is paid 2% of an Author's receipts from the motion picture sale.

Terms Sometimes Above Minimum

The Dramatists Guild Contract, which is, as I stated, a minimum basic contract, contains the minimum terms that you must give to an Author. There is nothing to prevent the Author's Agent, Attorney, or other representative from demanding more than the minimum terms, nor is there anything to prevent you from paying more. Some contracts are essentially upon the minimum basic terms. If the Author is a well-known personality, he may demand and receive a higher percentage of the gross box office receipts than the minimum for his royalty payments.

On a musical, if the Author, Composer, and Lyricist have never had a show produced before, the Contract may be on the minimum royalty terms of 6%. With veterans, it is more usual to pay a 7% or 8% royalty until Production costs are recouped, and then after that pay an extra 1%. Sometimes, however, the royalty on a musical is either a straight 7% or 8%.

There will be other areas where there may be a variance from the Minimum Basic Production Contract terms, and I will in each instance try to call these to your attention as we go along.

Guild Approval

The Minimum Basic Production Contract, after it is signed by the Producer and the Author, is forwarded to the Dramatists Guild, Inc. for its approval. If there have been changes which reduce the Author's rights or income below the minimums, then the Dramatists Guild, Inc. may not countersign the agreement and it will not be valid. There are certain established rules which the Dramatists Guild, Inc. will follow. There are, however, some occasions when they will vary in certain ways from the minimum terms to effect a contract, but there are limits to the extent of the variations permitted.

Contract Parts

The Dramatists Guild Minimum Basic Production Contract actually consists of three parts. There is the basic contract which is signed at the end by the parties to the contract. There is appended to the contract what is known as the "Schedule of Additional Production Terms." There is also appended to the contract an "Appendix A to the Schedule of Additional Production Terms" which consists of instructions to the Film Negotiator.

The contract in its section on definitions defines "Contract" as the Minimum Basic Production Contract plus the Schedule of Additional Production Terms. It is questionable whether or not the instructions are actually a part of the contract and binding upon the parties. Since they are instructions to the Film Negotiator, they are nevertheless important terms which, whether binding upon the parties or not, certainly affect the parties to the Agreement.

In addition to the three basic parts of the Contract, there is one paragraph, Paragraph TENTH, which is a blank paragraph that is filled in at the time the Contract is prepared and contains provisions which are specifically applicable to that particular contract. Paragraph TENTH contains variances from the printed form as well as additional provisions in the Contract.

Some Confusion in Contract

One of the reasons that the Dramatists Guild, Inc. Contract is very often difficult to read and is not easily understandable is that the Minimum Basic Production Contract will often make reference to certain items which are discussed in greater detail in the Schedule of Additional Production Terms. There are constant cross references from one paragraph to another or from one paragraph in the contract to a paragraph in the Additional Production Terms, with further reference back to a provision of the contract. In analyzing the Contract it may be noted which part of the Contract contains the term under discussion; however, although a term may be found in more than one part of the Contract or Schedule, it will be discussed as if it were all written into the Contract in one place.

Some Unresolved Questions

Some of the questions that are unresolved in this Contract and are in dispute will perhaps some day be settled. For an example: as we will learn later if a show runs for 21 performances, the Producer acquires certain very important rights. The question which is not clear in the Contract is from what date one counts the 21 performances. The League of New York Theatres takes the position that 21 performances must be counted from the first paid preview, whereas the Dramatist Guild takes the position that they must be counted from the official opening in New York City. It will serve no useful function for us to examine in detail the arguments on both sides. However, it is helpful to know this dispute exists and that perhaps some day it will be resolved.

Contract Is a License to Produce Play

The Dramatists Guild, Inc. Minimum Basic Production Contract is a license for the Producer to produce a Play on the speaking stage in the United States and Canada. If the Producer does produce the play in accordance with the terms of the Contract, then the producer shares in other proceeds of the Play and acquires certain other benefits.

Dramatic Production Contract

Option Cost

There are alternative ways of paying for the option. One contract provision provides that the Producer pay a minimum of $500. upon the signing of the Contract for the first 3 months, a monthly payment of $100. for each of the next 3 months, and $200. each month for the next 6 months. These payments constitute a non-returnable advance against royalties. A Producer may alternatively pay the sum of $200. each month for twelve consecutive months, which payments would also constitute a non-returnable advance against royalties. Not all option payments are advances against all royalty payments for there are certain royalty payments, which will be later discussed, for which option payments are not considered an advance.

There is no usual way of arranging the option payments, but perhaps the most common method is for an annual payment of between $2,000. and $2,500. This may be paid in various ways during the year, such as one-half on signing, and the other one-half after 6 months, or one-quarter every 3 months. Of course a neophyte for a first play may get the minimums provided in the Contract payable as therein provided. Which method of payment is used for the option, as well as for royalties, is agreed to by the parties or their representatives during the Contract negotiations.

Length of Option

The standard Minimum Basic Production Contract will run for a period of one year, which means that the Play must have a first-class performance before a paid audience on or before one year from the date of the contract or one year from the date of delivery of the completed Play. The Producer, of course, will want to make provision to extend the option to produce the Play after the one year period. If the year runs out and the Play has not been produced, he will have invested a great deal of time, energy, and effort in what will prove fruitless unless he can get an extension and get the Play on. It is not unusual to have a special provision in Paragraph TENTH which provides that for an additional payment of a certain amount of money, which may be an additional $200. per month, the option may be extended for a period of an additional six months. The Dramatists Guild, Inc. is reluctant to permit a Producer to extend an option except under certain circumstances. The Guild takes the position that the $200. per month is not as important to the Author as a production of the Play, and to tie the Play up, if there is little chance of it being produced, is not in the best interest of the Author. For this reason, the contract must provide that in order to extend the option beyond a year there must have been certain circumstances which prevented the Producer from getting the play on during the 1 year period. The clause may provide that extension of the option is conditioned upon the Producers having entered into a contract with a Star to appear in the show, or with a director to direct the show during the 6 month period that the option is extended, and the Star or director are unavailable to appear until the period covered by the 6 month extension. Such additional option payments are normally considered advances against the royalties in the same manner that the original option payments are deemed advances against royalties.

The Author's representative will try to include a provision in the agreement in Paragraph TENTH which provides that if the play is not in rehearsal by a certain date, all rights will revert to the Author. The basis for this is that if the option is for 1 year, and if the play has not gone into rehearsal at least 4 weeks before the expiration of the 1 year, it would be impossible for the play to open within the 1 year. If there is not an option extension, and it appears that it will be impossible for the Producer to get the Play on in time, the Author would want the rights to revert so that he may sell the option to another potential producer.

In the event that the Play has not been completed at the time the Contract is entered into, the 1 year runs from the date the completed Play is submitted to the Producer. A completed dramatic Play for the purposes of the Agreement means a minimum of one-hundred and ten pages single spaced.

Actually, pursuant to the Contract, the Producer is not obligated to pay any money until the date of delivery of the manuscript; however, payment is almost always made at the time the contract is signed, but the option time does not start to run until delivery is made.

Minimum Basic Royalty Payments

It should be noted that the minimum royalty payments to the Author (which is provided in the largest percentage of Contracts) are 5% of the first $5,000. of gross weekly box office receipts plus 7½% of the next $2.000. of gross weekly box office receipts plus 10% of the gross weekly box office receipts over $7,000. Bear in mind that these are the minimum terms, and under certain circumstances some Authors may demand and receive a straight 10% royalty, more or less, but rarely more.

Variances from Basic Minimum Royalty Payments

The contract provides for certain deviations from the minimum royalty payments of 5%, 7½%, and 10%. There are the following, each of which will hereinafter be discussed in detail:

1.) Reduced royalty to Author based on reduced royalty to other artistic personnel.
2.) Limitation of royalty during the first four weeks out of town.
3.) Alternative royalty payment for the first three weeks commencing with the official New York opening performance.
4.) Alternative royalty payment commencing with the fourth week following the official New York opening in New York City.
5.) Limitation on royalty payments for road companies after the New York run.

(There is an unanswered question as to whether the limitation would apply to a Road Company during the New York run. It may be argued that the contract limitation specifically states "after" the New York run, and not during. The argument may be answered that if the limitation does not apply to a Road Company during the New York run, then the royalty payments fixed in the contract also do not apply, since they too specifically refer to "after" the New York run. What generally happens is that the parties accept as applicable to a Road Company during the New York run both the royalty payment and the limitation as set forth in the Agreement applicable to a Road Company after the New York run.)

reduced royalty for all artistic personnel

If the Producer pays $200. each month for the option, then the Producer may elect a certain provision of the Contract which may become effective and permits reduced royalty payments to the Author if the other artistic personnel in the production accept similar reductions. This provision of the Contract was a result of long negotiations which took place between the Dramatists Guild, Inc. and League of New York Theatres in 1961 and the provision is complicated, somewhat difficult to comprehend, seldom used, but nevertheless part of the Minimum Basic Production Contract.

In effect, it provides that if the Producer makes similar arrangements with the director, actors, and with respect to the fees of the Producer himself, then the Author will accept compensation for not in excess of 17 consecutive weeks (including all out-of-town performances prior to the New York opening, New York preview performances, New York performances or performances after the New York run) commencing with the first paid performance of the play or until the "production expenses" are recouped (as production expenses are defined in the Contract), at the rate of one-half of the compensation otherwise provided, or 5% of the gross weekly box office receipts, whichever is greater. If the Producer is entering into a contract upon the minimum terms, then the one-half would mean 2½% of the first $5,000. gross weekly box office receipts plus 3¾% of the next $2,000. gross weekly box office receipts plus 5% of the gross weekly box office receipts over $7,000. so that in such event the alternative of 5% of the gross weekly box office receipts would be greater and would be the amount that would be paid. After payment of this compensation for 17 weeks or after the production expenses have been recouped, then the payments provided in the contract are made, so that if the contract is based on the minimum terms—5%, 7½%, and 10% would be paid. In the event that there are no out-of-town performances, then the 17 consecutive weeks commence with the first New York performance.

In determining whether production expenses have been recouped or not, one must take into account all income to the Producer derived directly or indirectly from the production of the Play, including not only income from the first-class performances but also from other activities such as the sale of souvenir gifts, payments from music publishers, and any share of net receipts to which the Producer may become entitled due to the disposition of any subsidiary rights in the Play during any such week, even though later received.

When it is said that comparable arrangements must be made with the director, with the actors, and with respect to Producer's fees, it means that during the period the Author accepts a reduced payment, the director must be paid an amount equal to one-half of the percentage of weekly box office receipts which he will receive during the New York run. However, he will not be required to be reduced below 1% of the gross weekly box office receipts. Each actor must also during this period receive one-half of the guaranteed salary and/or one-half of the percentage of weekly box office receipts which he will receive during the New York run. However, no actor during said period shall be required to be reduced below $1250. per week. No arrangement need be made with any actor who receives less than this amount who does not receive a percentage of the box office receipts. During this period any management fee or percentage of gross weekly box office receipts payable to the Producer will be one-half the amount of the management fee or percentage of box office receipts payable during the New York run. However, in no event will the management fee and/or percentage of weekly box office receipts exceed ½ of 1% of the gross weekly box office receipts. The Producer will not pay or make any charge for office expenses in excess of $300. per week during this period that the Author's payments are reduced. The Contract also provides that the director, actors, and Producer's fees need not be reduced proportionately more than the Author's fees are reduced during this period.

The Contract provides that the Producer will furnish the Author and the Dramatists Guild, Inc. with copies of all contracts with the director and actors, all contracts which concern the production or management fees, as well as all other documents and financial statements or reports which are issued by the Producer to the investors, within 10 days after Execution and no later than 2 weeks prior to rehearsal. There is further provision that the Guild or the Author may examine the Producer's books.

It must be understood that although the Producer may, at the time he enters into the Contract, if the Author agrees, select this alternative to take advantage of a reduced payment to the Author for seventeen weeks, or until recoupment, whichever is sooner, there is no obligation upon the Producer to actually do this. If, after he is into production, the Producer decides that these arrangements cannot be completed or are impractical or undesirable, then the Contract is effective but that particular provision of the Contract is inoperative, and the royalties would be paid in accordance with the Contract terms applicable as if this alternative had not been selected.

limitation of royalty during first four weeks out-of-town

As was noted, the most usual royalty arrangement is that the Author be paid 5% of the first $5,000. of the gross weekly box office receipts plus 7½% of the next $2,000. of such receipts, plus 10% of all such receipts in excess of $7,000. The contract also provides that such payments shall not exceed $750. in any of the first four weeks of the out-of-town performances prior to the New York opening. This restriction to $750. during that period is one of the provisions of the Minimum Basic Production Contract which the persons representing Authors sometimes try to have deleted. It sometimes is and it sometimes isn't. It also should be noted that this $750. limitation is not applicable if the previously discussed limitation of a reduced royalty for all artistic personnel is selected and becomes applicable.

alternative payments first three weeks in New York

In the event that the Producer has not elected to pay the reduced amount to the actors, director, and consequently to the Author, there is another alternative method of paying royalties which is provided for in the agreement. However, the Author's representative often will not permit the Producer to elect this alternative. It provides that for the first three weeks, beginning with the official New York opening, the sum of $3,000. shall be paid at least one week prior to the first rehearsal, which money is held by the Guild in escrow for the benefit of the Author. Immediately after the official New York opening the Guild turns this money over to the Author. If the Producer elects this alternative, and does not pay the $3,000. as provided in the agreement at least one week prior to the first rehearsal, then royalty payments will be at the 5%, 7½%, and 10% rate. However, the Author has the option of terminating the agreement if he so desires upon written notice to the Producer within three days of the default in payment of the $3,000.

If the Play is abandoned, and does not officially open in New York then the $3,000. is returned to the Producer. Although, as was noted, option payments are usually considered advances against royalties, this royalty payment is an exception, for if the Producer pays the sum of $3,000. for the first three weeks, then this royalty is in addition to the option payments. The option payments are not deemed to be advances against this royalty payment of $3.000. The opportunity to make the payment of $3,000. for the first three consecutive weeks is very important to the Producer for one reason. As we will later learn, the Producer acquires certain very valuable rights if the Play runs for a certain length of time. If the $3,000. payment is made, then the Play need only officially open in New York City for these rights to belong to the Producer. This will be discussed in detail later.

alternative royalty from fourth week in New York

The Contract also provides an alternative payment for each week commencing with the fourth week after the New York opening. However, this alternative cannot be selected if the Producer has elected to pay the author the reduced payments during the 17 weeks or until recoupment, as previously discussed. The alternative is a payment of $250. per week plus 25% of the weekly operating profits (as defined in the Contract) until the week in which the production expenses as defined in the Contract have been recouped. After the production expenses have been recouped, then the payments resume at the regular 5%, 7½%, and 10% rate. One should bear in mind that if this alternative is selected, the payments of $250. per week and the 25% cannot be credited against the advance which was paid for the option, but are payments in addition to the advance. After recoupment, however, if the advance has not been fully credited against royalties earned, any further royalties payable to the Author are credited against so much of the advance payments still uncredited.

its. Sometimes the size of type used for the Author's name will be designated, such as at least one-quarter, one-half, or three-quarters the size of the type used for the title of the Play. There may be a provision that the Author's name is larger than any other name or larger than any other name except the Star and a director of prominence. One must be especially careful as it is imperative that most Stars' names be larger—as well as some important directors. The Author may defeat his purpose by insisting that his name be larger if in so doing the Producer cannot hire the Star or director who would be right for the Play. The billing credits usually provide that the Author need not receive credit in so-called "ABC" and "Teaser" ads as well as shallow double ads, provided the Producer's name does not appear. The extent of the Contract provisions on billing credits varies. Some well-known Authors do not find it necessary to insist upon any specific billing credits, knowing that they will receive prominent billing as their names sell tickets.

Paragraph TENTH may also sometimes contain a provision that if there is a motion picture, a live or taped television program or series based upon the Play, the Author must use his best efforts to have credit given to the play Producer, to the effect that the Play was originally produced on Broadway by this Producer.

Author's Approval

The Producer in the Contract acknowledges that the Play is the artistic creation of the Author and agrees that the Author will have cast and director approval and where appropriate, conductor and dance director approval.

After opening any cast change or replacement of director, conductor, or dance director will also be subject to the Author's approval, which approval the Author may grant to another person who may act on his behalf. If the Author is outside the United States, then he gives up his approvals advances against royalties, this royalty payment is an exception, for if the Producer pays the sum of $3,000. for the first three weeks, then this royalty is in addition to the option payments. The option payments are not deemed to be advances against this royalty payment of $3.000. The opportunity to make the payment of $3,000. for the first three consecutive weeks is very important to the Producer for one reason. As we will later learn, the Producer acquires certain very valuable rights if the Play runs for a certain length of time. If the $3,000. payment is made, then the Play need only officially open in New York City for these rights to belong to the Producer. This will be discussed in detail later.

alternative royalty from fourth week in New York

The Contract also provides an alternative payment for each week commencing with the fourth week after the New York opening. However, this alternative cannot be selected if the Producer has elected to pay the author the reduced payments during the 17 weeks or until recoupment, as previously discussed. The alternative is a payment of $250. per week plus 25% of the weekly operating profits (as defined in the Contract) until the week in which the production expenses as defined in the Contract have been recouped. After the production expenses have been recouped, then the payments resume at the regular 5%, 7½%, and 10% rate. One should bear in mind that if this alternative is selected, the payments of $250. per week and the 25% cannot be credited against the advance which was paid for the option, but are payments in addition to the advance. After recoupment, however, if the advance has not been fully credited against royalties earned, any further royalties payable to the Author are credited against so much of the advance payments still uncredited.

road company limitation

It is not unusual for the Author's representative to try to include in Paragraph TENTH a provision that the compensation for road company tours after the New York run shall be 5% of the first $5,000. of gross weekly box office receipts, plus 7½% of the next $2,000. plus 10% of the receipts over $7,000. without the limitation that is provided in the Contract, to the effect that, if the payments would result in there being no operating profits for a particular week, the Author would receive only such compensation for that week so as not to result in an operating loss, however, in no event, less than $250.

Author's Warranties

guarantees of originality

In consideration of the payments to the Author, the Author guarantees that he is the Author of the Play and has the right to enter into the agreement, and that he will perform such services as may be reasonably necessary in making revisions. Since the warranties (a warranty is a guarantee) in the Contract are only to the effect that the Author is the Author and has the right to enter into the agreement, Paragraph TENTH may sometimes provide that to the best of the Author's knowledge the Play is wholly original with him and that use of the script will not conflict with or infringe upon the rights of any other person or corporation.

no warranty of title

In the case of the title, there is usually no warranty or representation by the Author of ownership as one may not own a title in the same sense that one may own other works that one creates and enters on a page. One cannot copyright a title. Therefore in Paragraph TENTH it may be provided that t Author gives a representation that he has not himself d anything which affects his right to use the title of the and that as far as he knows he has the right to use the

possible for a title, after continued usage, to become id d with a particular show and in such case, the title n ereafter have a protectable value which cannot be others. This is not the usual case with a Play title lay is being optioned for the first time. In the event re is a change in the title, it is not unusual to provide graph TENTH that the title change will become the y of the Author. Of course, no change may be made itle, just as no change may be made in any other part Play, without the Author's prior approval.

of Production Rights

Author grants the Producer the exclusive right to pro- ie Play in the United States and Canada and agrees will assist in selection of the cast and will consult and he Producer, director, dance director, conductor, and nd costume designers in all of the problems arising the production. He further agrees that he will attend sals of the Play as well as out-of-town performances to the New York opening of the play. However, he may xcused from attending out of town upon a showing of onable cause.

uthor's Billing and Credits

The Producer agrees to announce the name of the Author as the sole Author of the Play on all programs and in all advertising matter in which the name of the Producer appears.

Paragraph TENTH will usually elaborate on the Author's billing, listing the places where the Author will receive credits. Sometimes the size of type used for the Author's name will be designated, such as at least one-quarter, one-h or three-quarters the size of the type used for the title he Play. There may be a provision that the Author's na s larger than any other name or larger than any other except the Star and a director of prominence. One mu especially careful as it is imperative that most Stars' n be larger—as well as some important directors. The Au may defeat his purpose by insisting that his name be la if in so doing the Producer cannot hire the Star or dire who would be right for the Play. The billing credits usu provide that the Author need not receive credit in so-call "ABC" and "Teaser" ads as well as shallow double ads, pr vided the Producer's name does not appear. The extent the Contract provisions on billing credits varies. Some we known Authors do not find it necessary to insist upon an specific billing credits, knowing that they will receive prom inent billing as their names sell tickets.

Paragraph TENTH may also sometimes contain a pro vision that if there is a motion picture, a live or taped television program or series based upon the Play, the Author must use his best efforts to have credit given to the play Producer, to the effect that the Play was originally produced on Broadway by this Producer.

Author's Approval

The Producer in the Contract acknowledges that the Play is the artistic creation of the Author and agrees that the Author will have cast and director approval and where appropriate, conductor and dance director approval.

After opening any cast change or replacement of director, conductor, or dance director will also be subject to the Author's approval, which approval the Author may grant to another person who may act on his behalf. If the Author is outside the United States, then he gives up his approvals unless he has designated someone else who is in the United States to act for him.

In all cases, where the approval or consent of the Author is required, an unresolved disagreement among several Authors of the Play is resolved by a majority of the Authors, unless a different method of decision is provided for in the production contract. If there is a tie vote and the Authors cannot resolve the disagreement, the Schedule of Additional Production Terms provides that the President of the Guild upon the request of the Producer or the Authors, or either of them, may appoint a single arbitrator to pass upon the unresolved disagreement.

Changes in the Script

After delivery of the completed script, no addition, omission, or alteration may be made without the consent of both the Author and the Producer. The Author owns any changes in the Play. If the Producer feels that the Author is unreasonable in refusing to make changes or additions, he may complain to the Guild which will appoint a representative or representatives, and if they deem it advisable they will use their best efforts to prevail upon the Author to make the suggested changes. One must bear in mind however that the Guild does not have the power to compel an Author to agree to changes in his script.

The Author's right with respect to Play changes and approvals of cast and director shall similarly apply to any British production.

Rights Acquisition Time

The Producer by successfully producing the Play in a first-class production, makes a contribution to the value of the Play for other uses. Therefore, the Contract together with the Schedule of Additional Production Terms provides that if the Play runs for a certain length of time, the Producer will acquire certain rights which could prove to be very valuable.

These additional rights accrue if the Play is presented for one of the following: (1) 21 consecutive performances in New York; or (2) 64 consecutive performances in or out of New York (however traveling time out of New York does not break the continuity of consecutive performances so long as 64 of the performances are given within 80 days of the first performance) ; or (3) one performance in New York if the Producer has made the payment of $3,000. provided in the Contract for the royalty covering the first three consecutive weeks from the New York opening. Any one of these will be referred to as the "Rights Acquisition Time."

If the part of the Contract which permits the reduced payments to the Author if the other artistic personnel take similar cuts is selected and becomes operative, then each preview performance in New York within 10 days of the official opening in New York (even though not consecutive) will be considered a consecutive performance in New York for the purpose of determining whether the Play has been presented for the period of "21 consecutive performances in New York," provided that the Author is paid the compensation as set forth in the Contract and provided that the gross box office receipts of each performance is at least 65% of the capacity of the theatre (computed at the announced New York prices).

Additional Production Benefits

This measurement of the time necessary for the acquisition of additional rights is important in that if the production runs for the length of time as hereinabove stated the Producer: (1) acquires an interest in the subsidiary rights (the Contract refers to "Additional Rights" and the term "Subsidiary Rights" appears only once in the Contract, but is a colloquialism which has developed in the business to designate these Additional Rights) as set forth in the Contract; (2) acquires the right to do an English production in accordance with the contract terms; (3) may reopen the Show after it closes; (4) becomes entitled to special concessions which may under certain circumstances reduce the compensation to the Author; and (5) acquires a bargaining position with respect to the motion picture rights. Each of these rights will be discussed later in great detail. Of course, the Contract provides that all of the Producer's rights in the Play terminate unless the Play does run for this number of performances which was referred to as the "Rights Acquisition Time."

Interest in Subsidiary Rights

As we have noted, the Contract states that if the Producer successfully produces a Play, the production makes a contribution to the value of the uses of the Play in other media. Therefore, if the Play has been produced for the Rights Acquisition Time, namely for 21 consecutive performances in New York, or for 64 consecutive performances outside or in New York if the Producer made the payment previously discussed in the amount of $3,000. for the first 3 weeks royalties after the New York opening, the Producer acquires a percentage interest in the net receipts received by the Author from the sale or disposition of the property for other media. Bear in mind that the Author alone owns and controls the Play with respect to all other uses, and that any sale, lease, license, or other disposition will be by the Author. The Subsidiary Rights or Additional Rights here discussed are the rights to share in the proceeds and not the rights to control the Play. The Author does agree, however, that he will not permit, without the Producer's prior consent, any outright sale (as distinguished from a lease, license, or other disposition) for motion pictures throughout the world or within the United States and Canada, for radio, television, second-class touring performances, foreign language performances, condensed and tabloid versions, so-called concert touring versions, commercial uses, play albums of records, stock performances, amateur performances, off-Broadway performances and musical comedy, operetta or grand opera, based upon the play. In no event will there be an outright sale of any of such rights prior to the first class production of the Play, except that an outrights sale of motion picture rights prior to such first-class production of the Play may be permitted if made in accordance with certain terms set forth in the Schedule of Additional Production Terms which terms will later be discussed in detail.

basic rights covered

The rights in which the Producer may acquire a financial interest are the motion picture rights throughout the world and within the United States and Canada, radio, television, second-class touring performances, foreign language performances, condensed and tabloid versions, so-called concert tour versions, commercial uses, and play albums of records.

percentage interest

The Producer will receive 40% of the Author's net receipts, if any, if the above set forth basic rights are disposed of within 10 years after the last performance pursuant to the Contract; 35% if disposed of within the next 2 years; 30% if within the next 2 years; 25% if within the next 2 years; and 20% if within the next 2 years. Stock performance and amateur performances within the United States are also included, provided that the Producer has not elected the clause, and paid the director, actors, and the Author a smaller amount for the first 17 weeks or until the production has recouped its production expenses.

If that part of the Contract is selected and becomes operative which provides that the Author may be paid a reduced royalty during the first 17 weeks or until recoupment, then in lieu of the percentage above stated for stock and amateur performances, the Producer would receive 40% of the net receipts, if the stock performances and amateur performances (and off-Broadway performances are also here included) within the United States and Canada are disposed of within 5 years after the last performance under the Contract.

With respect to a first-class stage performance of a musical comedy, operetta, or grand opera based on a straight dramatic play, the Producer will receive 40% of the net proceeds received by the Author for any performances given within 18 years after the first-class run of the Play has ended.

The Producer will receive the percentage of the receipts as above set forth for the disposition of the motion picture rights; however, it should be borne in mind that if the original contract for the motion picture rights grants motion picture sequel rights upon payment of additional compensation, and if such additional compensation is paid, the Play Producer will receive one-half of the respective percentage for the sequels, as above set forth for the motion picture rights.

interest in British subsidiary rights

If the Play has been produced by the Producer in the British Isles in accordance with the terms of the Contract, then the Producer acquires the same financial interest in the net profits received by the Author for the subsidiary uses when exploited in the British Isles, exclusive of motion picture rights.

interest outside United States, Canada, and England

The Contract also provides that the Author has the exclusive rights to negotiate and contract for all performances or for other purposes outside the continental United States, Canada, or the British Isles. However, the Author agrees to pay the Producer 40% of the net proceeds which he receives from any such contracts so executed within 7 years after the New York opening.

The Contract nowhere specifically provides that the Producer's interest in the Author's share from productions outside the United States, Canada, or the British Isles is dependent upon the Play running for any particular length of time; however, it is most usual for Paragraph TENTH of the agreement to contain a provision to the effect that this interest is only acquired when the Producer acquires his interest in the subsidiary rights, that is, when the Play runs for the Rights Acquisition Time.

restrictions on other grants by author

The Contract in the Schedule of Additional Production Terms provides for certain restrictions on the Author's grant of rights in the Play. The reason for this is obvious as the Producer of a first-class production having invested a good deal of time, money, effort, and energy in the Play does not want to have to compete with television, film or other productions. Therefore, the Contract provides that the Author will not permit the release of stock presentations, amateur presentations, musical comedy, opera or grand opera based upon the Play, foreign language performances in the United States, radio, television, second-class touring rights, condensed and tabloid versions, concert tour versions, and off-Broadway performances at any time until after the end of the first-class run, provided however that selected songs from a musical production may be released for radio at any time. Commercial uses and mechanical reproduction of the music will not be permitted until after the initial first-class performance of the Play, and publication of the music may be simultaneously with, or at any time after, the initial first-class performance.

The Schedule of Additional Production Terms provides that the Author retains sole and complete title to all rights and uses except as otherwise specifically provided in the Contract and also reserves all rights and uses which may hereafter come into existence. However, the rights reserved by the Author will not be competitive with any of the Producer's rights and will be exercised by the Author only as specifically provided in the Contract. There is a provision that all Contracts for the publication of music and lyrics of a Play shall provide that the copyright be in the name of the Composer and Lyricist.

English Production

The Minimum Basic Production Contract further provides that if the Producer has produced the Play for the Rights Acquisition Time, the Producer acquires the exclusive right to produce the Play in the United Kingdom of Great Britain and in Ireland (referred to in the Contract as the "British Isles") upon the same terms and conditions applicable to a New York production. Within six months after the date of the New York opening, the Producer may without payment of any advance royalty payment send the Author written notice that he intends to produce the Play in the British Isles within said six month period. If the Producer wishes to extend the option to present the Play to open within an additional six month period, he may do so upon payment to the Author of $500. before the expiration of the initial six month period. He may further extend the option for a second six month period upon payment of an additional $500. prior to the expiration of the first extension of six months. These payments if made are considered non-returnable advances against the British royalty payments.

English royalty payments

The Producer agrees to make royalty payments to the Guild for the account of the author as follows: 5% of the first 750 pounds of gross weekly box office receipts; plus 7½% of the next 500 pounds of gross weekly box office receipts; plus 10% of the excess over 1250 pounds of gross weekly box office receipts.

The London theatre scene is somewhat unique, and it is almost imperative that an American Producer associate himself with an English Producer to present a play on the West End of London. The Dramatists Guild Minimum Basic Production Contract provides that the Producer may associate himself with an English producer or may produce the Play under a lease to a British producer, subject however to the Author's written consent.

Paragraph TENTH will sometimes include a provision that if the Play is produced in Great Britain by the Producer in association with a British manager or on lease to a British manager, and if the Producer receives an advance against royalties or profits, or a workable sum in lieu of royalties, then 50% of the amount received by the Producer must be paid to the Author as an advance against the Author's royalties for the British production. If this advance is larger than the advance provided for in the Contract provision covering a British production, then this payment shall be deemed inclusive of the original payment.

alternative interest in English production

If the Producer does not produce the Play in the British Isles within the period provided for in the Dramatists Guild Contract, then such rights revert to the Author. However, the Producer will still receive 25% of the net proceeds received by the Author as a result of any contract for the production of the Play in the British Isles made within 5 years after the

New York opening, which includes any proceeds received by the Author from subsidiary rights. Although the Contract is not explicit on this subject, it is assumed that before the Producer will receive this 25% of the net proceeds the first-class production must have run for the "Rights Acquisition Time," that is, for at least the 21 peformances, the 64 performances, or 1 performance with the $3,000. payment.

Right to Reopen Play

The Contract in the Schedule of Additional Production Terms makes provision for the Producer to reopen the Play, but this right is only acquired if the Play has run for the "Rights Acquisition Time."

This right to reopen is provided because the Producer may find it necessary to close the Play for vacations, to permit the Star to appear in another medium, or for any number of reasons. If the Play is closed at a time when it is still doing business and there is some reasonable probability that business would continue for some length of time, it should not be necessary for the Producer to start all over to again produce a Play which he has already successfully produced. If the Play has run the "Rights Acquisition Time," then the Producer may within 4½ months after the close of the initial first class run of the Play, notify the Author in writing that he wishes to reopen the first-class production of the Play in the United States and/or Canada. He must simultaneously with sending the notice pay the Author the sum of $100. plus $100. each month thereafter until the first performance of the renewed run takes place. The production must take place not later than 6 months after the date of mailing the notice to the Author; however, if the 6 month period expires between May 1 and September 14, the Producer may reopen the Play not later than September 15 of that same year.

If the producer does reopen the Play and the rerun is for a period of at least 21 consecutive first-class performances in

New York, or 64 first-class performances outside of New York or partly in New York and partly outside New York within a period of 80 days, then the Producer shall continue to be entitled to further reopenings, in each instance in accordance with the procedure above set forth. This means that the Producer may continue to open, close, reopen, close, reopen and so on, indefinitely, so long as each first-class production runs for at least 21 consecutive performances in New York or 64 performances within a period of 80 days either in or out of New York.

There are other provisions in the Contract for reopening the Play which one should be aware of. If the Play is first produced outside of New York in accordance with the terms of the Agreement, for at least 3 consecutive performances, and the Producer closes the Play within 1 month after the third performance, the Producer may reopen the Play provided he reopens it not later than 3 months after the closing and gives the Author written notice of his intention to do so within 30 days after the closing. No further payment is required for the Producer to reopen during the first month after the closing, but the Producer must pay $200. per month to reopen during each of the next 2 successive months. This reopening like the other reopenings above discussed may result in the Producer's acquiring the rights to further reopen the Play if the Play when reopened runs for the 21 consecutive first-class performances in New York or 64 first-class performances in or out of New York within the period of 80 days after reopening.

right to reopen English production

The Schedule of Additional Production Terms contains a similar provision for reopening a British production. If the British production has acquired exclusive first-class production rights by running: (1) for 21 consecutive performances in London if first produced in London; or (2) for a total of

64 consecutive performances within 80 days after the first performance partly in London and partly outside of London; or (3) if it is first produced outside of London and runs for at least 64 performances outside of London within 80 days after the first performance, then the Producer may within 3 months after the close of the initial first-class British run of the Play notify the Author in writing that he intends to reopen the first-class production of the Play in the British Isles. Simultaneously with the sending of the notice of intention the Producer must pay $100. to the Author plus $100. for each month thereafter until the first performance of the renewed run takes place. The production must take place within 3 months after mailing of the notice; however, if the 3 month period expires between October 1 and October 14, then the Producer may reopen the Play not later than October 15 of that same year.

If the Producer reopens the Play under the provisions above referred to and thereafter has a run of 21 consecutive first-class performances in London or 64 consecutive first-class performances outside of London within a period of 80 days, then the Producer will continue to be entitled to further reopenings in accordance with the procedure above set forth, until the first-class run in the British Isles ceases.

Special Concessions

The Contract in the Schedule of Additional Production Terms provides for certain special concessions which may be acquired by the Producer. If the Play has run the length of time we have referred to as the "Rights Acquisition Time," then after 8 weeks of out-of-town performances, it is possible for the Producer, with the written consent of the Author and the Guild, to reduce the royalties below the 5%, 7½%, and 10% which is provided in the Contract for out-of-town performances.

If the Play has run the "Rights Acquisition Time," a similar reduction may be agreed upon for the period commencing with the fourth week after the New York opening. You may recall that the Contract provides for a royalty payment during this time of either $250. per week plus 25% of the weekly operating profits until production expenses are recouped and then 5%, 7½%, and 10%, or in the alternative a minimum of 5%, 7½%, and 10%. If the Producer has elected the former payment in the amount of $250. plus 25% of the profits until recoupment, then the reduction may not be granted during the period of recoupment.

One reduction for not in excess of 2 weeks duration may be made without the consent of the Guild provided that the Author and Producer enter into an agreement in writing which is filed with the Guild, within a week after the reduction is agreed upon. No reduction is permissible during the period of reduced compensation for the Author if the contract clause is in effect which provides for reduced compensation to the Author if the director, cast, and Producer take similar cuts.

other concessions

There is a clause which provides that under certain circumstances certain concessions, other than financial, may be made. Any such concessions must be made in such a way that there is no discrimination, so that concessions granted to one Producer or Author will be made to others under similar circumstances. The Guild does not bind itself to follow prior decisions and reserves the right to adopt new or different policies from time to time. The Guild does, however, agree that when Guild approval is required it will not be unreasonably withheld, although the Guild may not be held liable in any matter involving the exercise of discretion.

Sale of Motion Picture Rights

If the play runs for the "Rights Acquisition Time," as has

been previously mentioned, the Producer acquires an interest in the share of the Author's net receipts from the disposition of certain subsidiary rights. Included among these is the motion picture rights. It is possible that conflicts might arise between a play and a movie of the same property.

A substantial portion of the Schedule of Additional Production Terms as well as the entire Appendix A to the Schedule is devoted to the procedure in connection with a film sale, and for good reasons, because the sale of motion picture right to a play can mean substantial income for both the Author and the production which shares the receipts. Because a production is sometimes financed by movie money, the Producer under such circumstances might find himself the seller on the one hand and the purchaser on the other hand. (An Author on the other hand might be tempted to make a movie deal that sells the property for less than it is worth, in exchange for an extravagant overpayment to the Author for writing or assisting with the screenplay. This, of course, would be unfair to the Producer who shares in the proceeds of the sale of the film rights but shares nothing of the revenue from the Author's services to the film company, independent of the script.)

It is important that a movie sale be consummated upon terms that are to the best interest of all of the parties. The Contract sets forth, in detail, terms which provide for the appointment, duties, and procedure of a Film Negotiator to represent the Author in the disposal of world-wide motion picture rights, in the hope that this objective might be gained.

prior disposition of motion picture rights

If the Author sells or leases the motion picture rights in a property prior to making a contract for its production as a play in the United States, then the Schedule provides that no contract may be made for the Play production until one year after the sale or lease of the motion picture rights.

In the event that the motion picture rights are disposed of after a Contract for the production of the Play has been entered into but prior to the production of the Play, then the motion picture contract must be signed before the beginning of rehearsals of the Play. Any such contract must be made on the basis of a minimum guaranty payment, or an advance plus, or on account of, percentage payments based on the picture receipts or the box office receipts of the Play, or both, and is subject to the approval of the Guild and the Producer.

play revival

If the Play is produced for the first time and the Producer is entitled to share in the motion picture proceeds but no motion picture rights have been sold, then before the Author grants any other Producer the right to revive the first-class run or before he himself revives it, the Author must offer the Producer who first produced the Play the right to revive the Play upon the same terms and conditions that the Author is willing to accept from another Producer, or if the Author wishes to revive the Play himself, then, upon the same terms as the original production. The offer must be made in writing to the Producer by registered mail. If the Producer does not accept the offer, in writing, within ten days after mailing of the notice by the Author, the Producer will be deemed to have rejected the offer and the Author may produce the Play himself or grant the rights to another producer within 90 days thereafter on terms at least as favorable to the Author as those offered to the original Producer who rejected them.

If the motion picture rights have not been disposed of within 5 years after the close of the first-class run, and the Producer has not exercised the option to revive the Play, then if there is thereafter a revival of the Play by a new Producer or by the Author, the percentage of the Author's profits to which the original Producer would be entitled is one-half of the share otherwise provided in the contract (if the Play runs the "Rights Acquisition Time" as discussed, the percentage payable to the Producer would normally be 40%, 35%, 30%, 25%, or 20% depending upon whether the rights are disposed of within 10 years, 12 years, 14 years, 16 years or 18 years after the last performance of the first-class run) from the sale of the movie rights. If the revival or new version runs for the "Rights Acquisition Time," then the Producer who produces the revival or new version shall receive the other one-half of the percentages specified as the Producer's share from the Author's receipts from the sale of the movie rights.

There is an unresolved question as to whether or not the original Producer and the revival Producer share the proceeds with the computation of the 10, 12, 14, 16, or 18 years computed from the termination of the revival or new version, or whether the original Producer's participation is computed from the termination of the original production and the revival Producer's participation is computed from the termination of the revival or new version. This question may or may not be resolved in the near future.

In the event that the revival or production of a new version does not run for the "Rights Acquisition Time," the original Producer would have full participation in the share of the Author's receipts from the disposition of the motion picture rights in the same manner as if there had not been a revival or new version.

The Film Negotiator - Duties

The Film Negotiator acts as the representative of the Author in connection with the disposition of the motion picture rights in a Play and has the rights to offer such rights to motion picture producers and to carry on negotiations for the sale or other disposition. The Negotiator has the right to consummate a sale or lease after consultation with the Producer (reporting details of all offers or proposed contracts) and approval of the Author, and to receive and distribute the monies received for the sale or lease. All contracts for the sale of the movie rights must also be countersigned by the Guild.

temporary replacement, alternate, or new negotiator

The Schedule of Additional Production Terms makes provisions for the replacement of a Negotiator and also for the appointment of a Temporary Negotiator if the Negotiator dies, resigns, or is unable to perform his duties. There is also provision for the appointment of an Alternate Negotiator (if the Negotiator is temporarily ill or away) and for the selection of a new Negotiator if required. If the Negotiator, in a sale, has a conflict of interest due to his relationship with the Producer, the Motion Picture Company or the Author, or upon the request of the Author or Producer—the General Advisory Committee of the Guild may replace him with a Substitute Negotiator.

no author conflict of interest permitted

The Author agrees to cooperate with the Negotiator, to promptly submit all offers to the Negotiator, and to make a full disclosure of all offers. He further agrees that unless the Producer consents, he will not insist on any commitment or agreement with a Motion Picture Producer for the Author's personal services either as Author, actor, director, or in any other capacity, as a condition of the disposition of the motion picture rights to such Motion Picture Producer

aggrieved producer's rights

If the Producer deems himself aggrieved by the disposition

of the motion picture rights the Producer's sole recourse is against the Author and then only for fraud or wilful misconduct. The Author's refusal to grant motion picture rights to make a sequel is no basis for the Producer's being aggrieved. The Schedule of Additional Production Terms specifically states that the Producer has no recourse against a purchaser or lessee of the motion picture rights or against the Negotiator, the Guild, or other producers who voted for the selection of the Negotiator.

Procedure Followed by Negotiator Varies

Appendix A (instructions to the Negotiator) sets forth specific procedures to be followed by the Negotiator in effecting a sale or lease of a Play for a motion picture production. The sales are divided into two kinds: (1) Plays produced by Producers independently of motion picture backing, and (2) plays which are financed by Motion Picture Producers either in whole or in part. The plays financed by Motion Picture Producers either in whole or in part include three kinds:

1. Those in which the Producer has disclosed in writing to the Author upon signing of the Dram Guild Contract the fact that the Producer is, or desires to be, motion picture financed;

2. Those in which the Producer does not make such a disclosure upon signing the production contract but makes it before the date of the Play's first rehearsal;

3. Those in which the Producer has made no such disclosure at any time but is not at the time of the negotiations for the Play's sale for motion pictures able to satisfy the Negotiator of his complete independence of motion picture financing.

The procedure is different in each instance.

The instructions to the Negotiator suggest the Negotiator should request that every Producer make a voluntary disclosure of any relationship which he may have which conflicts with the basic relationship of the Producer and the Author being jointly interested in the proceeds of motion picture monies.

Play Produced By Backers Independently of Motion Picture Backing

producer, author & negotiator joint effort

The Negotiator is instructed to offer the Producer a full opportunity to satisfy the Negotiator that the Producer is certain that no substantial part of the Play's backing is furnished directly or indirectly by any Motion Picture Producer. If the Producer does satisfy the Negotiator that no substantial part of the financing was derived from the motion picture industry, then it is recognized that the Producer's interest in securing the highest price and the best conditions of sale is identical with that of the Author and that it is to the Author's advantage to have the Producer's advice and experience throughout the negotiations for the screen rights to the Play.

If the Producer does not satisfy the Negotiator that no substantial part of the financing of the Play is motion picture money, then the Negotiator may use his best judgment as to the Producer's participation bearing in mind that the Negotiator is not responsible or liable for the exercise of his discretion.

Thus, in addition to acquiring an interest in the proceeds from the sale of the movie, if the show has run the "Rights Acquisition Time," and if the Producer is to participate, Appendix A instructs the Negotiator to call a conference to which the Producer is invited to help fix the price at which the Play will be offered for sale.

If the Negotiator, the Author, or the Producer deem it advisable to either raise or lower the price, the Negotiator is instructed to again call a conference to establish a new price. The price must not be changed in either direction without affording the Author and Producer an opportunity to confer. Any offer received by the Negotiator must be immediately communicated to the Author or his agent and to the Producer.

procedure if author's terms unacceptable to producer

It is, of course, most desirable that the sale price of the movie rights be mutually satisfactory to both the Author and the Producer. If the Author decides to accept a definite offer which is unsatisfactory to the Producer, and if the Producer is not associated with or employed by a Motion Picture Producer and has not been partly or completely financed by a Motion Picture Producer or an officer of a motion picture company, then the Negotiator must advise the Producer by telegram of the price, method of payment, and release date. Unless the Producer, within 24 hours (exclusive of Saturdays, Sundays, and holidays) of the giving of the notice, advises the Negotiator by telegram that the offer is rejected and the reason therefore, the Negotiator may accept the offer. If the Producer does reject the offer he must within 5 days from the receipt of the notice submit to the Negotiator a definite offer from a party of financial standing for a price in excess of the price acceptable to the Author and on other terms at least as favorable to the Author as those contained in the offer which the Author is willing to accept. If the Producer brings in such an offer within this time, this offer is accepted. If the Producer fails to bring in such an offer within the time, then the original offer acceptable to the Author is accepted. In the event that there is a disagreemeent between the Author and the Producer as to (1) the financial capability of the Producer's Offeror, or (2) the price, or (3) the terms being better than the original offer—then the Negotiator may in his sole discretion decide the issue or may request the American Arbitration Association to appoint two persons who together with the Negotiator will make the determination. If the Negotiator's relationship with one of the parties might be such that he would be unfairly influenced, then if requested by either the Author or the Producer, or upon the Negotiator's own initiative, he may ask the American Arbitration Association to appoint three persons to decide the issue. The determination, whether by the Negotiator or by the arbitrators with or without the Negotiator, is binding upon the parties.

If the determination is with the assistance of arbitrators, then the arbitration must take place on 2 days notice and the Author and Producer equally share the cost of the arbitration. The Negotiator is instructed that he has the right to make the decision himself except in such situations where the determination is a close one.

If, during the negotiations or after the sale, the Negotiator or the Author doubts the Producer's statement that he does not have financial backing from a Motion Picture Producer, then the Author or the Guild may demand an arbitration to determine whether or not the Producer has misrepresented.

Plays Financed by Motion Picture Producers in Whole Or in Part

As was above enumerated, there are three classifications with respect to plays financed by Motion Picture Producers.

(1) Procedure Where Producer Discloses Motion Picture Backing at Contract Signing

The instructions to the Negotiator set forth the fact that it is desirable that the Producer disclose in writing, prior to entering into the Production Contract, if his production is, or if he desires it to be, motion picture backed. If such disclosure is made, it is assumed that the Author in entering into a Production Contract for the Play is satisfied with such financing and the Motion Picture Backer should enjoy certain advantages.

If the Producer has produced the Play and it has run the "Rights Acquisition Time," then the Negotiator as the Author's representative determines when the Play will be offered for sale or lease, and after consultation with the Producer and Author arranges for the Author to fix a holding price. If the Negotiator suspects any collusion between the Motion Picture Producer and the Author, then the Negotiator is instructed to report such suspicions to the Council of the Guild as a violation of the Minimum Basic Production Contract.

offer to motion picture backer

After the price is fixed the Negotiator first offers the rights at this price to the Motion Picture Backer who has invested in the Play, with the stipulation that he will have 48 hours to accept or reject the offer. If the Motion Picture Backer does not accept the offer within 48 hours, the Play may be offered in the open market with the rejected price as a minimum and no further opportunity will be given to, or bids received from, the Motion Picture Backer to meet or better any other bids in excess of the price rejected by him. If the Play is not sold in the open market at the price fixed, or better, the Negotiator and the Author may reduce the holding price; however, if they do so, they must follow the procedure just outlined. They first must offer it to the Motion Picture Backer before placing it on the open market. It may be thereafter successively offered at a reduced price if found necessary, following the same procedure each time.

proof of motion picture backer's interest

After any rejection by the Motion Picture Backer, the Author and Negotiator may demand that the Motion Picture

Backer submit an offer as evidence of his interest in the property. In the event that the Motion Picture Backer does not submit an offer within 1 week of the Negotiator's request, then the Play shall be considered free and clear of any obligation to the Motion Picture Backer and may be offered in the open market without the further necessity of first offering it to the Motion Picture Backer or giving the Backer the opportunity to bid or better any price.

If the Motion Picture Backer wishes to express interest, he must do so by submitting a specific offer either as a fixed sum or as a fixed sum plus a percentage of receipts, together with a summary of the other terms of the proposed Contract. The Author would then have 1 week in which to accept or reject the offer. If the Author rejects the offer he may still use it as a minimum holding price at which to offer the property on the open market, but no bid will be considered from the Motion Picture Backer in excess of this holding price. If no offers are received in excess of this holding price, the Author may offer the Play in the open market at a sum at or below the price set by the Motion Picture Backer which was rejected by the Author. In such a case, however, the Motion Picture Backer will be free to file offers with the Film Negotiator in competition with any other motion picture company, but no bid from the Backer in excess of such minimum holding price will be considered in such competition. But if the Author receives a bid from any other motion picture company at the same price as that offered by the Motion Picture Backer, the Backer's bid (if kept open) will receive preference provided that the other terms offered by the Backer are as favorable as those offered by the other motion picture company.

In all cases of such a motion picture-financed-Play production, the Negotiator is instructed to keep the Author fully informed of all facts relating to the sale or lease, including offers received, steps in negotiation, etc., but to not reveal any of these facts to other than the Author and the Guild. The Negotiator should caution the Author against disclosing any such information to the Motion Picture-Backed Producer.

(2) Procedure Where Producer Discloses Backing After Signing But Prior to First Day of Rehearsal

If the Producer has made no written disclosure of motion picture financing upon signing the production contract but has made it prior to the date of the first rehearsal of the play, then the Author may instruct the Negotiator to: (1) follow the procedure as above set forth for a Producer who has given written notice upon signing the original production contract, or (2) to follow the procedure hereinafter set forth applicable to a Producer who has made no disclosure at any time but cannot satisfy the Negotiator of his independence of motion picture backing.

(3) Procedure Where Producer Makes No Disclosure But Cannot Satisfy Negotiator of Independence of Motion Picture Backing

Where the Producer has not at any time in writing disclosed to the Author that the Play has motion picture financing, or cannot at the time of the negotiations for the sale or lease of the motion picture rights satisfy the Negotiator of his independence of motion picture financing, or the Producer has received motion picture backing at some time after the date of the first rehearsal and prior to the offering for the sale or lease, whether such backing is disclosed or not, then the Negotiator is instructed to use his utmost efforts to secure a competitive open market for the picture rights to the Play without any of the advantages to the Motion Picture Backer previously discussed. The Author is, under such circumstances, doubly cautioned by the Negotiator to not disclose to the Producer any offers.

Compensation of Negotiator

The Guild determines the compensation of the Negotiator, which shall in no event exceed $20,000. per year. The Guild may also pay the Negotiator an amount up to $15,000. per year for his expenses.

The Guild retains 3½% of all monies received from the disposition of motion picture rights and if this 3½% exceeds $25,000., the Guild may pay the Negotiator an additional amount as compensation up to 1% of the gross picture proceeds of any pre-production lease of motion picture rights out of any surplus held by the Guild in its special account attributable to the Play for which such picture rights have been sold. The payments to the Negotiator for compensation and expenses shall in no event exceed the 3½% amount.

the 3½% fund disposition of proceeds

All monies received from the motion picture rights are deposited by the Negotiator in the Chemical Bank, New York Trust Company (or such other bank designated by the Guild), in a special account under the name "The Dramatists Guild Negotiator Account" and withdrawals from this account are signed by the Negotiator or by the Alternate Negotiator or by the Temporary Negotiator and are countersigned by someone designated by the Guild. Before dispersing the money the 3½% is deducted and delivered to the Guild and held by the Guild in a separate account.

At the end of each calendar year, a statement is prepared showing what part of the 3½% fund remains on hand after payment of the Negotiator's compensation and expenses, and any expenses of the Guild attributable to the fund. Any balance is apportioned to each play for which monies were received for the motion picture rights during that year and paid to the person or persons (Agent, Author, and Producer) in the same proportion that the contribution to the fund was originally made by such persons.

by whom 3½% contributed

As will later be discussed, an Agent may receive 10% of an Author's proceeds from the disposition of motion picture rights, and if the Agent also represents the Producer he may receive 10% as well from the Producer's share of the proceeds. In the event of such disposition, the 3½% payable to the Negotiator's fund is deducted from the Agent's commission if the Agent takes his commission from both the Author and the Producer. If the Agent receives a commission from the Author only and not from the Producer, then the 3½% is deducted from both the Agent's commission and the Producer's share of the film proceeds in accordance with the respective interests of the Author and the Producer in the entire proceeds from the sale or lease. If the Author had no Agent, then the Author and the Producer contribute to the 3½% Negotiator's fund in accordance with their respective interests in the film proceeds.

Producer's Defaults

In the event that the Producer is in default in making any payment to the Author, the Guild may file a memorandum with the Negotiator who will thereupon withhold that amount from the Producer's share of the film sale. Unless the Producer demands arbitration within 10 days after the Negotiator mails notice to him of the withholding of the funds, the Negotiator pays the amount due to the Guild on behalf of the Author.

If the Producer has furnished a bond which the Guild has drawn upon because of the Producer's default, the Guild may likewise give the Negotiator notice of this fact, and the Negotiator will withhold the amount necessary to replenish the bond from the Producer's share of the film sale. Similarly if the Producer, within 10 days after the mailing of the notice notifies the Negotiator in writing that he disputes the claim, an arbitration follows. If the Producer does not dispute the claim, the Negotiator will pay the amount to the Guild necessary to replenish the bond.

Debts by Author

On the other hand, if the Author is indebted to the Guild or to the Producer, the Guild may file a memorandum to that effect with the Negotiator, and the Negotiator will withhold the amount from the Author's share of the profits of the movie sale and pay the same either for the Guild or on behalf of the Producer.

Motion Picture Release Date Conflicts

The Schedule specifically provides that the release date of the motion picture must not interfere with either the New York or the road run of the Play. The Author, after fixing the film release date, notifies the Producer of this date by mail or telegram. If the Producer objects to the release date, he must notify the Negotiator within 3 days after the notice is sent or given to him, Saturdays, Sundays, and legal holidays excepted. The Producer should also state the reason that he objects to the release date, and the Negotiator will then give due consideration to the Producer's objections and fix a release date which is binding and conclusive on the parties.

Producer's Participation in Sequels

As was previously mentioned in our discussion of subsidiary rights, if the Motion Picture Producer in the original contract for the motion picture rights is granted the right to make sequels upon payment of additional compensation, then when the additional compensation is paid, the Producer is entitled to receive one-half of the percentage amount otherwise provided in the Contract for payment to the Producer as his share of the motion picture rights. That is, if additional compensation is paid for a sequel sold during the first 10 years after the last performance pursuant to this Contract, the Producer would be entitled to one-half of 40%, or 20%. If the additional compensation is paid for the sequel sold during the next 2 years, that is, within 12 years after the last performance, then the Producer is entitled to one-half of 35%, or 17½%. If the receipt is for a sale within the next 2 years, the Producer would receive one-half of 30,% or 15%, and if within the next 2 years, one-half of 20%, or 10%.

House Seats

Paragraph TENTH usually has a provision that the Author, or Authors if there be more than one, shall each be entitled to purchase a certain number of house seats. House seats are not free seats, but seats which are held for the Author and others involved in the production, to be purchased by them usually on or before 6 P.M. of the night before each evening performance and on or before 2:30 P.M. or 3:00 P.M. of the day before each matinee performance. It is not unusual to provide that for each performance each Author will be entitled to purchase either one pair or two pairs of adjoining house seats in the first 8 or 10 rows of the center section of the orchestra, nor is it unusual to provide that each Author will be entitled to either 6, 8, or 10 pair of house seats for opening night of the show.

Stage Manager's Script

Paragraph TENTH almost always provides that prior to the close of the Play or prior to 1 month after the New York opening, whichever is earlier, the Producer will furnish the

Author a legible copy of the "Stage Manager's Script" in the usual form which includes lighting, costume, and property plots and all other details and information to be found in a "Stage Manager's Script." This is an extremely valuable property, especially if the Play is a success, since all of the diverse elements that go into making up the Play and contributing to its success are contained in the "Stage Manager's Script" and nowhere else.

Author's Reservation of Rights in Foreign Grant

If the Author disposes of any foreign uses including uses in the British Isles, he must, in his contract, reserve for his own use all motion picture and television rights in such foreign territory, and the contract that he enters into for such production must provide that the exercise of such reserved rights, that is, the motion picture and television rights, by any other person in the foreign territory shall not be deemed competitive with any rights so disposed of.

Author's Agent

The contract authorizes the Author to employ an Agent and to pay the Agent up to 10% of the amount of the Author's receipts from any sale or lease of the property, except that the Agent may be paid up to 20% from a disposition for amateur performances.

author's agent may take share from producer

If the Producer consents to the Agent representing him with respect to other uses of the play, then the Agent's commission of 10% may be taken from both the Author's share and the Producer's share. It is, of course, to the Producer's interest to not permit the Agent to represent him with respect to the motion picture sale. This is not always easy since the Producer is dealing with the Agent in acquiring the production rights. If the Agent becomes insistent, and rest assured, he will, the outcome will depend upon the relative bargaining strength of the parties. There is also something to be said for the concept that the Producer ought to pay for the services of an Agent also, if the Agent's work accrues to the Producer's benefit as well. The authority to employ and use an Agent is set forth in the Schedule of Additional Production Terms; however Paragraph TENTH of the contract almost always additionally states who the Agent is and the fact that payments must be made to the Agent who may retain his 10%, or 20% in the case of amateur performances, from the amounts that the Author is entitled to. The amount of space required to set forth the Agent's duties and responsibilities depends upon the particular Agent and varies widely.

author & producer may not use same attorney or agent & other conflicts

The Contract provides in the Schedule that the Author must not appoint a Producer, or any corporation in which the Producer has an interest, or any employee of the Producer, or the Attorney for the Producer as his Agent or as his representative. No Author's Agent may act as Agent and Producer of the same Play.

Payments

All payments for the disposition of the motion picture and other subsidiary rights may be made to the Author's Agent but only if the Author's Agent is a member in good standing of the Society of Authors' Representatives, Inc. or of the Dramatists Play Service, Inc. Otherwise, the monies are paid to the Guild which pays the money directly to the Author, Agent, and Producer as their respective interests appear.

Neither the Author nor the Producer may make any claim for commissions in connection with any disposition of the Play for any purpose, nor will the Producer be reimbursed for any expenses or disbursements unless the Author prior to the expenditure agrees in writing to the payment of such disbursements and the agreement has been countersigned by the Guild. For this reason Producers should be careful in making any expenditures on behalf of an Author.

Arbitration

arbitration obligation

Any claim, dispute, or controversy arising between the Producer and the Author in connection with the Contract or its breach must be submitted to Arbitration as set forth with Schedule of Additional Production Terms with the exception previously noted that if any part of the Author's payments are withheld by the Producer, since they are deemed to be trust funds, the Author may at his option pursue any remedy at law or in equity without first going to Arbitration. The Guild receives notice of the Arbitration and has the right to be a party to the Arbitration.

arbitration procedure

Judgment upon any arbitration award may be entered in the highest court of the forum, state or federal, having jurisdiction, which means simply that the results of the arbitration may be made the ruling of a court and entered as an order of the court.

the complaint

The Schedule states that a Complainant must file with the American Arbitration Association 5 copies of a written complaint setting forth the claim, dispute, difficulty, misunderstanding, charge, or controversy to be arbitrated and the relief which the Complainant requests. One copy of the complaint is mailed by the American Arbitration Association to the party complained against and one copy is mailed to the Guild.

the answer

The party to whom the complaint is addressed has 8 days from the mailing to him in which to file 5 copies of a written answer with the Association. The Association mails 1 copy to the person who filed the complaint and 1 copy to the Guild. If the person to whom the complaint is mailed is more than 500 miles from New York, he shall have 3 additional days to file his answer. If no answer is filed within the period then it will be considered that he denies everything that the Complainant is complaining of.

guild participation

The Guild has authority pursuant to the Contract to file a complaint and demand arbitration with or without the Author's consent and in such event the Author becomes a party to the arbitration and cannot discontinue the arbitration without the consent of the Guild. If an award is rendered in an arbitration against the Author where the Producer is the complainant, the Guild may discipline the Author in the manner it deems advisable and this proposition is specifically set forth in the Schedule.

selection of arbitrators

Within 10 days of the mailing of the complaint, the Author, or the Guild if it has initiated the arbitration, appoints one arbitrator from the Author's Slate and the Producer appoints one arbitrator from the Producer's Slate. If either party fails to appoint an arbitrator within the 10 days, then such appointment is made for the Author by the Guild and for the Producer by the American Arbitration Association. Within 5 days after the appointment of the two arbitrators, the third arbitrator is selected from amongst the persons on the Public Slate by the two arbitrators who were chosen.

power of arbitrators

Arbitrators are empowered to award damages against any party in a controversy upon such terms as they deem fair and reasonable, to require specific performance of a contract, or to grant any other remedy or relief whether by injunction or otherwise which they deem equitable. Simply stated, an injunction is an order to someone to do something or to cease from doing something. Arbitrators may render a partial award before making a final award and will determine in their award who pays the cost of the arbitration.

immediate arbitration

There is provision for an immediate arbitration under certain circumstances set forth in the Schedule, in which case the entire arbitration proceeding is speeded up and a decision is quickly rendered. The necessity for speedy arbitration in the case of a theatrical production, under certain circumstances, is understandable. The conditions under which a speedy arbitration may be held are: (1) if the Complainant alleges a violation by the Author in not attending rehearsals of the Play, or out-of-town performances without having been excused for reasonable cause; (2) if the Producer fails to get the Author's approval for cast, director, and other approvals where appropriate, or for changes or replacements; (3) if the Producer fails to announce the Author's name as provided in the Agreement; and (4) if the Producer makes any alterations, additions, or omissions in the script without the Author's prior approval.

In an immediate arbitration the hearing is held within 3 days after the filing of the complaint. The copy of the complaint must be delivered or telegraphed to the party complained against, and he must file the 5 copies of the answer within 24 hours after receipt of the complaint. The Complainant must set forth in the complaint the name of the arbitrator selected by him and the other party similarly sets forth in the answer the name of his selection. Within 24 hours after receipt of the answer by the American Arbitration Association the third arbitrator is chosen by the two already selected.

Definitions

author

The Contract defines *Author* as each Dramatist, Collaborator, or Adaptor of the Play and each Composer, Lyricist, Novelist, or Author of any other literary or musical material used in the Play but not including a person whose service is only that of a literal translator.

commercial uses

Commercial uses are defined as toys, games, figures, dolls, novelties, or any physical property representing a character in the Play or using the name of a character or the title of the Play or otherwise connected with the Play or its title, provided that the Author has consented to such use.

end of first-class run

End of the first-class-run is defined as the time when the Producer loses his rights to reopen the Play or has in writing declared that he will not reopen it.

new york and off-Broadway

New York is defined as the theatrical district of the Borough of Manhattan in the City of New York, and *off-Broadway performances* are defined as performances in theatres located in the City of New York which are classified pursuant to the terms of the Minimum Basic Contract of Actors' Equity as "off-Broadway." The Actors' Equity Minimum Basic Contract defines off-Broadway as the Borough of Manhattan outside the area bounded by Fifth and Ninth Avenues, from 34th to 56th Street, and by Fifth Avenue to the Hudson River from 56th Street to 72nd Street. An off-Broadway theatre, in addition to being outside that area, is not more than 299 seats.

production expenses—weekly operating profits

In a previous discussion it was pointed out that it is possible for the Producer to elect a certain part of the contract which provides that for the first 17 weeks the Author, providing others have taken similar cuts, will receive a reduced royalty payment until the production expenses have been recouped, or for a maximum of 17 weeks. There is also a provision previously discussed which provides that during the week commencing with the fourth consecutive full calendar week, the Producer may elect, if the Author consents to it, to pay a royalty of $250. per week plus 25% of the weekly operating profits during each week up to and including the end of the week in which the production expenses have been recouped. For these reasons "Production Expenses" and "Weekly Operating Profits" should be and are defined.

Production expenses is defined as fees of designers and directors; cost of sets, curtains, drapes, and costumes; cost of props, furnishings, and electrical equipment; premiums for bonds and insurance; unrecouped advances to authors; rehearsal charges; transportation charges; reasonable legal and auditing expenses; advance publicity and other expenses actually incurred in connection with the production and presentation preliminary to the opening of the Play in New York, including any out-of-town losses, but there shall not be included any compensation to the Producer or to any person rendering the services of a Producer other than a charge for office expenses not to exceed $250. per week commencing 2 weeks before the opening of rehearsals and continuing until the New York opening. No items charged as "Production Expenses" shall be charged against operating profits, or vice versa.

Weekly Operating Profits are defined as the difference between the Producer's share of the box office receipts (after meeting any theatre minimum guaranty) and the total weekly expenses determined as follows: $250. (in the Dramatico-Musical Minimum Basic Production Contract this amount is $500.) for Author's compensation; salaries of the cast; business manager; press agent; orchestra; and miscellaneous stage help; compenseation payable to the directors; transportation charges; office charge not to exceed $250. (in the Dramatico-Musical Production Contract this amount is $450.) ; advertising; rentals; miscellaneous supplies; and all other reasonable expenses of whatever kind actually incurred in connection with the weekly operation of the Play as distinguished from production costs, but not including any compensation to the Producer or a person rendering the services of a Producer, nor any monies paid by way of percentage of the receipts or otherwise for the making of any loan or the posting of any bond.

gross weekly box office receipts

Production Expenses and *Weekly Operating Profits* are

defined in the contract. The Schedule of Additional Production Terms states that "gross weekly box office receipts" means receipts from all sources including sums over and above the box office prices of tickets received by the Producer or by anyone in his employ from speculators, ticket agencies, ticket brokers or other persons, and other additional sums received from the production of the play. If the play is performed by more than one company, the percentage compensation accruing from each company is computed and paid separately.

Paragraph TENTH may provide that although gross weekly box office receipts are computed as set forth in the Schedule of Additional Production Terms, in making the computation there should be deducted from the receipts any federal admission taxes or similar taxes imposed on admissions, any commissions paid in connection with theatre parties or benefits, and those sums equivalent to the former 5% New York City amusement tax, the net proceeds of which are now set aside for pension and welfare funds of the theatrical unions and ultimately will be paid to said funds. If the clause concerning the former 5% tax appears, there must be a sentence added stating that if the League of New York Theatres and Dramatists Guild, Inc. later agree on another definition of "Gross Weekly Box Office Receipts" it will be applicable.

Defense of Law Suits

Since a Play is a joint effort, and there are many contributions to the Play after what is originally put down on paper by the Author, there are certain specific provisions in the Schedule with respect to who is responsible for the Play in the event that there is a libel action or an action for infringement or interference with the rights of any other person. In the event of such an action, the Producer and Author jointly conduct the defense of the action and equally share the expenses, unless the infringement, libel, or other interference is found to have been caused by either the Producer or Author alone, in which case no part of the expense would be paid by the one not responsible. If the Producer furnishes the Author with an idea or material and the Author writes the Play based on this, then if an action is brought on the grounds of plagiarism, the Producer must defend the action at his own expense and pay any and all damages that may be assessed as a result of the plagiarism, as well as any judgment against the Author. The Author, of course, is not responsible for any material in the Play which is not written by him. If a suit is brought against either the Author or the Producer, the party sued must promptly inform the other one of the lawsuit.

Assignments of Contract

The Contract provides that it will be binding upon and inure to the benefit of the parties and their respective successors in interest, but that any assignments (an assignment is a transfer of the rights and obligations) of the Contract, with the exceptions hereinafter noted, will be effective only when approved in writing by the Author, countersigned by the Guild. The Schedule of Additional Production Terms contains a more specific provision to the effect that no assignment is effective without first obtaining the consent of the Author in writing and the countersignature of the Guild, except that an assignment may be made to a corporation in which the Producer has the controlling interest, or in which he is the directing head, or to a partnership in which the Producer is one of the General Partners. Any assignee must assume all of the obligations of the Contract, and the Producer who originally signed the Contract also remains personally liable for the fulfillment of the Contract in the same manner as though no such assignment has been made. A copy of the assignment must be filed with the Guild.

Adaptation

The Dramatists Guild, Inc. as well as protecting the rights of an Author of an original work also protects the rights of an Adaptor. There is a provision in the Schedule of Additional Production Terms that if an English language adaptation is made from a foreign language play or from another literary property, the Adaptor must receive at least one-third of the minimum compensation payable to the Author.

Repertory

If a play is produced in repertory, the percentage compensation is computed on the basis of 8 performances constituting a week. The times for payment or mailing must be agreed upon in the production contract; however, in no event can it be later than 4 days after the end of every calendar month in which the play is performed, regardless of the number of performances during that month.

Producer Cannot Offset Claims Against Author

The Schedule of Additional Production Terms contains a provision that the Producer may not deduct from the compensation owed to the Author any amounts which the Producer claims to be due to him from the Author (unless covered by a written Agreement between them) ; however, a deduction may be made if it is less than $100. and the Author has signed a memorandum which acknowledges his indebtedness.

Author's Expenses Out-of-Town and Transportation

The Contract in the Schedule of Additional Production Terms provides that the Producer must pay reasonable hotel and traveling expenses for the Author on trips outside New York City (or to New York City if the Author is a nonresident of New York City) to attend rehearsals, attend out-of-town performances prior to the opening, attend the New York opening, and at any other time when the presence of the Author is required by the Producer. It is most usual for Paragraph TENTH to set forth more precisely the amount payable for expenses on a daily basis. This additional provision will provide that the Author must receive payment for economy jet transportation and will sometimes provide that the Author will receive first-class air transportation. For each day that the author is in New York, away from his home, or outside New York if New York be his home, a per diem payment of $25. is sometimes paid, $30. or $35. is more usual, and $50. is demanded but almost never or very rarely paid. It will be provided that such living expenses are paid to the Author if he comes to New York from out-of-town only until opening night.

If there is a British production, then it is most usual for the Contract to provide that the Producer will also furnish the Author with round-trip transportation from his home to London, plus the equivalent amount of pounds sterling per day during the rehearsal tryouts and up until the opening of the first-class production in England. It should be borne in mind that if the Author is a resident of the New York City metropolitan area, the per diem payment is paid to the Author out-of-town during the out-of-town tryouts or at other times if the Producer requests the Author's presence for rewrites, for consultation, or for any other reason.

Author's Money Held by Producer in Trust

The Contract provides that all sums due the Author, which are in the hands of the Producer are deemed to be trust funds. The significance of this is that legally there is a very strict duty owed by one who holds trust funds. As noted previously, if there is a breach of trust and the funds are not paid to the Author, the Contract provides that in lieu of the arbitration procedure the Author may pursue his remedies at law or in equity.

To Whom Checks Payable and to Whom Sent

The Contract provides that all checks must be sent to the Guild. The checks in payment of the option, or to extend the British Isles option, and the check in payment of the $3,000. for the first 3 weeks royalties if this is applicable, are made payable to the Guild, and all of the other checks are made payable to the order of the Author, or the Author's Agent if the Author so instructs the Producer in writing, and if the Agent is a member in good standing of the Society of Authors' Representatives, Inc. or of the Dramatists Play Service, Inc.

Producer Furnishes Statements

The Producer agrees to forward to the Guild, within 7 days after the end of each calendar week, the amounts that are due as compensation together with the daily box office statements of each performance during the week, signed by the treasurer or treasurers of the theatre and countersigned by the Producer or his representative. Box office statements and payments for plays presented more than 500 miles from New York City may be furnished and paid within 14 days after the end of each week, and if the Play is presented in the British Isles, within 21 days. If the payment depends upon operating profits or losses, then the weekly operating statements must also be furnished to the Guild.

It is most usual that paragraph TENTH wil provide that copies of box-office and any other statements sent to the

Dramatists Guild pursuant to the contract will also be furnished to the Author's Agent.

Address of Notices

The Schedule provides that the Producer will supply the Guild, in writing, with his address. Notices are sent to the address furnished, and a notice sent by registered mail is deemed due notice to the Producer. All notices to the Author must be sent to him by registered mail to the address stated in the Production Contract, and a copy must be sent to the Guild.

Guild Countersignature and Corporate Producer

The Contract must be countersigned by the Dramatists Guild before it is effective. Any change or modification of the Contract must be in writing and also countersigned by the Guild. In the event that the Producer is a corporation, then an individual who is in control of the corporation, who owns a majority of the stock, or will be named as the Producer, must personally guarantee the Contract. One can understand the necessity for this if one realizes that a corporation need not be responsible in the same way that an individual is. If a corporation runs out of assets, it can simply go out of business. An individual would be more responsible, hence the Guild insists that an individual be personally obligated to the terms of the Contract, in addition to the corporation.

Author Approves Co-Producer

The Contract provides that the Producer may not use the name of any person, firm, or corporation as participating in the production of the Play without the Author's consent in writing.

Closing

When the Producer decides to close the Play he must immediately give written notice of this fact to the Author.

Termination of Contract by Author

If the Producer does not make any payments when due, or fails to fulfill any of the other terms of the Contract, the Author may send notice by registered mail or by telegraph requesting that the Producer correct such failure or breach within 3 days after the mailing or telegraphing. If the breach is not corrected within the 3 days, the contract ceases, and all rights revert to the Author. Sundays and legal holidays are not included in computing the 3 day period. If the Producer has his office or place of business more than 100 miles from where the notice is sent, the notice must be by telegraph.

Automatic Termination

All rights revert to the Author automatically if the Producer: (1) fails to produce the Play during the option period or the period as extended; or (2) the Play fails to run the number of performances which we have referred to as the "Rights Acquisition Time"; or (3) if the Producer does not make any option payment within 10 days after it is due; or (4) the Producer files a petition of bankruptcy or is adjudicated a bankrupt, or makes an assignment for the benefit of creditors or takes advantage of any insolvency act, liquidates his business, or a receiver is appointed for his property; or (5) if a corporate Producer without Guild consent is involved in a merger, consolidation, or reorganization; or (6) if the corporate existence of the Producer is terminated. In the event of a termination of the contract, the Producer must immediately return all manuscripts, scores, parts, and any other literary or musical material to the Author except for one copy of the manuscript which he may retain but not use or sell.

Contract Interpretation

If any part of the Contract is in conflict with any law of any state, the validity of any other portions or provisions are not affected.

Dramatico-Musical Minimum Basic Production Contract

Payment for Option

There are a few differences between the Dramatic and the Dramatico-Musical Production Contract. Although the dollar amount of the option minimums are the same, if the Producer elects the reduced royalty payments based on reduced royalty to other artistic personnel, and pays $200. per month for the option, it must be a payment of $200. each to the Bookwriter, Composer, and Lyricist. If the reduced royalty for artistic personnel is not selected, then the $200. each month is shared by the Bookwriter, Composer, and Lyricist. If a minimum payment of $500. for the first 3 months is made, the $500. is likewise shared by the Bookwriter, Composer, and Lyricist. What percentage each receives will have been decided based on the relative bargaining power of the parties.

Completed Book

A completed musical work is a book of at least 80 pages, single spaced, (it will be remembered that a completed dramatic work is at least 110 pages single spaced) plus a score consisting of music and lyrics for at least 12 songs.

Minimum Royalty Payments

The minimum weekly royalty payment payable to the Author (Bookwriter, Composer, and Lyricist) is in the amount of 6% of the gross weekly box office receipts.

Variances From Basic Minimum Royalty

reduced royalty for all artistic personnel

The provisions in the Contract which provide that the Author may be paid reduced payments if the director, actors, and the fee of the Producer are accordingly reduced in the Musical Contract also provides that the fees of the choreographer must be similarly reduced.

Comparable arrangements with the actors means that during the period each actor will receive one-half of the guaranteed salary and/or one-half of the percentage of weekly box office receipts which he will receive during the New York run; however, no actor during this period will be required to be reduced below $2,000. per week (in the Dramatic Contract it was $1,250. per week).

Comparable arrangements with the choreographer means that the choreographer must receive as compensation during the period one-half of the percentage of weekly box office receipts which he would receive during the New York run; however, the choreographer's compensation during this period need not be reduced below one-half of 1% of the gross weekly box office receipts.

The cash office charge may not be in excess of $350. per week during this period that the Author's payments are reduced, as distinguished from $300. per week in the dramatic Contract.

The payments to the Author under such circumstances is one-half of the payments otherwise provided for, or 4% of the gross weekly box-office receipts whichever is greater.

minimum royalty and limitation of first 4 weeks out-of-town

For the first 4 weeks of out-of-town performances before the New York opening the payments need not exceed $1,500. per week. The Dramatic Contract as noted limits this to $750. per week. As with the Dramatic Contract, this limitation does not apply if the reduced royalty for all artistic personnel is selected and becomes applicable.

alternative royalty payment for first 3 weeks in New York

The alternative royalty payment for the first 3 weeks beginning with the official New York opening which is in the amount of $3,000. in the Dramatic Contract is in the amount of $6,000. in the Musical Contract. Similarly, the other advantages accrue to the Producer if the $6,000. payment is made in that the Play need only run for 1 performance in New York as the "Rights Acquisition Time" for the Producer to acquire the additional rights previously referred to.

If the $6,000. is not paid, then the minimum royalty payment provided in the Musical Contract during this first 3 consecutive weeks, beginning with the New York opening, is in the amount of 6% of the gross weekly box office receipts.

royalty after fourth week

Unlike the Dramatic Contract, the Musical Contract does not offer alternative payments for the royalty payments commencing with the fourth consecutive full calendar week after the New York opening, but sets forth instead a minimum royalty for a musical of 6% of the gross weekly box-office receipts.

road company limitation

For each week of road performances after the New York run, the minimum royalty payment also is 6% of the gross weekly box office receipts. If, however, such payment would result in there being no operating profits for a particular week, then the Author is paid only such compensation as will not result in an operating loss, except that in no week will the Author receive less than $500. You will remember that in the Dramatic Contract this limitation is for not less than $250. for each week.

Royalties in British Isles

If a musical is done in the British Isles the royalty payment is also a minimum of 6% of the gross weekly box office receipts.

Author's Approval and Billing

The reference in the Musical Contract to Author's approvals include approval of the conductor and dance director. The Producer must announce the names of the Composer and Lyricist as well as the Bookwriter in the billing. There is a provision that where consent of the Author is required, Composers, Lyricists, and Bookwriters vote as separate units with one vote to each unit.

There is also a provision in the Musical Contract which does not appear in the Dramatic Contract to the effect that in any case where the Play has run for at least 3 weeks in New York City and the Producer, because of an emergency, requests the Author's approval to make changes or replacements, if the Producer is unable to obtain any Composers', Lyricists', or Bookwriters' response to such requests, then 72 hours after having sent telegrams to the individuals and to the Guild, the non-responsive parties' right to vote is forfeited and the vote of the others controls.

The Dramatic Contract provides that if the Play runs the length of time referred to as the "Rights Acquisition Time" the Producer will receive 40% of the Author's net proceeds from performances of a first-class stage musical, comedy opera, or grand opera based on the Play within 18 years after the first-class run of the Play has ended. Of course, no such provision is contained in the Musical Contract.

In the definition of weekly operating profits the weekly expenses are stated to be $500. for Author's minimum compensation (rather than $250. as appears in the Dramatic Contract) and the office charge is not to exceed $450. (rather than $250. as stated in the Dramatic Contract).

Interest in Subsidiary Rights

In the listing of the subsidiaries in which the Producer will share a percentage of the profits, if the Play runs the "Rights Acquisition Time" the Musical Contract includes "grand opera," but omits "play albums."

division of receipts

Paragraph TENTH of the Musical Contract will customarily contain most of the provisions which are contained in a Dramatic Contract and in addition should include a very detailed statement setting forth how the Bookwriter, Composer, and Lyricist (as well as the substitute bookwriter, if any, substitute composer, if any, and substitute lyricist, if any) share in the royalties and also specifically how they share in the subsidiaries. It is sometimes provided that the Bookwriter, Composer, and Lyricist share equally, so that if a royalty of 6% of the gross weekly box office receipts were paid, each would receive 2%. It is sometimes provided that the Bookwriter receives one-half and the Composer and Lyricist receive the other one-half which would mean that the Bookwriter would receive 3% and the Composer and Lyricist would share 3%. The sharing of the interest in the subsidiary rights is usually related to how the parties share royalties on the Broadway show. It is, however, most usual to provide that the Composer and Lyricist own and control the music and lyrics to the extent that they are usable separate and apart from the Play as an entity.

cast album

The interest that the Author, Composer, and Lyricist respectively share in the original cast album is always subject to sharp negotiation and the difference of opinion is accentuated by the argument that the recording is usually mostly music and lyrics. The Bookwriter's answer is that if it weren't for the book, there would not be an original cast album. It is not unusual that they share equally, that is, one-third of 60% to each, with the Producer receiving 40%.

Musical Schedule Terms

revue numbers

All of the provisions of the Schedule of Additional Production Terms are applicable to a Musical Contract. However there are some specific provisions of the Schedule which are applicable only to a musical.

There is a provision that any sketch or number from a revue, or any musical numbers in a musical play which have not been used on opening night in New York, or within 3 weeks thereafter, or are omitted for any 3 consecutive weeks, may be withdrawn by the Author and used by the Author for any purpose free of any claim by the Producer subject only to a participating interest in additional uses which the Producer may have previously acquired. If a sketch or song is omitted from a condensed or tabloid version of the Play, the Author whose work is omitted will nevertheless share in the proceeds from such version, provided that his contribution has been included in at least one-half of the prior presentations in New York. In such case, the Authors would share in the profits of such a condensed or tabloid version in the same proportion that they shared in the original production.

producer furnishes score of music

The Producer agrees to furnish all orchestral scores, conductor's scores, orchestra parts, or vocal parts at his own expense which thereafter belong jointly to the Lyricist and Composer. Such scores and parts may be used by the Lyricist and Composer at any time after the close of the first-class run of the Play.

producer may get reimbursed up to 50% for score

There is provision in the Schedule for the Producer to reimburse himself for an amount up to 50% of his expenditure for the orchestral score, conductor's score, orchestra parts, and vocal parts. The Producer may deduct from the compensation of the Composer and Lyricist (but not from the payment for the option, not from the $3,000. for the first 3 weeks beginning with the New York opening if this is provided for in the Contract, and not from the royalties for the road performances after the New York run) up to $100. each week as payment toward the 50% of the cost. The Producer must pay the monies so deducted to the Guild until the Producer has presented evidence to the Guild of such expenditures for which the Guild will then return the amount up to 50% to the Producer. The deduction unless otherwise agreed upon is borne by the Composer and Lyricist according to their respective percentages of compensation. The provision that the score and parts will belong to and may be used by the Lyricist and Composer after the close of the Play is not conditioned upon the deductions provided for having been completed. The Composer and Lyricist may at their option at any time pay the Producer an amount equal to 50% of the amount which he spent for the score and parts, or the balance which may then be unpaid.

composer and lyricist control publishing

The Composer and Lyricist alone have the right to contract for the publication of the music and lyrics without prejudice to the right of the Producer to arrange for separate payment to him by the publisher. The Composer and Lyricist alone may permit reproduction of the music and lyrics by phonograph records, tapes, or other devices

musical score available to guild

The Producer must, upon the request of the Composer and Lyricist, or the Guild, make the orchestral score available to the Guild as soon as possible after the opening, for the purpose of making a copy. Upon the close of the run of each company, the Producer agrees to deliver the complete orchestral score, conductor's score, orchestra parts, vocal parts, and prompt book to the Composer and Lyricist. The Producer may retain a copy of these items but not for use or sale.

song for movie use

The Schedule provides that a separate song or sketch from a revue may be disposed of for motion picture purposes only after 18 months from the close of the first-class run, except that if the Producer within 5 days after notice to him objects to such disposal, then the approval of the General Advisory Committee of the Guild must first be obtained. The Authors' share of the profits is shared only by the Authors of the song or sketch so disposed of unless there is specific agreement to the contrary.

no publishing until first performance

As has been stated above, the Schedule provides that the Author will not without the Producer's consent in writing, release publication of the music nor will he permit publication of the music or mechanical reproduction of the music until after the initial first-class performance of the play. We have also already noted that all contracts for the publication of the music and lyrics of any play shall provide that the copyrights be in the names of the Composer and Lyricist.

Waivers on a Musical

On most Musicals, the Bookwriter, Composer, and Lyricist enter into a letter agreement with the Producer wherein they defer collection of a certain percentage of their royalties under certain circumstances. They do not usually waive the royalties, but instead agree to take less during certain weeks and recoup the deferred amounts at some later date if the show makes money. A typical letter agreement of this kind might provide that if the show grosses below $35,000. during a week, then the Bookwriter, Composer, and Lyricist would collect 75% of the royalty otherwise provided for; if it grosses below $34,000. then they would receive 50% of the royalty otherwise provided for; if it grosses less than $33,000. then they would only receive 25% of the royalty otherwise provided for; and if it grosses less than $23,000. then they would defer collection of the royalty completely during that week. Bear in mind that these figures are arbitrary and subject to negotiation and could be in amounts higher or lower than above stated.

Other Dramatists Guild Inc. Contracts

There are three other less commonly used Dramatists Guild Contracts:

Revue Production Contract

The "Revue Production Contract" with the supplemental provisions recomended by the Dramatists Guild for incorporation in the "Revue Production Contract" is used for a musical revue. At the present time, musical revues are out of vogue on Broadway. When and if the form is used, it is necessary to complete a form with a good number of blanks which have to be filled in. The supplemental provisions set forth certain recommendations of the Guild which may or may not be incorporated into the Revue Contract. All in all the form may prove helpful in suggesting areas that should be covered in a Contract.

Collaboration Contract

The Dramatists Guild "Collaboration Contract" is a form that is suggested for use by persons collaborating on the writing of a play.

The necessity for its use is very often avoided by incorporating all of the terms of the collaboration into the "Minimum Basic Production Contract" entered into with the Producer. If the parties are collaborating on a property to be written which has not as yet been sold to a Producer, they may wish to use this form.

Stock Try Out Production Contract

The Dramatists Guild, Inc. also has a "Stock Try Out Production Contract". If the Contract is used, it is prepared together with a Dramatists Guild "Minimum Basic Production

Contract," which is annexed to the "Stock Try Out Production Contract." If the play is produced in stock, then the producer has an option for not more than 30 days from the opening performance to enter into the "Minimum Basic Production Contract" upon the terms set forth in the annexed Contract as prepared.

CHAPTER 3

MOVIE DEALS

Investors Expect to Share in Movie

As later discussed in detail, most generally the Investors in a show share in the proceeds from the sale of subsidiary rights if the Play runs for a certain length of time. This means that if there is a sale of the Motion Picture rights or the Television rights (among other rights), that the Author will get his share and the Producing Company will get its share, part of which will go to the Limited Partners, the Investors. This is not true of all shows, as some Producers presenting a Play written or composed by a famous name may have no trouble financing the Play by offering the Investors a share of the box office receipts only and no part of the proceeds from the subsidiaries.

Most Investors have come to expect a share of the proceeds from the additional or subsidiary rights and therefore it is of importance that the Author and Producer be in a position to offer to share these proceeds.

If a Play is adapted from a work that has already been made into a Movie, then the movie right have already been disposed of and unless the rights have reverted to the Owner (which is not likely in most instances), some kind of a deal has to be made with the Company owning the movie rights.

Film Company May Also Own Basic Play Rights

A Play and a Movie may be based on the same work, or a Producer or Adaptor may want to base a Play on a Movie. The Movie may have been an original, or it may have been based on another work that the Moving Picture Company acquired all rights to, including the dramatic rights. In either event appropriate arrangements should be made. The only basic difference in these two instances is that if the Play is to be based on a Movie, then the Motion Picture Company will expect a larger payment, for in addition to permitting the Adaptor to deal with the Play to make a Movie sale based on the Play, they are also granting the basic rights to do the Play based on the Movie. The Motion Picture Company would be in a much stronger bargaining position than if they did not own the basic rights on which the Play will be based. You may ask why anyone would want the rights to base a Movie on a Play based on the Movie. The answer is simple. The Play, although based on the Movie, may become a totally different property. Especially if the Play is a Musical Adaptation of a Dramatic Movie, then there is surely a market for a Musical Movie if the Play is a success.

One should be prepared to bargain for the motion picture rights so that if the Play is a success it may then be made into another Movie.

Dramatic Rights

If the Motion Picture Company owns the dramatic rights, then that part of the negotiations is the same as negotiating with anyone else for the dramatic rights, which has been discussed in detail. Except as has been noted, the other party may be bargaining from a strong position.

Film Rights—Option of First Refusal

For the most part, apart from the dramatic rights, one may expect that the Company owning the film rights will want an option of first refusal to make a Movie based on the Play for one-third less than any other bona fide offer. There may also be a fixed amount set forth in the Agreement for which they may purchase the movie rights such as $50,000. plus an amount equal to 2% or 5% or 10% of the first year's gross box office receipts for the Play, but in no event more than another fixed amount which might be $500,000. These, of course, are hypothetical figures and could vary greatly in either direction.

share of sale to other film company

In addition, if the Motion Picture Company chooses not to make the film and the rights are sold to someone else, they will expect one-third of the proceeds of the film sale. They may want one-half, the Producer or Adaptor may get by with one-fourth, but one-third is most usual.

The Motion Picture Company will expect a certain percentage of the box office receipts from the Play such as 2%, 5%, or 10%. 5% is not unusual. Tey might also insist upon a payment, at the time that the Agreement is entered into, as an advance against the box office receipts, or merely as a fee. This amount may vary between $1,000. and $5,000. but so very often is not even demanded, agreed to, or paid.

film company may want cast album and publishing

An Owner of the motion picture rights may try to get the

rights to publish the music and to make the Original Cast Album if the Play is a Musical. Many of the major film studios have associated companies which do publishing and recording. It is not advisable for a Producer or an Adaptor to permit them to have these rights unless it is unavoidable. The Producer may have to rely on a large investment from a record company in exchange for the rights to the Album, and if these rights have been tied up and are not available, the Producer may lose this large investment source. It is more in order to give the Motion Picture Owner an option of first refusal on these rights, so that at the very least he will have to match any other bona fide offers.

Sometimes the Motion Picture Owner will agree to cease distribution of the original Movie, and at other times will not. In most instances they will cooperate in every way, including making copies of the print available for viewing, for in fact at this point, if a deal has been made, they will have a vested interest in the outcome of the Play.

The negotiations would be similar whether the Play will be a Musical or a Drama, except with a Drama there would be no discussion of music publishing. A Drama Cast Album is a possibility but of much less importance so that it is less a subject of sharp bargaining. The dollar amounts and percentages might vary, but not substantially. But more important, bear in mind that by and large, most adaptations are for Musicals rather than for Dramas.

CHAPTER 4

THE PRODUCING COMPANY

Partnership or Corporation

Why a Limited Partnership?

tax benefits

For the most part Limited Partnerships are used as the producing entity rather than a corporation, a joint venture, or a General Partnership. Although there are various complicated schemes for using corporations to accomplish certain specific purposes, by and large, the tax advantages of a partnership, namely that the profits are only taxed once, and in the event of a loss, the loss can be offset against ordinary income, are advantages that most Investors look for, expect, and sometimes even insist upon. With a corporation the profits are first taxed as income to the corporation, and then when paid out to the Investors as dividends are again taxed to the Investors. If there is a loss, since the Investors have purchased common stock in the corporation, the loss is a capital loss which can first be offset against capital gains and the balance if any may then be offset against up to $1,000.

of ordinary income. Most theatre investors have more need of a loss which can be offset against ordinary income than they have for a capital loss.

It is also possible to arrange for the Investors to make loans to a corporation in which the Producer is the sole stockholder. Up until 1942 when the Internal Revenue Code was changed, this was a common procedure. This was abandoned for the reason that a non-business bad debt, unless by a corporation regularly engaged in the lending business, is considered a capital loss rather than an ordinary loss.

limited liability

A General Partnership is seldom used as the producing entity because it does not give the Investors the protection of limited liability which is the essential feature of a limited partnership. A Limited Partner's liability is limited to the amount of hs investment.

A joint venture is a fancy name for a kind of General Partnership. The Investors under such circumstances would be considered General Partners with all of the liability of a General Partner. There have been some producing companies (one rather well known) which have used Joint Venture Agreements where the Investors were led to believe that they enjoyed limited liability. Although he may not have to expend his own funds above the original investment, as a matter of fact, a joint venturer does not enjoy limited liability and is exposed to the same liability as any other General Partner in a general partnership.

Corporation May Be a General or Limited Partner

The laws of the State of New York were changed effective September 1, 1963, to provide that a Corporation may be a

General Partner or Limited Partner. This, of course, means that it is possible to combine the advantages of a Corporation and the advantages of a partnership by having the Producer or Producers first organize a Corporation which becomes the General Partner of the Limited Partnership. In this way the Investors, being Limited Partners, would have all of the tax benefits of a partnership and the Producer at the same time, as well as the Investors, would enjoy the advantage of limited liability since the Producer, as a stockholder, would not be exposed to general liability. If the Corporation has large assets and is substantial, there may be good reason why one ought to do this. If, however, a Corporation is organized solely for the purpose of becoming a General Partner of a Limited Partnership and the Corporation has no assets to speak of, then there is an unresolved question as to whether or not the Internal Revenue Service would consider the producing company to be a Partnership or to be a Corporation for income tax purposes. I am informed by eminent theatrical accountants that to date there is not a specific ruling on this issue.

There is respectable opinion which holds that if the Limited Partnership Agreement provides that the partnership will be dissolved upon the death of one or more officers of the Corporation, or dissolution or bankruptcy of the corporate General Partner, and if the agreement further provides that partnership interests may not be assigned without the consent of the General Partners, that in such an instance the partnership would be considered a Partnership for tax purposes even with a single Corporation as the sole General Partner.

Of course, there is nothing to prevent an affluent Producer from convincing one of his less affluent Co-Producers to be the General Partner of the Limited Partnership, together with a Corporation belonging to the affluent member. So long as there is an individual who is one of the General Partners, then there is no problem with any number of corporate General Partners. The Internal Revenue requirements would be complied with if there is this single partner, and the Partnership would be taxed as a Partnership rather than a Corporation, no matter how rich or how insolvent the individual partner is.

Characteristics of Corporation for Tax Purposes

In order for the Partnership to be taxed as a Partnership and not as a Corporation, it must in fact have certain basic characteristics. There are four characteristics of a Corporation which distinguish it from other entities. They are: (1) continuity of life; (2) centralization of management; (3) free transferability of interests; and (4) limited liability.

(1) It is for this reason that the Limited Partnership Agreement will generally provide that the partnership will end upon the death or insanity of a General Partner or of one or more corporate officers. Such a provisions is adequate to avoid continuity of life.

(2) The Agreement will almost always state that the management of the affairs of the Partnership shall not be centralized in one or more persons acting in a representative capacity. In fact, the Internal Revenue regulations actually provide that a Limited Partnership organized under the Laws of the State of New York does not have centralized management unless substantially all of the interests in the partnership are owned by the Limited Partners.

(3) Under a Limited Partnership, if properly drawn, a partner may assign the right to receive a share of capital and/or net profits but ought not grant the right to become a member of the Partnership in his place. It is usually desireable to limit an assignment of a Limited Partner's interest

by requiring the consent of the General Partner.

(4) The Limited Partners in a Limited Partnership have limited liability, and for tax purposes if the General Partner is an agent acting on behalf of the Limited Partners, then the partnership is deemed to have limited liability.

It is not easy to set forth fixed rules always applicable in determining whether the entity will be considered a Partnership or Corporation for tax purposes. Each of the characteristics of a Corporation has relative importance and in making a determination all of the factors are taken into consideration. There is no doubt but that if all four characteristics of a Corporation were present, it would be considered a Corporation for tax purposes. If less than all four of the characteristics are present, it may or may not be considered a Corporation, depending upon a number of factors which it is impossible to set forth here in detail. Suffice it to say that one must be aware of the problem so that the Partnership does not inadvertently end up being treated as a Corporation for tax purposes.

Limited Partnership Agreement

There is no standard theatrical Limited Partnership Agreement. There is a printed form which some attorneys use and adapt for each particular show. The printed form omits some provisions which should be included, and the job of properly adapting it can be extensive. For this reason some attorneys who do this kind of work use their own form which will contain some of the provisions that are found in the printed form.

Basic Provisions

There are certain basics which all or most all Limited Partnership Agreements used in theatre production have in common. It is usually these few important elements which the Producer knows and discusses with the Investor. Many Investors who have invested in theatre before are aware of these basic provisions. For example, almost all theatrical Limited Partnership Agreements provide that the first profits of the Partnership are used to repay the Investors their original investment, and after the Investors have recouped their original investment, all net profits are shared equally with the Producer. The Producer receives 50% and the Investors share 50% proportionately, in accordance with the amount of their respective investments. Most Limited Partnership Agreements provide that the Investors will share in all of the profits of the producing company which includes profits from subsidiaries. There are, however, instances where the Producer will share only the box office receipts with the Investors just as there are rare instances where the Producer will give the Investors 60% of the profits, rather than 50%.

The Limited Partnership Agreement is usually signed by the Investor at the time the investment in the production is made. After all of the Limited Partners have invested, and the production is completely financed, the Attorney for the production will prepare a conformed copy of the Partnership Agreement (a conformed copy is a duplicate of the original with the signatures of each partner duplicated) and will forward a copy to each of the Investors.

Usual Provisions

The discussion which follows will cover most of the terms, items, and provisions found in most Limited Partnership Agreements. There will be some things discussed which might not appear in some agreements. For all practical purposes, however, this discussion includes the terms in some measure found in most agreements, although not all agreements will contain all the terms discussed.

One should bear in mind that each General Partner assumes all of the obligations and liabilities of the producing company. As between them, the General Partners may have any arrangement for sharing the liabilities, but as to creditors, each General Partner is responsible for all obligations.

If additional funds are needed after the Limited Partners' money is used up it must come from the General Partner. In exchange for the obligations of the partnership, the General Partner has the right to make all of the decisions for the partnership. He is, and should be, responsible since he is making decisions.

The Limited Partnership Agreement will state that it is being made between the Producer and those persons who sign the partnership agreement as Limited Partners. It will set forth the main address of the partnership as well as the name and address of the Attorney for the Partnership.

Definitions

Most Limited Partnership Agreements contain certain definitions.

"the play"

Since "The Play" is referred to throughout the agreement, it is most usual in the beginning to define "The Play" as the specific play or plays that the partnership will be producing.

"contributions of limited partners"

The term "contributions of Limited Partners" is generally defined in the agreements as the amounts which the Limited Partners contribute to the partnership.

"aggregate limited contributions"

The term "aggregate limited contributions" means all of

the contributions of all of the Limited Partners required to be made by them.

"sinking fund"

After a show opens, even if it is making money, the Production Company should not disperse all of the profits to the Partners because of the nature of theatre business. It is not unusual to have a period of very successful business followed by several weeks or more of difficult times. If all of the profits have been paid to the Partners, then there would be nothing in the Partnership to get over the rough times. Accordingly, most agreements provide that a "sinking fund" may be established and retained by the Partnership. The amount of the sinking fund is defined in the agreement and will usually be between $20,000. and $60,000., the amount depending upon the show's total weekly expenses.

"estimated production requirements"

The amount of money that the Producer intends to raise for the Production is known as the "estimated production requirements." The "estimated production requirements" should be defined as the amount of cash which together with any bonds or guarantees furnished, totals the specific dollar amount which the Producer will attempt to raise. As we shall later see, it may be possible for the production to commence with something less than the estimated production requirements, for it may be possible to produce the show for a smaller amount. However, under all circumstances the agreement should state the minimum specific dollar amount which must be raised for a Production, before the Investors' money can be used. Investors want to know that when an investment is made, it will be used only if enough money is raised to produce the show. The estimated production requirements of a dramatic show will range between $75,000.

and $300,000. ($150,000. is not unusual) and for a musical will range between $350,000. and $750,000. ($500,000 to $600,000 is most usual) .

"gross receipts, expenses, production expenses, running expenses, other expenses, and net profits"

In order to define "net profits" it is necessary to also define "gross receipts" and the various kinds of expenses which includes "expenses," "other expenses," "running expenses," and "production expenses." "Net profits" is defined as the excess of "gross receipts" over all expenses of all kinds. The definition of "gross receipts," "production expenses," "running expenses," "other expenses," and "expenses" may be found in the copy of the Limited Partnership Agreement which is reproduced with the other forms at the back of this book.

"author"

"Author" is defined as the author, adaptor, and/or owner of the play and includes the singular or plural as the case may be. A person may inherit or otherwise acquire the rights to produce the play, and would be the owner, although not the author of the play. An owner may sell the production rights to the producer.

Miscellaneous

There is usually a provision which states that the phrase "General Partners" shall be construed to mean the plural, if more than one person signs the agreement as General Partner, and all pronouns shall be deemed to refer to the masculine, feminine, neuter, singular, or plural as the identity of the person or persons, firm or firms, corporation or corparations may require.

Representations and Warranties by the General Partner

The General Partner warrants and represents (which simply stated means that he guarantees) that he has acquired the first class production rights in the Play by contract under the terms of a Minimum Basic Production Contract of the Dramatists Guild, Inc. If the terms vary from the Minimum Basic Production Terms, then the Agreement must set forth the variance. Most usually the Agreement states that the limitations, restrictions, conditions, and contingencies of the Partner's right to produce the Play is as set forth in said Minimum Basic Production Contract, and that a copy of the Contract is on file at the office of the Attorneys for the Partnership and is available for inspection by the Limited Partners.

The General Partner further warrants and represents that, in his opinion, the total cost of opening a first class production of the Play including all bonds, cash deposits, production expenses, and the cost of an out-of-town trial run, if anticipated, will not exceed the amount which is set forth as the estimated production requirements.

Formation of Limited Partnership

The Agreement will state that the parties do form a Limited Partnership pursuant to the Partnership Law of the State of New York, for the purpose of managing and producing the Play and for the purpose of exploiting all rights held by the partnership in the Play. The rights which the Production Company owns are the rights which were originally obtained by the General Partner when the General Partner entered into the Dramatists Guild Contract. The Dramatists Guild Contract is assigned (an assignment is a transfer of rights and obligations) to the partnership after the partnership is formed by the General Partner who acquired the rights.

Term of Partnership

The Agreement will usually provide that the partnership will commence on the day when the Certificate of Limited Partnership is filed in the office of the County Clerk and will terminate upon the death, insanity, or retirement of any individual General Partner or upon the dissolution of a corporate General Partner. The Certificate of Limited Partnership is a document which must be filed in the County Clerk's office in the county in which the partnership is organized. The Agreement usually provides that the General Partner will file such a certificate after, but not before, the aggregate limited contributions have been paid into the Partnership and will immediately thereafter publish the Notice of the Limited Partnership, which means publishing a copy of the Certificate or a digest of the Certificate once a week for six weeks in two publications in the County. The partnership may also be terminated when all rights of the partnership in the Play have terminated. Upon termination, the General Partner must immediately liquidate the affairs of the Partnership.

Death of Limited Partner

If a Limited Partner dies, his Executors or Administrators, or if he becomes insane, his Committee or other representative, will have the same rights the Limited Partner would have under the Agreement until the termination of the Partnership. The share of such Limited Partner in the assets of the Partnership is subject to all of the terms, provisions, and conditions of the Agreement as if the Limited Partner had not died or become insane.

General Partner May Add General Partners

The Agreement provides that the person who executes the Agreement as General Partner is the General Partner of the Partnership. However, the General Partner may nevertheless enter into agreements with other persons to undertake the obligations and the privileges of General Partners. The Limited Partners consent to the General Partner entering into such an Agreement, providing that the General Partner is not relieved of any of his obligations under the Agreement.

Rights in Play Assigned to Partnership

The General Partner agrees to assign to the Partnership all of the rights held by him or any rights acquired by him in the Play.

General Partner's Expenditures

The General Partner is generally reimbursed for all legitimate expenditures made prior to the formation of the General Partnership. The General Partner may not be reimbursed for expenses incurred in raising money, but may be reimbursed for the cost of the option agreement, Attorneys' fees, Accountants' fees, script duplication costs, and similar expenses. The agreement may state an exact dollar amount which the General Partner has expended to date, or it may simply state that he is to be reimbursed for such expenditures he may reasonably spend or incur, including but not limited to advances to the Author.

Use of Funds Invested

Each Limited Partner in the agreement agrees to contribute a specific amount which is set forth in the Agreement to the capital of the Partnership, which money may be used by the Partnership for the payment of production, running, and other expenses.

Investment of Bond or Theatre Guarantee

In lieu of a cash contribution, a Limited Partner may make his investment in the Partnership by furnishing a bond to Actors' Equity Association or one of the other associations, or by furnishing the theatre guarantee. The Agreement provides that such an investment is the same as a cash investment by the Limited Partner. If the play closes before the Limited Partner's contributions have been repaid to them in full and the Partnership has paid any of the obligations covered by the bond deposit, then each Limited Partner who furnished a bond must pay the Partnership the full principal amount which was originally pledged by him as a bond or guarantee, less any amounts which he may already have been called upon to pay, and actually paid. There is an advantage to furnishing a bond or guarantee since an association will accept an investment in a savings bank account if it is given together with an assignment to the association to be held as security. Under such circumstances a party putting up bond money does not lose the bank interest, whereas all other investors in the producing company would receive no interest on their investment. This provision of the agreement is intended, however, not to substantially discriminate in favor of such bond-furnishing investors, so that in the event that the Play closes and the other Limited Partners have lost part or all of their investment, a proportionate share will be taken from the Bond-Furnishing Limited Partners to the extent that the bond is not used and is returned to them.

There is also a provision in most agreements that the General Partner may arrange for the deposit of bonds or other deposits based on an agreement which provides that the first net profits received shall be paid to the association or theatre holding the bond for the purpose of releasing the bond to the Investor who put up the bond. This would mean in effect that such an Investor would have a distinct advantage over the other Investors in that his funds are first returned to him. It is most usual for the contract provision to provide that such an arrangement may not reduce the percentage of net profits payable to the other Limited Partners. This means that the General Partner will have to compensate such person who furnishes the bonds by giving him a share of the Producer's profits. If a Producer is having difficulty raising the last money needed for the show, and he is very close to financed, he may under such circumstances make such an arrangement for the furnishing of the bond. Most General Partners do not want to prefer one Limited Partner over another, but if it means getting the last $20,000. necessary for the production to go on, and it might not otherwise go on, then the General Partner might be more inclined to make such an arrangement.

Use of Funds—Smaller Capitalization Finally

The General Partner agrees that he will not use the funds given to him by the Limited Partners until a specified amount of money has been raised, which amount the Producer states is sufficient to produce the show.

Bear in mind that the Producer will of course try to raise the estimated production requirements. However, the estimated production requirements, although a more desirable amount, may be an amount in excess of the amount which is actually needed to produce the show. The Producer may, for example, try to raise $165,000. which will be set forth in the Partnership Agreement as the estimated production requirements, but may, however, be able to get the production on for $150,000. with a somewhat smaller reserve. The Partnership Agreement will provide that the partnership will be formed when between $150,000. and $165,000. has been raised and that under no circumstances may any of the Limited Partner's investment be used without prior written approval from such Limited Partner, until at least $150,000. has been raised and the Partnership is formed. If the Partnership is not formed, the General Partner agrees to return all of the funds collected to the respective Limited Partners.

If the Play is finally capitalized for less than the estimated production requirements, then instead of returning money to the Investors, each Limited Partner will end up with a larger percentage of the show for his investment. For an example: if a Limited Partner would invest $3,400. for a 1% interest in the profits of a $170,000 show and if the Producer later decides to capitalize the show for $155,000., then the $3,400. investment would purchase 1.09% of the net profits of the production, and the Investor would receive this share. An Investor is investing a fixed dollar amount, and he may get more than 1% for his $3,400. investment in such case, but he may not get less than 1% for such an amount.

Overcall

The Partnership Agreement may provide that each Limited Partner must upon demand of the General Partner make an additional contribution of 10%, 15%, or 20% of his original contribution. The Agreement will usually also provide that if the Limited Partner fails to make the contribution when demanded, the General Partner may bring an action against the Limited Partner, and he will be responsible for such unpaid additional contribution, plus all disbursements, costs, and expenses (including reasonable Counsel Fees) of bringing and maintaining the action to collect this amount.

Investment Held in Special Bank Account

It is most usual for each Limited Partner to make the

investment at the time that he signs the Limited Partnership Agreement, but this may not in fact happen. If the Agreement is signed and the contribution is not made, then the Limited Partner must make his contribution when demanded by the General Partner. The General Partner on the other hand agrees that he will keep all of the funds received by him in a special bank account in trust (sometimes these funds are held by the Attorney for the production and sometimes they are held by the General Partner) and the funds may not be used until the amount necessary to produce the show has been raised.

The General Partner further agrees that after the Partnership is formed he will open a special bank account or accounts in the name of the Partnership in New York City in which all of the capital and all of the gross receipts of the Partnership (and no other funds) will be deposited. The funds in these accounts may be used solely for the business or the Partnership .

Books of Account

The General Partner agrees to keep or cause to be kept full and faithful books of account in which all the partnership transactions will be fully and accurately entered. The books of account as well as the box office statements received from the theatre (or theatres) are available for inspection and examination of the Limited Partners or their representatives. The General Partner further agrees to deliver to the Limited Partners a complete statement of production expenses not later than 60 days after the opening of the Play in New York City, a monthly unaudited statement of operations, and such other financial statements as may be required by the New York Theatrical Syndication and Financing Act and Regulations. The Limited Partners are furnished with all information necessary to prepare their Federal and State Income Tax Returns.

General Partner's Services

The General Partner agrees to render the services customarily and usually rendered by theatrical Producers, and to devote as much time as necessary to the production. It is understood that the Producer may engage in other businesses, including other theatrical productions.

The Agreement will state that the General Partner has complete control of production of the Play and the exploitation of all rights in the Play. The Limited Partners' liability is limited, but so are the Limited Partners' rights with respect to management of the Production.

General Partner's Fee and "Cash Office Charge"

The Producer is paid a Producer's fee for his services which is usually in the amount of 1% of the gross weekly box office receipts or a fixed amount generally ranging between $200. and $500. each week. The Producer will also reimburse himself for office facilities furnished to the production which includes office space, secretarial services, telephone service, stationary, and like facilities. The amount which the Producer takes as reimbursement is known as the "cash office charge" and is usually an amount between $250. and $450. each week. The cash office charge does not cover long distance telephone calls, and if there are unusual expenses which would cause the Producer's cost to exceed the amount set forth as the cash office charge, the Producer would most usually be entitled to reimburse himself for these additional charges.

The Producer will generally receive the cash office charge and his Producer's fee beginning 2 weeks prior to the first rehearsal and continuing through the week after the close of the Play. Of course, if the Producer's fee is based upon a percentage of gross box office receipts, he would not receive the Producer's fee until there are box office receipts.

Fee and Cash Office Charge If More Than One Company

In the event that there is more than one Company, the fee and cash office charge is also payable for each additional Company for the period beginning 2 weeks prior to the first rehearsal of such additional Company and continuing until 1 week after its close.

Additional Limited Partners

The Agreement will very often provide that additional persons may become Limited Partners after the aggregate limited contributions have been obtained. In such case if the General Partner needs money above the original amount intended as the total capitalization, he may not take additional Limited Partners and reduce the respective shares of the original Limited Partners, so the General Partner must pay such Additional Limited Partners from the General Partner's share of the net profits, just as the General Partner would pay for a bond deal from his share of the profits.

Advances and Loans

The Agreement will usually provide that the General Partner has the right to make or receive loans to the partnership which loans will share a certain advantage. If all of the production money has been expended and additional funds are needed to get the show on or to keep the show running, then the General Partner may make a loan to the Producing Company or obtain a loan from someone else, which loan may be repaid in full prior to the return of any of the contributions of the Limited Partners. It is most usual, however, that the

Agreement provide that the partnership may not incur any expenses in connection with any such loan or advance and that the percentage of the net profits payable to the Limited Partners must not be affected by such an arrangement.

Additional Services by Producer

The Limited Partnership Agreement should contain a provision that if the Producer finds it necessary to perform any services that would otherwise be performed by a third person, then the Producer may, if he so desires, receive reasonable compensation in the amount that the third person would have received for such services. It may just happen that the Producer has to fill in and direct the show, act as Stage Manager, or serve in some other vitally important capacity, and unless this provision appears in the Agreement he could not be paid for such services no matter how well performed and no matter how important to the company.

Share of Profits

As was previously stated, it is most usual for the Limited Partners to share the profits equally with the Producer after the Limited Partners have recouped their total investment. The agreement usually states this as: the Limited Partners shall each receive that proportion of 50% of the net profits which his contribution bears to the aggregate limited contributions, excluding, however, from such Limited Partners all persons who may be entitled to compensation as Limited Partners only from the share of the General Partner in such net profits and excluding from such aggregate limited contributions, the contributions as Limited Partners so made by such persons. Simply stated this means that each Limited Partner shares the 50% of the net profits with the other Limited Partners, pro-rata in accordance with the size of the investment of each Limited Partner. The excluded Limited

Partners for their excluded contributions, as we have stated, would receive compensation from whatever part of the General Partner's profits the General Partner has agreed to pay them.

To cover the contingency we previously referred to—that in the event the Play is finally capitalized for less than the Estimated Production Requirements—then in lieu of returning any part of the capital contribution of a Limited Partner, the percentage of the net profits is accordingly increased so that each Limited Partner will receive that proportion of 50% of the net profits which the contribution made by the Limited Partner bears to the reduced aggregate limited contributions, excluding the same Limited Partners (and their contributions) who are compensated from the Producer's share of the profits. This means simply that if the capitalization of the show is less than anticipated, then the Limited Partners' specific dollar amount will purchase a larger percentage than originally anticipated. Each Limited Partner still shares part of the 50% of the net profits, and his share is pro-rata in accordance with the size of the investment; however, if the total budget decreases, his same dollar amount invested is then a proportionately larger percentage of the smaller reduced capitalization. It will be remembered that this was discussed previously under the heading "Use of Funds—Smaller Capitalization Finally" where it was pointed out that $3,400. purchases 1% of the net profits of a $170,000. production and the same $3,400. purchases 1.09% of the net profits of a $155,000. production.

Limited Partners' Limited Liability

The Agreement specifically states that Limited Partners will not be personally liable for any debts, obligations, or losses of the Partnership except from the capital contributed by them.

Payments in Cash

Unless agreed to, the Limited Partners have no right to demand and receive property other than cash in return for their contributions.

Return of Contributions

Contributions of the Limited Partners are returned to them after opening of the Play in New York City, after the partnership has accumulated a cash reserve in the amount of the sinking fund (plus a reasonable amount for initial expenses in the event that the original company is sent on tour, and plus an amount for any additional company or companies which the Producer wishes to organize to present the Play), and after the payment of all expenses and provision for contingent expenses. If an Investor instead of investing cash has given an obligation to Actors' Equity Association or to a similar organization, then in lieu of paying that particular Inverstor's share to him the Partnership will set aside the amount of each distribution until there is a sum sufficient to release the bond to the Limited Partner and will then substitute the amount for the Limited Partner's obligation and release the bond security to such Limited Partner.

Distribution of Profits

The Agreement will provide that after the Limited Partner's contributions have been returned to them, after accumulating the cash reserve in the amount of the sinking fund plus any reasonable amount for additional companies, and after payment of all expenses and provision for contingent expenses, the net profits are to be paid monthly to the Limited and General Partners in accordance with their respective interest in the profits. The monthly financial report prepared by the Accountants for the Partnership is used to determine whether or not any contributions are to be repaid or net profits distributed.

Distribution upon Closing

Upon the closing of all Companies and abandonment of further intention of producing the Play, the assets of the Partnership are liquidated as promptly as possible. The cash proceeds are used first for the payment of all debts, taxes and obligations, for the creation of reserves for all contingent obligations, then to the repayment of the capital contributed by the Limited Partners if they have not been repaid. The balance is then divided among the Limited and General Partners in the proportion that they share in the net profits.

The agreement will probably provide that all physical assets of a saleable nature belonging to the Partnership must be sold at public or private sale, but that no assets other than the physical assets have to be sold. Any Limited and/or General Partner may purchase the physical assets at such sale.

After the completion of the run of all Companies under the management of the Partnership, the General Partner has the right to sell or otherwise dispose of the Production Rights and the Partnership's interest in the subsidiary rights other than the motion picture rights. The Limited and/or General Partners may be the purchasers at any such sale provided that the amount paid by them as purchasers is a fair and reasonable price. The Agreement will sometimes provide that if there is a dispute as to the fairness and reasonableness of the offer, then the President of The League of New York Theatres will make the determination.

Return of Contributions or Profits to the Company

Most Limited Partnership Agreements provide that if any contribution or distribution of profits is returned to the Partners and funds are thereafter needed by the partnership, the General Partner may demand the return of any part of the profits or contribution distributed. The General and Limited Partners must first repay any profits received by them, and if such profits are insufficient, then the Limited Partners must return their capital contributions. The return to the Partnership of profits and contributions by each Partner is in proportion to the respective amounts received as profits by the parties.

Abandonment

The Partnership Agreement will provide that the General Partner has the right whenever he deems it necessary to abandon the production at any time prior to its New York opening for any reasonable cause. In such event the production will liquidate all of its funds or accounts and the gross receipts will be distributed in the same manner that they would be distributed if there were no abandonment of the production. This provision is an essential part of any agreement, because although the Producer agrees that he will produce the show and fully intends to do so, show business, like no other business, has unpredictable possibilities which could preclude proceeding with a production.

If the General Partner, after the first public performance of the Play, determines that continuation of the run is not in the best interests of the Partnership and should be abandoned, he has the right to make arrangements with any person to continue the run of the Play on such terms that he feels are to the best interests of the Partnership.

Substitute Limited Partner

A Limited Partner may assign his interest in the Partnership to someone else who would be then known as an Assignee. It is not unusual for a Partnership Agreement to provide that an Assignee may not become a Substitute Limited Partner in the place of his Assignor. Under the Partnership Laws of the State of New York, there is a provision that one may become a Substitute Limited Partner in accordance with certain procedures. The Producer must be in a position to choose his Limited Partners and would not want to end up with a Limited Partner who is undesirable to him, hence the limitation appears in most agreements.

Additional Company to Produce Here or in Great Britain

use of company funds

The Partnership Agreement may provide that the General Partner may organize an additional company or companies to present the Play in the United States, Canada, or Great Britain (if the rights to produce the Play in Great Britain accrue to the Partnership). Under such circumstances the net profits are not distributed until there is further accumulated in the bank account, in addition to the reserve (sinking fund) provided for, a sum which in the opinion of the General Partner will be sufficient to pay the production expenses of each such additional company. In the event that there is more than one company being presented at the same time, the reserve (sinking fund) provided for shall be maintained for each separate company before the repayment of contributions or distribution of net profits.

general partner's involvement in other company

It is not unusual for the Agreement to also provide that the Partnership may enter into an agreement concerning the disposition of the British production and subsidiary rights of the Play with any partnership, corporation, or other firm in which the General Partner may be any way interested, provided that such agreement must be on fair and reasonable terms.

There is also likely to be a provision that the General Partner may be associated with any person, firm, or corporation which produces or co-produces a second company of the play and may receive compensation for doing so, without any obligation to account to the Partnership or to the Partners of the Original Producing Company, provided that the Original Company receives from any such person, firm, or corporation the customary fees and royalties payable to it as the Producer of the Original Company.

The General Partner may have the right in the Contract, at his discretion, to make arrangements to license the road rights to any other party or parties he may designate, provided that the Partnership receives reasonable royalties, or other reasonable compensation, and the Partnership assumes no obligation in connection with any loss or expenses of the company to which the license is granted. The Limited or General Partners are not disqualified from participating in the company to which the rights are licensed, by investing their funds, or otherwise, as a separate enterprise. In such event the reasonableness of the royalties or other compensation payable to the Partnership for the license will be passed upon by the then President of The League of New York Theatres. A General Partner may render services to the entity licensing the rights in connection with the exploitation of such rights.

general partner's acquisition of rights after termination of partnership

If after the termination of the Partnership, the General Partner purchases the production rights of the Play for the United States or Canada, either with or without the physical production of the Play, and with or without the Partnership's interest in the proceeds of the subsidiary rights of the Play, then the amount which the General Partner pays for such rights must be the fair and reasonable market value, or an amount equal to the best offer obtainable, whichever is the higher price.

Motion Pictures

It is not unusual for the Agreement to contain a provision to the effect that the Parties acknowledge that one or more of the Limited Partners may be a Motion Picture Company, or person nominated or otherwise controlled by a Motion Picture Company and that such Company may acquire the Motion Picture Rights in the Play. In such event the Partnership must be free to deal with the Motion Picture Company without liability on the part of the Motion Picture Company to account to the Partnership or to the General Partner or Limited Partners for any profits it may derive from, or in connection with, the rights which it acquires.

Execution of Agreement

There are certain provisions in the Agreement which are designed to simplify the execution of the Agreement and the filing of the necessary documents. For an example, there is a provision that the Agreement may be executed in counterparts, all of which taken together shall be deemed to be one original. This avoids the necessity of all Partners actually signing the same copy of the document. Each of the Partners agrees that the original of the Agreement (or set of original counterparts) may be held at the Office of the Partnership; that a Certificate of Limited Partnership be filed in the Office of the County Clerk and that a duplicate original (or set of duplicate original counterparts) be held at the office of the Attorney for the Partnership; and that each Partner shall receive a conformed copy of the Partnership agreement. In addition the Limited Partners give any one of the General Partners a power of attorney in his place to make, execute, sign, acknowledge, and file: (1) the Certificate of Limited Partnership and to include in the Certificate all information required by the Laws of the State of New York, (2) such Amended Certificates of Limited Partnership as may be required, and (3) all papers which may be required to effectuate the dissolution of the Partnership after its termination.

Arbitration

The Limited Partnership Agreement will almost always contain an Arbitration Clause which provides in effect that if there is a dispute in connection with the making or validity of the Agreement, or its interpretation, or any breach of the Agreement, then such dispute is determined and settled by arbitration in New York City pursuant to the rules of the American Arbitration Association. Any award rendered by the Arbitration Association is final and conclusive upon the parties and a judgment may be entered in the highest court of the forum, state or federal, having jurisdiction. Such a provision cannot, however, affect the rights of the Limited Partners under the Federal Securities Laws (later discussed) which Laws govern offering of a security (a Limited Partnership interest is considered a security) to the public for sale.

Certificate of Limited Partnership

The Certificate of Limited Partnership previously referred to is the document that is filed in the County Clerk's office in the County where the partnership will have its office and do business. The partnership agreement usually provides that the partnership will come into existence when the certificate is filed.

The certificate must be signed by all of the partners both

general and limited. The Limited Partnership Agreement contains a specific provision designed to simplify the signing of the certificate by the limited partners, for if there are 40 or 50 limited partners, it could be a troublesome chore to obtain all of their signatures. For this reason, the Limited Partnership Agreement contains a provision that each limited partner appoints a general partner as his Attorney in Fact to sign the Certificate of Limited Partnership, any amendments and the Certificate of Dissolution of the Partnership. So the general partners will sign as general partners, and one general partner will sign for all the limited partners pursuant to this Power of Attorney.

Contents of Certificate

The certificate will contain the following information:

1. The name of the partnership.
2. The nature of the business of the partnership which is usually stated to be: to act as theatrical producer and to turn to account all rights held in the play.
3. The principal place of business.
4. The date that the partnership commences business and the date of termination.
5. The time when the contribution of each limited partner is returned to him.
6. The name and place of residence of each member, general and limited partners being respectively designated, the amount of cash and a description of and the agreed value of any other property contributed by each limited partner, and the percentage of individual profits to be received by each limited partner.
7. Additional contributions, if any, agreed to be made by each limited partner and the times at which or events on the happening of which they will be made.
8. If a limited partner may substitute an assignee as con-

tributor in his place, then this must be set forth together with the terms and conditions of the substitution.

9. The right, if given, of partners to admit additional limited partners.

10. The right, if given, of one or more of the limited partners to priority over other limited partners as to return of contributions or as to income and the nature of such priority.

11. The right, if given, of the remaining general partner or partners to continue the business on the death, retirement, or insanity of a partner.

12. The right, if given, of a limited partner to demand and receive property other than cash in return for his contribution.

Publication of Certificate

Immediately after the certificate is filed, a copy of the certificate or a notice containing the substance of the certificate must be published once a week for six successive weeks in two newspapers in the county in which the original certificate is filed. The County Clerk will designate the newspapers, and one is always the New York Law Journal. The cost of publication of the substance of a certificate for a theatrical Limited Partnership will cost between $200. and $1,000., depending upon the number of investors, that is limited partners, and the other complexities of the certificate. It is most usual that the cost with thirty or forty investors would be approximately $750. Naturally, a Producer would like to save this expenditure if possible. With a Broadway production, where the total budget for a straight play will be between $75,000. and $200,000., and for a musical will be between $350,000. and $750,000., no Producer should balk at the expenditure of $800. or $900. necessary to give his Investors the protection to which they are entitled, and which they deserve.

CHAPTER 5

CO-PRODUCERS and ASSOCIATE PRODUCERS

Either before or after the Option is acquired, the Producer may decide to produce the Play together with a Co-Producer. Producing a Broadway show is a large venture and it may be advisable to have assistance in the raising of the money, in handling the business details, and in the many areas of decision.

What one gives the Co-Producer and what one receives in exchange depends upon the relative bargaining power of the parties.

Co-Producer a General Partner

Bear in mind that a Co-Producer will ultimately also be a General Partner of the Limited Partnership. As a General Partner he may bind the Partnership. Furthermore, each General Partner as stated, in obligating the General Partnership, at the same time obligates all of the General Partners personally to the payment of a debt. The Partners, as between themselves, may agree to share the obligations of the

Partnership in any fashion, but a creditor of the Partnership may seek payment in full from any one of the General Partners.

Co-Producers Operate As a Joint Venture

Before the Limited Partnership comes into existence, the Producer and Co-Producer will be operating as an entity—usually a "Joint Venture." A Joint Venture is a kind of a partnership and each of the joint venturers is a General Partner, and thus personally liable for all of the acts of the Joint Venture.

Joint Venture Agreement

basic terms

The Joint Venture agreement will state that the Co-Producers own a property which they wish to produce, that they are going to endeavor to raise the money for the production, and when the money is raised, they will be the general partners of a limited partnership which will be formed. This agreement will set forth the basic terms which will be incorporated into the Limited Partnership Agreement. There will also be set forth the amount of the budget, the method of sharing profits and losses by each of the partners, whether or not the partners' profits are related to the amount of money that each Producer raises, how the Producers' fees are to be shared, how the cash office charge is shared, and so forth.

sharing of profits by co-producers

The Co-Producers may agree that they will share equally in the profits of the company irrespective of which partner is responsible for the raising of most of the money for the show. On the other hand, sometimes Co-Producers wish to relate the share of the profits more directly to the amount of money which each one raises. If one is going to relate the sharing of the profits to the amount of money that each Co-Producer raises, one ought also to relate the other important contributions to the production to the sharing of the profits. For an example: the partner who discovered the property could claim a larger percentage of the profits for this contribution, the party influencing the star could claim something extra for that, and so on. The next logical step is an attempt to balance all of the items that each of the Co-Producers contributes, and to relate the share of the profits to the relative importance of each contribution. So very often, when Co-Producers sit down and try to balance the contribution that each one makes to a production, they discover that the importance of each contribution is difficult to measure. As a result they end up sharing equally in the profits and losses, with all parties agreeing to contribute their best efforts to the production in all ways.

who makes decisions

The Joint Venture agreement will also set forth how decisions are to be made and what happens if there is a deadlock. It is very important that there be some quick resolution in the event that there is a disagreement. In the case of an artistic decision, two Co-Producers may provide that in the event of a dispute by them, the Director will make the final determination. They may also provide that in the event of a business dispute, the question will be settled by the attorney, the accountant, or anyone else whose business judgment both Producers would respect. Other possibilities exist for settling such disputes and are as various as one's imagination.

who signs checks and agreements—billing credits—arbitration

The Agreement should also set forth who may sign checks

and who may sign other obligations of the Joint Venture. The ever-prevailing question of credits must be dealt with in this agreement, that is, whose name comes first. It is usual to provide that wherever the name of one Co-Producer appears, the name of all Co-Producers will appear in type of the same size, prominence, and boldness. Billing credits are usually in alphabetical order in the absence of other more pressing considerations. An arbitration clause may be included which, as we know, means that in the event of a dispute, rather than going to court, an impartial person would make the determination.

personnel agreed upon

The Joint Venture agreement should also set forth the personnel the Producers have agreed upon who will be employed by the show, namely; the attorney, the accountant, the general manager, as well as any other personnel that there is agreement upon at this stage.

termination of joint venture

The Joint Venture will cease upon the organization of the Limited Partnership unless the parties abandon the Play and decide to terminate it sooner.

Associate Producers — Money

An Associate Producer is sometimes part of a production, and almost always means that he makes a contribution of money. Associate Producers rarely have any say-so in the business, although a smart Producer will always consult with the Associate, even if he ignores the Associate's advice or suggestions.

The Associate, in addition to getting billing credit, will generally get a percentage of the Producers profits. It is not unusual to give the Associate 1% of the Producer's share of the profits for each 4% (it could be for each 3% or 5%—4% is more usual) of the Producing Company purchased by an investment for which the Associate Producer is responsible.

Front Money

Amount Needed and Uses

It may be necessary or advisable to take a Co-Producer or an Associate Producer to assist with front money. Usually one may expect to need a minimum of $10,000. front money for a Broadway show, and if the Producer is putting a big Musical together, it is not difficult to spend between $25,000. and $50,000. of front money. Front money is money that is used for the production prior to the receipt of the total capitalization and release of the investors' fund. It is generally used to acquire the property, to engage a Star and Director, to print scripts, to make a payment to the General Manager and the Attorney, and such usual pre-production expenditures.

Reimburse Producer for Front Money Not Used to Raise Money

Front money expended is reimbursed to the Producer after the Play is financed to the extent that the front money was not used to raise money. One may not reimburse oneself for money spent to raise money. Thus the cost of auditions and the like must be borne solely by the Producer and may not be recouped as a pre-production expense.

Agreement Should Set Forth Facts

Sometimes a Co-Producer will contribute all of the front money in exchange for the other Producer furnishing the property. The facts should be set forth in the Co-Production Joint Venture Agreement as to who is responsible for the front money, and what the party receives for it.

Front Money Arrangements

An arrangement for front money must not be confused with the assignment of profits in exchange for raising capital for the Production. Front money is risk capital and as stated can be used prior to the capitalization of the show. If the show is not produced, then the front money investor loses the money spent by the Producer, and to that extent has a tax loss. The person furnishing the front money will usually get 1% of the Producer's share of the profits, for each 1% (or sometimes 2%) of the Producing Company that that particular amount of money would buy from the Limited Partner's share of the profits.

A front money investor might also be given Associate Producer billing in addition to the percentage interest. Of course if the front money is left in the production after the budget is raised, that is if the amount of the budget is reduced by the amount of the front money and that front money was not used to raise money, the front money investor will receive a share for the amount of the front money from the Limited Partner's profits, as well as what he receives from the General Partner's share. If the front money investor wants his money returned to him at the time the show is fully financed, then he is left only with his share of the Producer's profits since he leaves none of his money in as an investment as a Limited Partner.

CHAPTER 6

RAISING MONEY – NECESSARY FILINGS – THE SECURITIES AND EXCHANGE COMMISSION AND ATTORNEY GENERAL

The Securities and Exchange Commission and Attorney General

Before funds may be raised, the Production must file certain documents with the SEC and with the Attorney General of the State of New York, if funds will be raised from the public outside of the State of New York. If funds are to be raised solely in the State of New York, then the filing with the SEC is unnecessary, but one must still file with the Attorney General.

If the offering exceeds $300,000., a full registration is in order in accordance with what is known as Form S-1. The full registration is a detailed, complicated chore and requires careful preparation, for it is important that there be no misleading statements in the documents filed with the SEC.

If the total offering price does not exceed $300,000., then instead of a full Securities and Exchange Commission registration in accordance with what is known as Form S-1, it is possible to file for an exemption from registration pursuant to Regulation A. The fact that the offerer is "exempt" from registration does not mean that the offerer is exempt from filing. The filing which must take place is a simpler and less complicated kind of filing than the full registration and usually may be accomplished in less time.

It bears repeating that if funds are being raised outside the state in which the business is to be conducted and if the funds are being raised from the public, then one must either file a full registration or, if the offering is for less than $300,000., then an exemption from registration. The Securities and Exchange Commission presumptions favor a conclusion that an offering is being made to the public, if there is any doubt as to whether or not it is a public offering.

The penalties for non-compliance with the Securities Act are severe: For example, in addition to possible criminal penalties, a Producer may be held responsible for the total budget if there is non-compliance. This means that he may raise money, open the show, close the show, lose the entire investment for the investors and then have to reimburse the investors for the total budget. For this reason, if there is any doubt as to whether a filing should be made, it is wise to resolve the decision in favor of filing.

The Securities and Exchange Commission is careful to point out that they do not actually approve of the facts as submitted to them. What the Securities and Exchange Commission does is accept or reject a filing. If it is not accepted, appropriate changes must be made in the documents submitted so that the documents will be accepted. They must accept the documents before an offering may be made to the public. However, the SEC makes the fine distinction that acceptance of a filing does not constitute "approval" of the filing.

A person should bear in mind that no sales material of any kind may be given to a prospective investor unless it is filed and accepted by the Securities and Exchange Commission. Each prospective investor must be given an offering circular or a "prospectus" as it is sometimes called.

S.E.C. Exemption from Registration

Documents to Be Filed

In order to obtain an exemption from registration, certain documents must be prepared and filed with the Securities and Exchange Commission. These documents are: (1) Form 1-A – Notification under Regulation A; (2) the Offering Circular; (3) a copy of the Limited Partnership Agreement; (4) a consent and certification by the attorney; (5) any other pertinent documents or agreements.

Form 1-A—Notification under Regulation A

The Notification under Regulation A, like all of the other documents, is submitted to the Securities and Exchange Commission in quadruplicate.

This document must set forth the name of the producer, and the name of the producing company which will be organized, to produce the play, the date that the company will be organized, the state in which it will be organized, and the state in which the principal business will be carried on.

The offerer must set forth any predecessors, affiliates, and principle security holders of the issuer as well as their addresses and the nature of the affiliation. The name of any person owing 10% or more in the producing company must be set forth as well as the amount of such interest.

The name and residence of each director, officer, and promoter of the offering company must be set forth.

One should bear in mind that many of these requirements are particularly applicable to a corporation and are inapplicable to a limited partnership agreement, which would be the producing company in most theatrical ventures. For example, a limited partnership which would be the issuer or offerer would have no officers or directors.

The name and address of the counsel for the issuer and the counsel for the securities underwriter, if there is an underwriter, must be set forth. For a theatrical limited partnership offering, an underwriter is not used so this would also be inapplicable. The issuer must state if the issuer, his predecessor, or any affiliate issuers have been convicted of any crime or offense involving the purchase or sale of securities; is subject to any order, judgment, or decree of any court temporarily or permanently restraining or enjoining such persons from engaging in or continuing any conduct or practice in connection with the purchase or sale of securities; or is subject to a United States Post Office fraud order.

The Notification must list information concerning the promoter, general partner or principle security holder of the issuer and must state whether or not any of them have been convicted of any crime or offense involving the purchase or sale of any security or arising out of any such person's conduct as an underwriter, broker, dealer, or investment advisor; are subject to any order, judgment, or decree of any court enjoining or restraining such persons from engaging in or continuing any conduct or practice in connection with the purchase or sale of any security, or arising out of such person's conduct as an investment advisor, underwriter, broker, or dealer; have been or are suspended or expelled from membership in any national or professional security dealers' association or national security exchange or Canadian securities exchange; or are subject to a United States Post Office fraud order.

There must be set forth where, that is, in what states or provinces the offering will be made, and if it is to be made by advertisements, mail, telephone, or otherwise, the method which will be employed in those particular states or provinces.

There must be set forth information as to any unregistered securities issued by the issuer or any of its predecessors or affiliated issuers within one year prior to the filing of the Notification.

Whether or not the issuer or any affiliated issuer is presently offering or contemplates offering any other securities in the United States or Canada must also be described in detail.

The Notification will set forth a list of the other exhibits which are being submitted together with the Notification such as the offering circular and limited partnership agreement.

The Prospectus or Offering Circular

The prospectus which is prepared, filed, and used in an exemption from registration as well as the prospectus which is used for a full filing pursuant to S-1, are both intended to detail the terms of the agreement between the investor and the Producer. Hence, one may discern a good deal of repetition in the discussion of the prospectus in that it restates the Limited Partnership Agreement terms, which we have already discussed in detail. In addition to the Limited Partnership Agreement terms, the prospectus is intended to inform the prospective investor of the inherent risks in investing in theatre.

The offering circular which must be filed with the Securities and Exchange Commission is patterned after a form which was arrived at as a result of discussions between the Securities and Exchange Commission and the League of New York Theatres. The present form of offering circular leaves much to be desired from a theatrical point of view, but it is a vast improvement over the circular previously used. The circular formerly used was created for the purpose of protecting investors from dishonest promoters of oil wells, nonexistent steel companies, and the like, but did not have any relationship to the theatrical business and its own peculiar attendant insecurities.

front cover

In the present form of the offering circular, in addition to setting forth the amount of money which is being raised, the name of the company, and the name of the play, the following must appear on the outside front cover page in capital letters and in type as large as that generally used in the body of the circular:

THESE SECURITIES ARE OFFERED PURSUANT TO AN EXEMPTION FROM REGISTRATION WITH THE UNITED STATES SECURITIES AND EXCHANGE COMMISSION. THE COMMISSION DOES NOT PASS UPON THE MERITS OF ANY SECURITIES NOR DOES IT PASS UPON THE ACCURACY OR COMPLETENESS OF ANY OFFERING CIRCULAR OR OTHER SELLING LITERATURE.

the offering

The circular will set forth the name of the producer and the fact that he will be the general partner. It will state what financial contribution, if any, is made by the general partner and how the profits and losses will be shared. It will state the minimum amount that each limited partner may invest and the maximum amount that will be raised. If the partnership may be formed before the total budget is raised, then this must likewise be set forth.

The name of the Attorney for the production is usually set forth.

the risk to investors

The offering circular must set forth the fact that the risk of loss is especially high in this business and the investor should be prepared for the possibility of a total loss. It will state the fact that during the last season a certain percentage of plays resulted in loss to investors; depending upon the season, this will vary between 70% and 80% which have resulted in loss to investors. Information must be furnished as to how long the play must run at capacity to return to the limited partners their initial contributions. The percentage of plays which have run this long during the last season must also be set forth.

subscriptions

The agreement sets forth to whom the investment is to be given and the fact that the funds will be held until an amount sufficient to present the play has been raised. It is usual to state that if the amount necessary to present the play has not been raised by a certain date, then all funds will be returned to the investors.

It usually says that an investor may consent to the producer using his funds prior to the total budget being raised. If this is stated, it is also pointed out that there is no advantage to the investor in giving this permission and in fact, there may be a disadvantage. The producer reserves the right to pay any investor an additional percentage of the profits so long as it is paid from the producer's share of the profits.

overcall

A limited partnership agreement, as noted in the discussion of such agreements, will sometimes set forth the fact that the limited partners must contribute an additional 10%, 15%, or 20% above the initial investment if called upon by the producer to do so. If such is the case, this must be set forth in the offering circular.

the producer

Detailed facts are set forth concerning the producer. The Securities and Exchange Commission is careful to make sure that only ascertainable facts are set forth and that there are not any misleading statements or an overabundance of superlative adjectives. Information must be given about all previous plays produced by the producer and it must state the names of the plays, the opening and closing dates, the number of performances, and the percentage of gain or loss per dollar invested.

the play

A brief outline of the play or other details about the play must be set forth.

the author

Details about the author and his previous works must be set forth. If this is the first play produced by the author, then it must be so stated.

the director

Information about the director and past works must be set forth, if the director has been hired. The offering circular must also state the fee payable as well as any royalty payments.

the cast

The names and information about any important cast

members who are signed must be set forth together with the details concerning their salaries.

theatre

If a contract for the theatre has been entered into, all of the details must be set forth. If not, it must be stated what the estimated capacity of a probable theatre will be and what the estimated costs will be.

scenic designer

Appropriate information about and the compensation of the scenic designer must be set forth if he has been signed.

compensation of general partner

This section must state the amount of the producer's fee, the amount of the cash office charge, and the fact that the producer will receive 50% (or whatever percentage is to be received) of the net profits of the company, as well as any other compensation to which he would be entitled. It is wise to set forth the fact that if the producer does perform any services of a third person, then the producer may, if he so desires, receive reasonable payment in the amount that the third person would have received for these services. In the absence of such a provision, if the producer with directing ability found it necessary to direct the show to save it, he could not be compensated for the directing.

use of proceeds

A detailed production budget must be set forth showing the proposed expenditure of the funds raised.

estimated weekly budget

The total weekly costs at capacity must be set forth and the number of weeks that the play must run at full capacity to return the original investment.

net profits

Net profits are defined and the offering circular here sets forth any payments from the gross weekly box office receipts which are deducted in the computation of net profits. Since the limited partners will receive net profits, they should want to know if a large percentage of the gross box office receipts will be payable to a star, author, or director and thus deducted from the gross receipts in computing what constitutes net profits.

return of contributions—share of profits

The circular must set forth how the profits are shared, which is usually 50% for the limited partners and 50% for the general partner. It will also state when the contributions will be returned to the partners.

production and subsidiary rights

It will briefly be stated what rights in the play the production owns and the extent of the interest in subsidiary rights.

other financing

The circular must state whether or not any one has advanced anything of value toward the production of the play.

financial statements

Since the partnership will later be formed, there are no financial statements available to furnish to prospective investors and this will be stated. A statement will also be made that the limited partners will be furnished with all financial statements required by the New York law. The name of the accountant may be stated.

production personnel

The offering circular will sometimes set forth the names of the general manager, the press agent and the production supervisor or stage manager.

In addition to the notification, the prospectus and the Limited Partnership Agreement, the submission will include a document signed by the attorney consenting to being the attorney and any other exhibits that are pertinent, such as the contractual arrangements.

S.E.C. Full Registration Pursuant to Form S-1

The registration statement consists of a facing sheet of the form, the prospectus containing certain specified information, certain other information required which is largely inapplicable to a theatrical financing, and the exhibits.

The Facing Sheet

The facing sheet sets forth the name of the Issuer, that is, the name of the limited partnership and the general partner or general partners, since it is the limited partnership, through the general partners, which is offering the securities (limited partnership interests). In addition, the nature and amount of securities being offered is indicated. Thus, for example, if the partnership is capitalized at $500,000.00, $500,000.00 in limited partnership interests would be stated. If the General Partner is entitled to 50% of the net profits of the company and the Limited Partners the other 50%, then the price per unit is, for convenience, figured on the basis of 50 units. In a partnership capitalized at $500,000.00, each unit would cost $10,000.00 and would represent a 1%

interest in the partnership. The filing fee and the name and address of counsel to the Issuers are indicated and a statement is added that the approximate date of the proposed sale is as soon as possible after the effective date of the prospectus (the date of clearance with the S.E.C.).

The Prospectus

The Prospectus (also referred to as an Offering Circular) being the basic sales document used in connection with the sale of securities to the public must contain all of the relevant facts concerning the offering, and no sale can be made unless prior to the sale a Prospectus is shown to the potential investor. The Prospectus must be prepared with great care and accuracy since misstatements, even though unintentional, may be serious.

Although no sales may be made until after the Prospectus has been cleared with the S.E.C., while the S.E.C. is processing the offering, a "red herring" prospectus may be distributed to potential investors. After the Prospectus is initially filed with the S.E.C., a legend in bold red ink is printed across the top of the first page as follows:

> PRELIMINARY PROSPECTUS — ISSUED
>
> A registration statement relating to these securities has been filed with the Securities and Exchange Commission, but has not yet become effective. Information contained herein is subject to completion or amendment. These securities may not be sold nor may offers to buy be accepted prior to the time the registration statement becomes effective. This prospectus shall not constitute an offer to sell or the solicitation of an offer to buy nor shall there be any sales of these securities in any State in which such offer, solicitation or sale would be unlawful prior to registration or qualification under the securities laws of any such State.

This red herring prospectus (which may be used with a full registration but not with an exemption from registration) may be sent to potential investors to advise them that an offering is being processed and that sales will be made in the future. It is important that a detailed record be kept of when and to whom the "red herring" is distributed as such information will be requested by the S.E.C.

Contents of the Prospectus

The Prospectus will contain all of the facts of the Partnership Agreement, information about the persons involved in the Production, and facts which the S.E.C. Regulations require which are designed to make investors better informed.

introductory

Initially there is stated a set of statistics concerning the speculative nature of the offering: approximately 80% (this figure may vary from year to year) of the plays produced in the past year resulted in loss to investors; based on estimated expenses, this play would have to run "X" (the number is inserted depending upon the facts) number of weeks at capacity merely to recoup the capitalization and "X"% (the % amount is inserted depending upon the facts) of the plays produced in the past year failed to run that long; of those that did, most did not play to capacity. The investor is reminded that there is no ready market for the partnership interests being offered, that no assignee of a limited partner may become a substituted limited partner, and that there is no right to withdraw from the partnership except in the event the entire capitalization is not raised by the outside date set forth in the limited partnership agreement.

Some general statements are made concerning the nature of the partnership: the limited partners furnish all of the capital of the partnership and bear all of the losses up to the amount of their partnership contributions, in return for which they are each entitled to their proportionate share of 50% of the net profits of the partnership; if there is to be an overcall, that is stated; the general partner, who makes no cash contribution to the partnership, receives 50% of the net profits, a percentage of gross receipts as a management fee (usually from 1 to 2%), and a weekly office expense charge for each company presenting the play (usually from $300. to $500. per week) ; limited partners take no part in the control of the business or affairs of the partnership, and the general partner makes all decisions relating to the conduct of partnership business. The investor is advised that to an extent the success or failure of a play depends on the ability of the producer to secure suitable talent and a suitable property and that considerable competition exists among producers in the acquisition of talent and properties. He is further reminded that ultimately it is the professional drama critic and the audience who determine whether the production will be a commercial success or failure.

the producer

The name and principal place of business of the producer is indicated. In addition, a brief outline of the producer's background in the theatre and his past record is set forth. The record indicates, in table form, the plays he has produced during the last ten years, their opening and closing dates in New York, the number of performances run in New York, and the profit or loss to the investors per dollar invested.

acquisition of property

A few sentences briefly stating the nature of the play appear here, with an indication of the size of the cast which will be required and the number of major roles.

The date and parties to the Dramatists Guild Minimum Basic Production Contract are set forth in addition to the royalties payable to the Authors (which would include the bookwriter, lyricist, and composer if it is a musical). In addition, if the play is based on a book or a movie or some other underlying work, the date and parties to the underlying rights agreement are given together with the royalty payable to the owners of the underlying rights. A general outline of the Dramatists Guild Minimum Basic Production Contract provisions with respect to the right of the partnership to share in subsidiary rights income is also set forth. There is a statement that the contracts are on file and available for inspection at the offices of the attorneys for the partnership and that copies are on file with the S.E.C. in Washington, D.C. Finally, reference is made to the fact that, upon formation of the partnership, the general partner will assign the contracts to the partnership.

estimated cost of production and aggregate contributions being offered

A statement is made as to the estimated total cost of producing the play (usually the capitalization of the partnership). Reference is made to an overcall if there is to be one and a statement is made that if funds are required in addition to the capitalization of the partnership, the general partner may make loans to the partnership, without interest, which are repayable prior to the return to the limited partners of their contributions.

An explanation of the share of net profits to which each limited partner would be entitled is again included and also an indication of the minimum amount which may be invested by each limited partner. "Net Profits" are defined usually as the excess of Gross Receipts over all Production

Expenses, Running Expenses and Other Expenses as defined in the limited partnership agreement.

return of contributions if partnership not formed

A limited partnership contribution is payable at the time of execution of the partnership agreement. All contributions are held in a special bank account in trust until employed for production or pre-production purposes or until returned to investors. (This clause is essential in the limited partnership agreement as it is a requirement of the N.Y. State Attorney General's Regulations.) If the entire capital is not raised by a specific date, each limited partner will receive the return of this contribution unless it was expended pursuant to his written consent and he specifically waived the return of his contribution. It should be stated that his contribution will be returned "without interest." Monies advanced by the General Partner personally for partnership expenses are deemed a cash contribution to the partnership if the general partner elects not to have the money reimbursed to him.

general nature of offering plan of offering interests to public

The prospectus will state how the contributions will be offered to the public. That is, it will usually say the offering will be made through the mails, by telephone, and personal solicitation by the producer. It will almost always state that the producer intends to solicit motion picture and record companies for substantial contributions to the capital of the limited partnership.

subscription to limited partnership

This section of the prospectus will state that in order to subscribe, the Limited Partners must sign copies of the Limited Partnership Agreement and deliver this together with the amount of the investment to the producer. The producer has the right to accept a subscription or not.

restriction on right of limited partner to withdraw from the partnership

The offering circular will state that upon signing the partnership agreement, the party is obligated to become a Limited Partner of the partnership when formed, and has no right to withdraw from the partnership or reduce his contribution. If the partnership is not formed because the total budget is not raised, then of course, the contributions will be returned to the prospective limited partners.

right of assignee of a limited partner

There will be set forth the fact that an assignee of a limited partner will not have the right to become a substituted limited partner. It may also state that the partnership is not bound by any assignment of less than the entire interest of a limited partner unless the General Partner consents to the assignment.

use of proceeds

There is here set forth a pre-production budget setting forth how it is estimated the proceeds will be used. It will also usually state that the estimate is not necessarily based on any bids of third parties, and the general partners are not limited in their use of the funds as set forth, but may make changes in the allocation which may be deemed necessary or advisable. There is likely to be a statement also that the estimate includes some expenditures which have already been made and others to which the general partner is committed.

purpose of partnership

The prospectus will state the purpose of the partnership and the language used will probably be to the effect that the purpose is to manage and produce the play and to exploit and turn to account all rights at anytime held by the partnership in connection with the production of the play.

commencement of partnership

It will be stated that after all the capital has been contributed, the general partner will form a partnership in accordance with the Partnership Law of the State of New York, and will open up a partnership special bank account in which all of the funds of the partnership will be deposited. The partnership monies will be used solely for the business of the partnership. There may also be a reference to the effect that the monies invested prior to the formation of the partnership are to be held in a special account in trust as described in another section of the offering circular.

contracts and assignments thereof

There will be here set forth all agreements which have been and will be entered into in connection with the production of the plays, as well as agreements which are anticipated. It is stated that the producer will assign to the partnership all of the contracts entered into in connection with the play.

sources of partnership income

The prospectus will state that the partnership income will come from turning to account all rights in the play.

If there is a pre-production recording contract, all of the terms of such contract will be set forth.

expenses of conducting business

"Production expenses" and "running expenses" are defined. There is also attention called to the fact that running expenses in addition to certain stated items will also include any percentage of the net profits or of the gross receipts which are payable to an author, member of the cast, scenic designer, costume designer, director, choreographer, or any other person offering services for the play. It will also include the percentage of the gross receipts paid as the producer's fee, as well as the payment to the producer for the weekly cash office charge.

disposition of partnership income; return of contributions; profits and losses

The prospectus will here set forth the terms outlined in the limited partnership for the repayment to the investors of their contributions pro-rata after payment of all expenses and establishment of a cash reserve in a stated amount. There is also herein set forth the fact that losses are borne entirely by the limited partners in proportion to their respective contributions, until net profits have been earned, and after net profits have been earned the general partners and limited partners share losses in the same proportion that they are entitled to share in the net profits. There is also the statement contained in the limited partnership agreement that contributions and profits paid to the partners may have to be returned to the partnership if required.

net profits

It is here pointed out that the producer may enter into contracts providing for payment of shares of the net profits and the remaining net profits are then divided between the limited and general partners. It is not unusual to have to pay a percentage of the gross receipts or net profits to the star or director.

As of the date of the prospectus, there is set forth the specific percentage payments of gross weekly box office receipts and net profits which are deducted prior to computing the net profits payable to the partners.

effect of federal income taxes

The offering circular may state that in the opinion of counsel for the partnership, for Federal Income Tax purposes, the net profits are treated as ordinary income and any losses as ordinary losses deductible from ordinary income.

additional funds

The offering circular may state that the general partner, if additional funds are needed, may loan money to the partnership or borrow money from others for this purpose. Such loans may be repaid prior to the repayment of contributions to the limited partners. Also, union and theatre bonds and guarantees may be furnished instead of using partnership funds for this purpose, and the amount of such bonds and guarantees may also be repaid prior to repayment of the limited partners' contributions.

additional companies

If the limited partnership agreement contains provision for the partnership to produce other companies of the play, then these facts must be set forth. It may state that funds of the original company may be used for this purpose.

theatre tickets

A complete detailed list of everyone entitled to purchase house seats is set forth in this section of the offering circular.

control by general partner

It will here be stated that the general partner has complete control of the production and that he agrees to render such services as is customarily rendered by a theatrical producer. He may of course engage in other businesses, including other theatrical productions.

remuneration of general partner

There is here set forth the fee payable to the producer. It is not unusual for the producer's fee to be an amount ranging between one and two percent of the gross box office receipts.

reimbursement of general partner

There will be here set forth the amount which the general partner has laid out for the production for which he will be reimbursed after the partnership is formed.

interest of general partner in certain transactions

There is here set forth the fact that the general partner will furnish office facilities and what these will consist of, as well as a statement that he will be reimbursed by payment to him of a specified amount known as the cash office charge. If the Limited Partnership Agreement authorizes the partner to deal with the partnership or to function in any way so that his interests are adverse to the interests of the partnership, then these facts must be set forth.

abandonment of production

The general partner may abandon the production at any time prior to the New York opening for any reason whatsoever, and this fact is set forth in the offering circular.

the creative elements

The names and biographical credits of the author, composer, lyricist, director, choreographer and star is detailed as well as information about any other creative personnel who are signed for the production.

termination of partnership

There is here set forth details as to when the partnership will terminate and the fact that the partnership may continue after a limited partner dies with his executors or administrators having the same rights that he would have.

underwriting

Any facts concerning arrangements for underwriting all or any part of the investment must be set forth here in detail.

miscellaneous

The names of the attorneys for the production are set forth. It is also stated that there are no financial statements available since the company has not yet been formed, but upon formation of the company, the limited partners will be furnished with financial statements as required by law.

other s.e.c. information required

There is a large mass of information which must be accumulated and furnished to the S.E.C. for their purposes, which information does not appear in the prospectus. Much of this information is intended to inform the S.E.C. about the conditions surrounding offerings other than theatrical offerings and is particularly applicable to corporate offerors. For this reason many of the items are inapplicable to a limited partnership, and especially inapplicable to a theatrical production, so the information is furnished by stating that the items are inapplicable. The exact information required is carefully prepared by the attorney for the Production, and a detailed itemization is somewhat beyond the scope of this book.

The Attorney General

If the money is going to be raised only in the State of New York, then an S.E.C. filing may be avoided. In all cases, however, there must be a filing with the office of the Attorney General.

New York like all of the other states in the union, has what is known as "Blue Sky Laws." In addition to the New York Law, there are the New York State Theatre Financing Regulations which govern a theatrical financing. It may be necessary to file in other states in which money will be raised. The production attorney will make this decision as to where filings are necessary.

If a filing has been made with the S.E.C., then, the filing with the Attorney General is greatly simplified, since the Attorney General will accept the offering circular filed with the S.E.C. with one or two minor additions which will have been included at the time the S.E.C. filing is made.

If there is no S.E.C. filing and money will be raised solely in the State of New York, and, if the offering is for less than $100,000, the producer may file and use a prospectus (an offering circular) and a limited partnership agreement, or may choose to simply file and use a limited partnership agreement setting forth all of the terms of the agreement with the limited partners. If more than $100,000 is being raised, an offering circular must be filed and used. If it is possible to avoid the use of an offering circular, I usually recommend it, as the Attorney General's offering circular, like the S.E.C. form, must contain some provisions likely to discourage investment.

If the offering is to be made to less than 26 persons, then

it is possible to avoid filing with the Attorney General if each of the investors expressly waives in writing the right to have offering literature filed and the right to receive information that would be contained in such an offering circular.

CHAPTER 7

THE LEAGUE OF NEW YORK THEATRES

The Broadway Producer must deal with a number of different craft unions and associations. The Producers and Theatres Owners founded their own association on January 30, 1930, which is known as the League of New York Theatres, Inc. The League has offices at 226 West 47th Street in New York City. It is interesting to note that whether a person owns 1 theatre or 17 theatres and whether a person is the Producer of 1 show or 7 shows, he is entitled to only 1 membership in the League.

Purpose of the League

The objectives of the Association as stated in their bylaws are to conserve and promote the general welfare of the legitimate theatre and the common interests and welfare of theatre owners, lessees, or operators and producers of plays and to afford an organization which enables them to act for their common purpose and interest. The primary duty of the League is to act as bargaining representative for theatre owners and producers with the various craft unions and associations. Each contract is negotiated and entered into for a specified limited period. There are usually some changes, sometimes minor, when each contract is negotiated.

Dues

The Dues paid by Producers and Theatre Owners is $50. per week during each week that a show is running in a first class theatre whether it is in or out of New York City.

Collective Bargaining Agreements Negotiated

The League has negotiated and signed collective bargaining agreements with many associations and craft unions which can for our purposes be divided into three categories. There are the agreements between the Unions and the Theatre Owners or Lessees. There are another group of contracts between the Unions and the Producers. There are a third category of agreements which are entered into by the Unions with both the Theatre Owners or Lessees, and the Producers. Bear in mind that those contracts between the Theatre Owners and Unions are, of course, as important to the Producers as the contracts which the Producers make directly with the Unions, for these contracts directly affect the Producer.

agreements for theatre owners or lessees

The contracts negotiated by the League for the Theatre Owners or Lessees are with the following:

Theatrical Protective Union, Local No. 1, IATSE, which represents the basic house crew of a theatre covering the carpentry, electrical, property, and other related work including "taking in" and "taking out," handling, assembling, and dismantling all equipment used in the show. This would cover the Curtain Men, Sound Men, Fly Men, as well as the Carpenters, Electricians, Property Men, and the like.

Treasurers and Ticket Sellers Union, Local No. 751, which as the name implies covers Treasurers, Assistant Treasurers, and other box office personnel involved in ticket selling.

Legitimate Theatre Employees Union, Local No. B-183, which covers employment of Ushers, Directresses, Chief Ushers, Front Doormen, the Ticket Takers, and the Backstage Doormen.

Theatre, Amusement and Cultural Building Service Employees, Local No. 54, which covers building service employees such as Porters, Elevator Operators, Cleaners, and Matrons.

Local Union No. 30, International Union of Operating Engineers, affiliated with the AFL-CIO which covers the employees engaged in the operation and maintenance of heating boilers, heating systems, mechanical refrigerating systems, air circulation which is part of the mechanical refrigerating system, standpipes, and fire pumps.

Agreements for Producers

The contracts with the Producers negotiated by the League (with the exception of the United Scenic Artists, with which the League has no Bargaining Agreement) include the following:

Actors' Equity Association which covers Actors and Stage Managers.

Theatrical Wardrobe Attendants Union, Local No. 764, which covers the wardrobe crew consisting of Wadrobe Supervisors and Dressers.

The Society of Stage Directors and Choreographers, which as the name clearly states, covers Directors and Choreographers.

The Dramatists Guild Minimum Basic Production Contract previously discussed in detail is also negotiated by the League for the Producers.

The United Scenic Artists which covers Set Designers, Lighting Designers, and Costume Designers.

agreements for both theatre owners and producers

The contracts negotiated by the League which are entered into by both the Theatre Owners and the Producers (only under certain circumstances, however, will the Producer contract with the Musicians Union) are the following:

Association of Theatrical Press Agents and Managers, Union No. 18032, AFL-CIO, which as the name states covers Press Agents (which would be hired by the Producer or the Theatre Owner, but most usually just the Producer), Company Managers (which would be hired by the Producer), and House Managers (which would be hired by the Theatre).

Associated Musicians of Greater New York, Local No. 802, American Federation of Musicians, which as the name states covers the Musicians. A Theatre may contract with the Union for a guaranteed minimum number of Musicians in that Theatre in which case the Theatre guarantees payment of at least the number of Musicians contracted for. The number of Musicians required in a particular Theatre will vary depending upon whether the show is a Drama or Musical. The Contract is for the season (1 year) and each Theatre decides whether or not to enter into the Contract for the ensuing season. If the Theatre elects not to contract with the Union and a Dramatic Show without music goes into the House, no payments need be made to the Union. If, however, a Musical (or Dramatic which uses music) goes into a non-contracted House, then the rate of pay to the Musicians is much greater than if it were a Contracted House. Theatres without an annual Contract are during the Non-Contract Season sometimes referred to as "Penalty Houses." Whether or not a particular production needs Musicians in excess of the number contracted for, payment of the Musicians is usually shared by the Theatre and the Producer, and the basis of the sharing, as later discussed in detail under the section on Theatre License Agreements, is a subject of negotiation at the time the Lease or Theatre License Agreement is entered into.

Agreements Made with League

The older Agreements entered into by some of the Unions and Associations were entered with the League of New York Theatres Inc. and with the Shubert Theatrical Interests. The Shubert Theatrical Interests have since become members of the League and the later agreements are by the Association or Union with the League of New York Theatres, Inc. only.

Employer and Employee Also Sign Agreement—Term of Employment

The League has entered into a Bargaining Agreement with all the above listed Associations and Unions with the exception of the United Scenic Artists. Those with a Bargaining Agreement will still have a separate agreement which must be entered into between the Employee and the Employer. The Theatre generally hires employees under a 1 year Contract during a season which is usually, roughly, the period from Labor Day to Labor Day. A Producer will enter into an agreement with an employee for a particular production.

The Contracts entered into with the Theatres will be discussed separately from those entered into with the Producers and those entered with both the Producers and the Theatres.

Terms in Common

union sole bargaining agent

All of the Contracts have some things in common. For an example; all of the Agreements, with one exception, have language to the effect that the Producer (Producer is referred to as "Manager" or "Management" in many of these Agreements) recognizes the Union as the sole and exclusive bargaining agent for all employees who perform work under the jurisdiction of the Union. The one exception where there is not a recognition clause makes it quite implicit even though it is not specifically stated.

employee must join union—no strikes or lockout

All of the Agreements state in similar language that an employee doing the kind of work covered by the Union Contract must become a Union Member within a specified time, usually within 30 days after his employment. The contracts will almost always provide that there will be no strikes or walkouts, nor will there be any lockouts.

scope and jurisdiction

All Agreements have a clause setting forth the scope of the Agreement and the jurisdiction of the Union. Of course, the language differs with each Agreement since each Union or Association has a different jurisdiction, that is, some are applicable only to legitimate theatre while others cover revues, night clubs, ballet, etc., as well. The geographic jurisdiction varies also with the different Unions and Associations.

rates—pension and welfare

The Schedule of rate payments differ as do the hours of employment. With one exception there is a provision for welfare payments and/or pension payments in all of the Agreements. The only exception is the United Scenic Artists.

business agent may enter theatre

Some Contracts provide for a payment of dues (checkoff) by the Theatre and Producer directly to the Union. It is most usual to find a provision that the business agent of the Union (or other representative) may be admitted to the Theatre at all times for the purpose of verifying conditions.

grievance procedure and arbitration

All of the Contracts have a provision for grievance procedure and/or arbitration to settle any disputes. The contract dates vary from 1 year to 10 years. In several cases there is provision for vacation benefits to employees.

pension and welfare chart

The following chart will be helpful with respect to certain items contained in all contracts so that a comparison can be made.

CONTRACTS WITH THEATRE

	Local #1 Carpenters Electricians Property	Local #751 Treasurers & Ticket Sellers	Local B-183 Ushers Directresses Front & Back Doormen	Local #54 Building Service Employees Elevator Men Cleaners Matrons, Etc.	Local #30 Heat & Air Conditioning Maintenance ***
Contract Dates	Aug. 1, 1967 to July 31, 1970	Sept. 1, 1967 to Aug. 31, 1970	Sept. 3, 1968 to Sept. 7, 1971	Labor Day 1966 to Labor Day 1969	Dec. 21, 1966 to Dec. 21, 1969
Pensions*	4% gross earnings*	6% gross earnings*	3% gross earnings*	5% gross earnings*	$6.20 per employee per week*
Welfare	3% gross earnings			$109.02 per employee semi-annually**	$7.00 per employee per week
Vacation	4% gross performance salary & 1st 8 hours take-in	4% gross earnings	4% of weekly salary	30 weeks worked 1st year gets 1 week	2 week vacation if work 52 weeks in any year

* First paid out of money allocated from the 5% of gross NYC amusement tax no longer paid to the city or such greater amount as is so allocated to the Union.

** If insurance carrier rates increase, Employer will increase semi-annual payment to cover the increase.

*** ½ of 1% of payroll at straight time rates payable to an apprentice training fund.

CONTRACTS WITH PRODUCER

	Actors' Equity Association	Local #764 Wardrobe Supervisors & Dressers	Society of Stage Directors & Choreographers
Contract Dates	June 2, 1968 to June 1, 1971	Sep. 1, 1967 to Aug. 29, 1970	Aug. 13, 1962 to Aug. 12, 1972**
Pensions	3% of gross weekly payments*	5% of gross earnings*	–0– (may be reopened at next negotiations)
Welfare	120 day Blue Cross GHI Plan C, HIP or similar $3000 Life Ins.***	$1.50 per week for Blue Cross, HIP or GHI	———
Vacation	4% after 6 mos. of performances; up to $250.00 1 week per 6 mos. omit 2 consecutive weeks.	4% gross weekly salary	———

* First paid out of money allocated from the 5% of gross NYC amusement tax no longer paid to the city or such greater amount as is so allocated to the Union.

** Although contract is for 10 years, the Union agrees to waive negotiation of certain specified items for a period of 20 years.

*** Eligible only after Probationary Period. 6 mos. coverage less than 8 weeks employment; over 8 weeks but less than 6 mos. employment then coverage is for period of employment plus 6 weeks; over 6 mos. employment coverage is for period of employment plus 9 mos.

CONTRACTS WITH THEATRE AND WITH PRODUCER

	Association of Theatrical Press Agents and Managers Union No. 18032	Local #802 American Federation of Musicians
Contract Date	August 28, 1965 to August 30, 1969	September 6, 1966 to Labor Day 1969
Pensions	3% gross salary outside NYC and 1st 21 performances in NYC. 5% after 21st performance in NYC.*	5% gross payroll*
Welfare	$80. semi-annually per employee**	$1.70 per week per employee and $1.00 per week per employee for major medical insurance
Vacations	4% of gross weekly salary	1/25th of weekly salary paid to Union Vacation Fund***

* First paid out of money allocated from the 5% of gross NYC amusement tax no longer paid to the city or such greater amount as is so allocated to the Union.

** If cost of benefits purchased by contribution is increased, Employer will pay additional cost.

*** Union pays amount to Employee after each year with Employer or sooner if show closes or employment terminated.

CHAPTER 8

CONTRACTS WITH THE THEATRE

Hiring Personnel

In hiring the crew, a Producer ought to try to find a group that is compatible socially, as well as on a working basis. There are certain persons in the business who most usually work together. A certain electrician may work with a particular carpenter most of the time as a team, so a Producer would hire both together. This is desirable since it is to the advantage of a Production to have persons on the show who know the working habits of their fellow workers. Liking the people one works with is also most helpful, especially in Theatre when often times the work is under extreme pressure and in close quarters.

Theatrical Protective Union, Local #1, I.A.T.S.E.

Jurisdiction

As I have mentioned, this Union has jurisdiction over carpenters, electricians, property men and includes "taking in" and "taking out," handling, assembling, and dismantling of any and all equipment, property, chairs, seats, furniture, hardware, all electrical fixtures and appliances, staging, scenery, masking, unloading, loading of vehicles, and the like. The minimum basic house crew for each Theatre consists of a Head Carpenter, Head Electrician, Head Property Man, and Curtain Man, and in the Mark Hellinger and Winter Garden, the basic crew in addition includes an Assistant Electrician.

Term of Employment

Although the employment is for the term of the agreement with the Union the employee need not be paid during the period that the theatre is dark, subject to any other specific provisions of the contract.

Work Week

The work week commences on Sunday and ends with the following Saturday night's performance. All men work on a weekly salary basis with a few minor exceptions which are specifically set forth in the Agreement.

Wage Rates

The weekly payments are as follows:

	July 28, 1968– Aug. 2, 1969	Aug. 3, 1969– Aug. 1, 1970
(a) Heads of Department	$199.00	$204.00
(b) Assistants	176.00	180.00
(c) Flyman and Front Light Men	165.00	170.00
(d) Portable Board Operators, Public Address Men, Keymen, Soundmen, House or Traveler Curtain Men, Flying, Rigging, Traps, Turntable or Winchmen	153.00	156.00
(e) All other men	136.00	156.00

Pro-rata performance rates of pay:

(a) Heads of Departments	$ 24.90	$ 25.50
(b) Assistants	22.00	22.50
(c) Flyman and Front Light Men	20.60	21:25
(d) Portable Board Operators, Public Address Men, Keymen, Soundmen, House or Traveler Curtain Men, Flying, Rigging, Traps, Turntable or Winchmen	19.10	19.50
(e) All other men	17.00	19.50

Hourly Rates of Pay:

(a) Heads of Department		
Mon. to Sat.	$ 6.85	$ 7.15
Sun. & Hol.	7.35	7.65
(b) Assistants		
Mon. to Sat.	6.70	5.90
Sun. & Hol.	6.70	6.90
(c) Flyman and Front Light Men		
Mon. to Sat.	5.20	5.40
Sun. & Hol.	6.20	6.40
(d) Portable Board Operators, Public Address Men, Keymen, Soundmen, House or Traveler Curtain Men, Flying, Rigging, Traps, Turntable or Winchmen		
Mon. to Sat.	$ 4.65	$ 4.85
Sun. & Hol.	5.65	5.85
(e) All other men		
Mon. to Sat.	4.65	4.85
Sun. & Hol.	5.65	5.85

Key Men

Whenever the term "Key Men" is used, it means those men who perform cues in front of an audience in a black-out or otherwise, or who operate equipment that moves in front of an audience in a black-out or otherwise. After August 31, 1969, the term "Key Men" will be meaningless since as can be noted in the wage schedule, after that time, there will be no distinction made between "Key Men" and other men with respect to wages.

Take-In and Take-Out

There are detailed terms covering the take-in and put-on of an attraction as well as the take-out of an attraction. The take-in provisions include for example: the fact that all men must be called for not less than a minimum call of 8 hours on a take-in and put-on of a show during the first day, and all calls after that must be for not less than a minimum of 6 hours. The men must receive 1 hour off for meals between 12 noon and 1 pm; between 6 pm and 7 pm; between midnight and 1 am; and between 6 am and 7 am; or be paid double the hourly rate for such hours.

Regular Work Week Hours

The contract states that during the regular attraction, the regular work week for Heads of Departments and Assistants consists of 8 performances, 6 evening performances occuring during the hours of 7:30 pm to 11:30 pm, Monday through Saturday evenings, plus 2 matinee performances occuring during the hours from 1:30 pm to 5:30 pm on Wednesdays and Saturdays. The hours are slightly less for other persons. The Heads of Departments must work as well as direct the Department. A Carpenter cannot operate the curtain but may assist the Curtain Man in one scene shows.

Minimum Hours and Repertory

All calls unless otherwise specifically provided for in the contract shall be a minimum of 4 hours duration, and there is provision that repertory productions must negotiate with the Union on the terms applicable to them.

Extra Performances and Sign Work

The Agreement contains specific provision for 9 or more performances per week and seventh day performances, as well as regular Sunday, special Sunday, Holiday performances, and Midnight performances. It is also provided that the men must be paid a full weekly salary even if an attraction operates on a fixed policy of less than 8 performances per week. There are special provisions covering work on the theatre signs.

Vacation and Temporary Closings

Men on vacation must be replaced by the Union during their vacation. The men must be paid one-half of their regular salary during a period of voluntary closing, which is considered the interuption of a show in order to permit a Star a leave of absence, or for some other similar reason.

Fire Proofing and Inspections

There are specific provisions that the respective Head of a Department must be employed on at least a 4 hour call for fire-proofing of scenery, drops, props, equipment, or material; that the 3 Heads of Departments and the Curtain Man must likewise be employed on a similar call for annual fire inspection; and that the Head Electrician will be given a 4 hour call to obtain or renew the standpipe license or permit for the Theatre.

Discharge for Cause — Severance Pay

Except in the case of discharge for drunkeness, dishonesty,

or incompetence, Heads of Departments and Assistants employed for at least 1 year are entitled to severance pay in the event of termination of their employment. They are entitled to 1 weeks pay at the rate being received at the time of termination for each year of service, with a maximum of 5 weeks pay.

Rehearsals and Construction Work

There are detailed provisions concerning rehearsals at Rehearsal Halls and Theatres as well as detailed terms concerning closing performances. The rates of pay for theatre rehabilitation and construction work is set forth in detail. This includes work in the pit, platforms, stage work, flooring, rigging, loading and unloading of cars, etc.

Dark Houses & Safe Conditions & Photos

The Agreement also covers work in dark houses and the reduction of manpower as a result. There are provisions that the working conditions will be safe. Specific provision is also made for the taking of all commercial pictures.

Treasurers and Ticket Sellers Union, Local #751

Jurisdiction

As the name implies, this Union governs the hiring of Treasurers and Ticket Sellers within the five Boroughs of the City of New York. The League members must negotiate special terms, wages, and hours for Theatres outside this area.

Wage Rates

The wage scale provided in the agreement is as follows:

	Sept. 1, 1967 to Aug. 31, 1969	Sept. 1, 1969 to Aug. 31, 1970
TREASURERS, for week of six (6) days (Monday to Saturday inclusive) not less than	$205.00	$220.00
ASSISTANT TREASURERS, for week of six (6) days (Monday to Saturday inclusive) not less than	$175.00	$185.00

SUNDAYS, Box Office is to be open from 12:00 Noon to 10.00 P.M. All members of the Box Office staff shall receive, in addition to their weekly salary, not less than one-quarter (1/4) of weekly salary for two performances or not less than one-sixth (1/6) of weekly salary for one performance, without any offset or deduction for taking a substitute day off during the week.

MIDNIGHT PERFORMANCES, not less than one-sixth (1/6) of weekly salary.

The above scales provide for up to 4 matinees from Monday through Saturday. One-eighth (1/8) extra shall be paid for any matinees in excess of four during that period.

Advance Sale — Extra Attractions
Other than Current Attraction

TREASURERS, when performance given on Sunday (regardless whether tickets sold in advance or not) for one performance, not less than $40.00
for two performances, not less than 55.00

ASSISTANT TREASURERS,
when performance given on Sunday (regardless whether tickets sold in advance or not) for one performances, not less than 32.50
for two performances,
not less than 45.00

Advance Sale and Benefits

For handling the advance sale of a current attraction on weekdays and for a weekday matinee, the salary may not be less than one-sixth of the weekly wage for each day. The parties must also be paid a salary, pro-rated at the weekly rate, for advance sale and for benefit performances during a period that the Theatre is normally dark.

Refunds

If more than $400. has to be refunded, the Treasurer and Assistant Treasurer must be retained for that purpose and must be paid at the rate of one-sixth of the weekly salary for each day, but in no event longer than 1 week unless the Employer decides to retain the staff. After the amount of the refund is reduced to less than $400., further refunds may be handled without additional compensation at any box office which is staffed by members of the Union. If the Theatre has a following attraction, then the Treasurer and Assistant Treasurer must make refunds with no extra compensation to them, providing that the continuity of employment is not interrupted.

Contract for Season

A standard individual Contract is entered into with each Employee which provides the Theatre at which he is employed, and the period of employment, which may not be less than a season, except in cases of extra box office help. There is also an exception in that the employment may be for less than a season if the lease of the Employer terminates before the expiration of the season and/or the Employer loses control of the Theatre. In such event the Contract of employment is for that portion of the season that the Employer is in control of the Theatre. The Employer must designate the box office staff not later than August 1 of each year that the Theatre is open, and if the Theatre is dark, he must designate the box office no later than September 1, regardless of when the Theatre thereafter opens. Although the hiring is seasonal, even during the season unless otherwise specifically provided in the contract, the employee is not paid if the Theatre is closed.

Season, Box Office Staff, Subscription, and Benefits

"Season" as it is used in the Contract means such time as the theatre is open from September 1 to August 31 the following year. The Box Office Staff of each Theatre consists of a Box Office Treasurer and at least two Assistants, except that during a refund week it consists of those staff members under contract. There is negotiation procedure outlined in the Agreement for determining whether Theatres seating over 1,000 should be required to employ yet another Assistant Treasurer at Assistant's salary. No person other than the Treasurer or his Assistants may handle ticket sales to the public or a broker. Extra help may be engaged to handle subscriptions and benefits at places other than in the box office. All reservations at the Theatre must be handled by Employees covered by this Agreement. The Employer or his Representative, the Producer or his Representative, the Treasurer or his Assistant Treasurer and Ticket Sellers are the only ones permitted in the box office.

Minimum Hours

Treasurers and Assistant Treasurers must be called to service at least one-half week prior to opening of the Play and 1 day must be added to the one-half week for each paid preview in advance of the public opening. The Treasurer outlines the hours of Box Office Employees which may not exceed 8 hours in any one calendar day, of which 1 hour must be a meal period. Work for advance sales, less than a full week is pro-rated. Time and a half is payable for certain holidays as set forth in the Agreement, and the Employees receive an additional one-sixth of their weekly salary for "settlement," at the end of a run.

Bonding of Treasurers and Assistants

Box Office Treasurers and Assistants must be bonded and the bond is paid for by the Employer. The money and tickets for which the Treasurer and his Assistants are responsible can be handled only by them.

Termination of Employment

Either party, by written notice, may terminate the Contract of a Box Office Employee during the first week of employment. This, however, may not be done where that Box Office Employee was employed for the previous season for the same Employer and did not receive notice of termination before May 31; he is automatically reengaged for the following season.

Transfer of Theatres and Closing Notice

House Staff Employees may be transferred from one Theatre to another during the season, providing that the continuity of the operation is designated in the individual Contract of Employment. If the attraction has run more than 4 weeks, then closing notice given by the Employer to the Box Office Employees before the closing of the box office on Monday night shall be effective to constitute 1 weeks notice of closing as of the following Saturday night. If the Employer fails to give notice he must pay 1 weeks compensation in lieu thereof. If the attraction has run 4 weeks or less, then notice of closing is not necessary. However, if the attraction closes during a calendar week, the box office staff is entitled to a full week's compensation.

Discharge for Cause

An Employee may be summarily dismissed for cause without prior notice. Cause means intoxication on duty, dishonesty in the discharge of duty, disorderly conduct in the performance of duty, or inability to secure a bond. There is provision in the Contract for review of a summary dismissal.

Notice if Theatre Sold

If the theatre is sold, the Box Office Employees' employment may be terminated on 2 weeks notice or 2 weeks pay in lieu of the notice.

Miscellaneous and Riot, Fire, Strikes, etc.

There are specific provisions in the Contract for negotiations in the event that the Theatre is leased for less than a year by the same Employer or by a different Employer for other than legitimate theatre purposes. Employees are not paid during the period that a production is closed because of fire, accident, strikes, riots, act of God, the illness of the Star or a principal featured performer, or action of a public enemy which could not be reasonably anticipated or prevented.

Ticket Cannot Be Sold for More Than Stated Price

The Contract specifically states that neither the Employer nor the Employee may accept any charge or fee in excess of the amount designated on the ticket as the ticket price.

Legitimate Theatre Employees' Union, Local #B-183

Jurisdiction

This Union agreement controls the hiring of Ushers, Front Doormen (Ticket Takers), Directresses, Chief Ushers, and Back Stage Doormen. The Union shop provision is to the effect that the Union will supply the Employer with applicants in the operation of "legitimate" Theatre or Theatres and Vaudville or Motion Picture Theatre or Theatres having a "reserved seat" policy, as distinguished from a "grind" policy, in the City of Greater New York. If the Union cannot supply help, then the Employer may engage help in the open market.

Term of Employment

If an employee is retained for 4 weeks the employee may not be replaced before the following Labor Day except for just cause. If there is a dispute as to what constitutes just cause which the theatre and the local union cannot settle, then the League of New York Theatres and the general office of I.A.T.S.E. (the parent Union) settle the matter.

Prior employees must be recalled for the following season unless they are given notice of termination at least 30 days before Labor Day.

Although the hiring is for the season, the employee need not be paid during a period when the theatre is closed unless otherwise specifically provided in the contract.

Wage Rates

The weekly and daily wage rates are as follows:

	1st Year	2nd Year	3rd Year
Ushers	$46.64 (5.83)	$49.28 (6.16)	$51.92 (6.49)
Directresses	50.09 (6.26)	52.93 (6.62)	55.77 (6.98)
Chief Ushers	57.50 (7.19)	60.75 (7.59)	64.00 (8.00)
Front Ticket-Takers	77.17 (9.65)	80.84 (10.10)	84.51 (10.56)
2nd Balcony Ticket-Takers	54.33 (6.79)	56.91 (7.12)	59.49 (7.44)
Backstage Doormen	80.34	84.18	88.02

Eight Performance Week

The scale of employment is based on an 8 performance week (except Back Stage Doormen) and the Employees substituting for Regular Employees are paid a proportionate share of a week's work. Performances in excess of 8 are at the rate of time and a half, except where a show opens with a policy in excess of 8 performances.

Back Stage Doormen Week

Back Stage Doormen's work week is 6 days but not exceeding 40 hours in a week. Over 40 hours per week is paid at the rate of time and a half with a minimum overtime call of 7 hours. Back Stage Doormen receive no extra compensation for extra performances.

Overtime (Other Than Back Stage Doormen)

Extra time required for Ushers, Chief Ushers, Directresses, or Tickets Takers in excess of the regular hours is paid at the hourly rate, with a minimum of 1 hour. All midnight performances are paid at the rate of time and a half. For work performed on Sunday, each employee is paid fifty cents extra.

Program Insertions and Cancelled Performances

Employees are paid $2. extra per week whenever they insert printed material (other than cast changes or show publicity) in the Theatre Programs. Employees must be notified at the prior performance in the event of a cancellation, or they must be compensated for the performance.

Time Employees May Leave Theatre

With the exception of opening night, one-half of the Employees (excluding Back Stage Doormen) are permitted to leave work 20 minutes after the curtain goes up. If a Theatre has only one Ticket Taker, this does not apply to him.

Special Uniforms

If the Producer requires that an Employee wear any special uniform, and black dresses by ushers, then such apparel must be furnished by the Producer. While collars for Ushers must also be furnished by, and laundered at the expense of, the Producer.

Notice of Discharge

An Employee on a weekly salary must be given 2 weeks notice in writing of discharge and Employees wishing to terminate must do the same. If the Theatre closes or the policy of the Theatre changes then only 1 week notice is required. If an attraction closes after having run less than 4 weeks, no notice is necessary, nor is it necessary for an employee discharged for drunkeness or dishonesty.

Theatre, Amusement and Cultural Building Service Employees, Local # 54

Jurisdiction

This Agreement covers Porters, Roundsmen, Elevator Operator, Cleaners, and Matrons.

Wage Rates

The minimum weekly wages are as follows:

Head Porter (If the theatre has only one porter, he shall be considered as Head Porter) shall receive:
A minimum weekly wage of $97.00 for the period commencing Labor Day 1968.

Porters shall receive:
A minimum weekly wage of $89.50 for the period commencing Labor Day 1968.

Roundsmen shall receive:
A minimum weekly wage of $89.50 for the period commencing Labor Day 1968.

Elevator Operators shall receive:
A minimum weekly wage of $89.50 for the period commencing Labor Day 1968.

Head Cleaners shall receive:
A minimum weekly wage of $67.50 for the period commencing Labor Day 1968.

Cleaning Women shall receive:
A minimum weekly wage of $60.00 for the period commencing Labor Day 1968.

Matrons shall receive:
A minimum weekly wage of $59.00 for the period commencing Labor Day 1968.

Extra Matinees – Pick-up for Head Cleaner:
commencing Labor Day 1968 – $3.75 per pick-up.

Extra Matinees – Pick-up for Cleaning Women:
commencing Labor Day 1968 – $3.10 per pick-up.

Basic Crew

The Basic Crew employed in a Theatre is the same number of employees employed in the Theatre on the first day of August, 1955, or if closed on that date, then the last open date before then. New theatres opened since then have a Basic Crew consisting of the number of employees used on the opening of the Theatre.

Discharge for Cause

An Employee may not be discharged except for intoxication while on duty or an act of dishonesty. The Contract contains provision for investigation and review of a discharge.

Seasonal Employment

Employment in a theatre is on a seasonal basis and an Employee is employed for a period from Labor Day to Labor Day of each year. The Employer must give written notice to an Employee and to the Union prior to August 1 in the event that the Employee is not engaged for the ensuing year.

Although the hiring is seasonal subject to any other specific contract provisions, the Employee need not be paid during a period when the theatre is dark.

Sunday Performances

The entire crew (normal complement of workers) must be employed in the event of a Sunday performance or performances and each Employee receives $1. in addition to his regular day's pay. If the Sunday is the seventh consecutive day of work then the Employee receives time and a half for the Sunday work in addition to the payment of $1. per performance. The $1. additional is also provided for certain holidays which are set forth in the Contract.

Hours of Work

standard week & overtime

Porters work a standard 40 hour week consisting of 6 days not exceeding 8 hours per day. Overtime for work in excess of 8 hours per day, or 40 hours per week, is at the rate of one and one-half the regular straight time hourly rate. If a porter is required to work in excess of 3 evening performances a week, then he must be paid time and a half for all hours worked during such performances. The regular Head Porter of the House must be at the Theatre when the box office is open to the public, even though the House is not in operation.

cleaning women's standard week and overtime

Cleaning Women work a standard week of 26 hours consisting of 6 days not exceeding 4 hours each day performed between the hours of 7 am and 1 pm with 1 additional hour each matinee day at the conclusion of the matinee performance. The overtime rate for Cleaning Women is one and a half the regular rate and is paid after 4 hours of work per day, or after 6 days per week or after 24 hours per week, except when there are matinee pick-ups, in which event overtime commences during that week after 26 hours.

matrons' standard work and overtime

Matrons' standard work week consists of 8 performances per week within a 6 day period. The maximum time of each performance is 4 hours. All time worked in excess of 8 performances per week or 4 hours per performance is considered overtime and is paid at the rate of time and a half.

Uniforms and Equipment Supplied

The uniforms, work clothes, and equipment required to be worn or used by the employees is supplied and maintained by the employer.

Local Union #30 of the International Union of Operating Engineers

Jurisdiction

Local # 30 is the Collective Bargaining Agent for Employees engaged in the operation and maintenance of the heating and air conditioning systems in the theatres.

Work Week

The work week consists of 5 straight time days and a sixth day at the rate of time and a half. All work in excess of 8 hours in any day or in excess of 40 hours during a week is at the rate of time and one half.

Wage Rates

The minimum wages of the Employees covered by this Agreement for the period from December 21, 1968 until December 21, 1969 is an hourly rate of $3.4808 ($3.4808 times 40 = $139.23) plus 8 hours for the sixth day at time and a half ($3.4808 times 12 = $41.77) making a total of $181.00 per week.

Holidays and Vacations

The Employer agrees that Employees will be paid for New

Year's Day, Independence Day, Labor Day, Thanksgiving Day, and Christmas Day. Employees required to work on a holiday must be provided with 8 hours work at double the regular rate, plus time and one half for everything in excess of 8 hours. The Employer further agrees that a replacement will be hired to replace each man while he is on vacation.

Season

Employees are employed on a seasonal basis from October 15 (unless the Theatre opens later) to April 15 which is the guaranteed employment period. An operator must also be hired during the air conditioning season to operate the equipment.

CHAPTER 9

CONTRACTS WITH THE PRODUCERS

Actors' Equity Association

Casting

Uusually the Stage Manager and the Casting Director (if one is hired) take charge of the casting, so that the Director, Author, and Producer are insulated from seeing persons totally impossible for the parts. The good possibilities are brought back for the Director, Author, and Producer to see and a decision is then made. The decision, as it should be, is largely the Director's, but all cast must be approved by the Author (and Composer and Lyricist if it is a Musical) and the Producer who does the hiring.

In most instances the negotiations for the Cast are carried on by the General Manager for the Production. Equity requires that there be an open call at which any Equity member so desiring may audition for any part.

Star and Director

Probably the most that a Star will be paid is $10,000. per week. A Star might also get a smaller amount as payment against a percentage of the gross box office receipts and maybe also a percentage of the net profits, so that the Star on good weeks could end up getting paid something more than the flat $10,000. per week.

If a Director or Star gets a percentage of the net profits, although it is a share of the "net" profits, it nevertheless comes off of the top and is considered an operating expense. It is thus not payable from just the Producer's share of the profits, but from the profits before they are shared by the Investors and Producer.

Three Standard Contracts

The Actors' Equity Association Contract covers the hiring of the Cast and Stage Managers. There are three basic contracts: (1) a Standard Minimum Contract for Principal Actors, (2) a Standard Minimum Contract for Chorus, and (3) a Standard Run of the Play contract. The minimum contract for Principals and the minimum contract for the Chorus are almost identical, with a few minor differences.

Contracts Include Agreement with League and Equity Rules

The Actors' Equity Contracts are very simple one page documents. The Standard Minimum Contracts are on 8½ by 11 inch paper and the Run of the Play Contract is 8½ x 13 inches. The type is small but easily readable. However, each of these Agreements states on it that all of the provisions contained in the basic agreement entered into between Equity and the League, and the Equity Rules governing employment, is part of the Agreement as if it were set forth at length. The Equity Rules governing employment are set forth in a small pamphlet of 80 pages which has seven and one half mimeographed pages of changes which became effective June 2, 1968, which will be incorporated into the Rules. The Rules are very detailed and set forth most of the provisions governing the employment of an Actor.

Deputies

One of the members of the cast is elected as the deputy to represent the Equity members in dealing with the Producer in connection with any breach of the Agreement or other employment terms. If a Chorus is employed, then there is a deputy for Chorus singers and deputy for Chorus dancers.

Minimum Salaries

The minimum salaries which became effective June 2, 1968, are as follows:

Actors	*Point of Origin*		*Road*	
1968	$145.00	Plus Cost-	$195.00	Plus Cost-
1969	$150.00	of-Living	$200.00	of-Living
1970	$155.00	Increase	$205.00	Increase

Rehearsal experise money is the amount of the minimum salary plus the cost of living increase, no matter what the actors' contract salary is.

Stage Manager — Dramatic

1968	$242.45	Plus Cost-	$292.45	Plus Cost-
1969	$247.45	of-Living	$297.45	of-Living
1970	$252.45	Increase	$302.45	Increase

Stage Manager — Musical

1968	$293.05	Plus Cost-	$343.05	Plus Cost-
1969	$208.05	of-Living	$348.05	of-Living
1970	$303.05	Increase	$353.05	Increase

1st Assistant Stage Manager — Dramatic

1968	$181.70	Plus Cost-	$231.70	Plus Cost-
1969	$186.70	of-Living	$236.70	of-Living
1970	$191.70	Increase	$241.70	Increase

1st Assistant Stage Manager — Musical

1968	$212.10	Plus Cost-	$262.10	Plus Cost-
1969	$217.10	of-Living	$267.10	of-Living
1970	$222.10	Increase	$272.10	Increase

Origin Point

The Contract has designations for either New York, Los Angeles, or Chicago as the points of origin for a show. In the case of any other city, Equity has the right to designate the point of origin. While performing in the City designated as the point of origin, New York conditions apply. In all other cities, road conditions apply. The point of origin remains the same after it is designated.

Cost of Living Increase

The cost-of-living increase is computed by multiplying the U.S. Government Cost of Living Index by the minimum salary. The Index in March of 1968 was 3.9% so the Actor's minimum of $145.00 multiplied by 3.9% equals the minimum with the cost of living increase, in the amount of $150.65. The minimum will be adjusted again in March, 1969, effective as of June, 1969, and each year thereafter when the new Index figure is available.

For the year from June, 1968, to the end of May, 1969, the salaries including the cost of living increase are as follows:

	Point of Origin	Road
Actors	$150.65	$202.60
Stage Manager		
Dramatic	$251.90	$303.85
Musical	$304.50	$356.45
1st Assist. Stage Manager	$188.80	$240.75
Dramatic	$188.80	$240.75
Musical	$220.35	$272.30

Rehearsal Payments

The Producer agrees to pay rehearsal expense money for a

period of 4 weeks for a Dramatic Production and for 5 weeks for a Musical Production and Revue.

If the Producer wishes to extend a rehearsal period he may do so by paying for each of the first 3 days, one-sixth of the weekly rehearsal expense money amount; for the next 7 days at the New York or road company minimum, whichever is applicable; and after 10 days, rehearsal payments are at the full contracted salary. If the Chorus is used in a dramatic production, the rehearsal period is limited to 4 weeks plus the 10 days extension provided.

Certain Extra Payments for Chorus

Dance Captains must be paid not less than an additional $50. per week. If a member of the chorus is required to play a part, speak lines, sing a song, or do a dance that is individual in its character and which is understudied, then such person must be paid an additional $7.50 per week. If such assignment is not understudied, then the person will be paid not less than $5. per week in addition.

Televising, Recording, and Motion Pictures

There are detailed provisions set forth in the Rules for television, recordings, and motion pictures. It is provided that each Actor engaged in a television, motion picture, or sound recording of a Play, in full or in part, must be paid a minimum of 1 weeks salary for each day or part of a day employed on such production.

If 1 weeks salary for each day or part thereof is less than the minimum rate required by the American Federation of Television and Radio Artists, or by the Screen Actors Guild, then the Actor must receive not less than the AFTRA or SAG minimum. If an Actor is employed to make a television spot commercial of 1 minute or less duration using material from the Play, then Equity will waive the 1 week payment required, however; the Actor must receive no less than the AFTRA or SAG minimum for such work. Closed circuit or paid television is not covered by the Rules and the Producer agrees that there will be none, without prior negotiations and agreement with Equity as to the payments and working conditions. The Producer may make a non-commercial filming or recording (to be used in the Production) using Chorus only by paying one half the weekly salary for each day or part thereof. The foregoing (both commercial and non-commercial) is applicable whether the televising, recording, or filming is done at the Theatre or elsewhere.

Show Album

On the Show Album the Producer must use the Actor who sings or verbalizes the part in the show. A Producer must give the Actor at least 1 weeks notice of the making of a recording. A day's recording session is limited to 8 out of 9 hours with a 1 hour break after no more than 5 hours, and must be completed not later than 6:30 P.M. when it occurs on a day of performance. The Stage Manager must be used for the recording session.

Broadcast of Part of a Production

If the Producer gives permission for a broadcast of any part of a production, the Producer must pay a minimum of one eighth of a week's salary to each actor for any day or part thereof that the Actor is engaged in the broadcast or in rehearsing for the broadcast, or the American Federation of Television and Radio Artists minimum for such broadcast, whichever is greater.

Number of Performances

8 performances constitute a week work and may be given

only during a period of 6 out of 7 consecutive days except for road tours in those cities where Sunday performances have customarily been given as of May 1, 1924. Commencing June 1, 1970, a week's work will consist of 8 performances in no more than 6 days, even on road tours, the only exception being Las Vegas where performances may be given 7 nights a week. The Actors must be paid a week's compensation even if less than 8 performances are given in any week and they must be paid a sum equal to one-eighth of the weekly compensation for each performance in excess of 8 during each week. If admission is charged (except bona fide benefits endorsed by the Theatre Authority or Equity) then they are counted and considered as performances for which the Actor is to be paid.

If more than 2 performances are given or begun in any 1 day, the third performance is paid for as an extra performance even though the total number of performances given during that week is 8 or less. Any performance begun before 2 P.M. and/or after 11:00 P.M. is counted as an extra performance and is paid for at the rate of two-eighths of the Actors' weekly salary. If Sunday performances are lawful, then an Actor may perform on Sunday provided that he is given at least 1 full day of rest in each calendar week free of rehearsals and performances and providing further that the Actor is paid two-eighths (one-eighth in New York City) of his contractual salary for each and every performance given by him on Sunday. A Sunday performance counts as 1 performance in computing the number of performances during a week, even though extra payment may be required. Sunday rehearsals count as part of the rehearsal period.

Performances Lost

There is specific provision in the Contract for the payment of Actors in the event of performances lost as a result of an act of God, riot, public enemy, fire, accident, etc.

Rehearsal Hours and Recesses

during rehearsal period and prior to NY or road tour opening

During the rehearsal period there must be a recess of one and a half hours after each 5 consecutive hours of rehearsal. The Chorus and Principals working with Chorus must be given a 5 minute break during each hour.

During each calendar week of rehearsal period, the Actors must be given 1 day off, except during the last 7 days prior to the first public performance when none is required.

Rehearsal hours prior to the New York or road tour opening must not exceed 7 out of 8 and a half consecutive hours a day which includes the 1 and a half hour recess above referred to.

final week of rehersals prior to 1st public performance

The maximum rehearsal time above described does not apply during the final week of rehearsals prior to the first public performance. During that week the rehearsals must not exceed 10 out of 12 consecutive hours a day including recesses, except for the final day before opening. If the company does not rehearse for the full week before opening on the 12 consecutive hour basis, then when it returns to New York it may use that number of unexpended days of the week prior to the New York opening on a 12 consecutive hour basis, provided that there is still unexpired rehearsal time.

after opening—recesses

After opening of the Play, there must be a 1 and a half hour recess after any period of 5 consecutive hours of performances and/or rehearsals combined. The break must be for at least 1 and a half hours including the one half hour call before curtain and if the break is for less than 1 and a half hours excluding the one half hour call, then the Producer must furnish the actors with food if requested.

after 1st performance but prior to NY opening — maximum hours

After the first public performance outside New York City and before the New York opening, rehearsals including recesses and performances must not exceed 12 hours on any 1 day while the company is out of town. If there is unused rehearsal time there is provision, with certain limitations, for using it upon the return to New York.

during pre-Broadway tour — day off every three weeks

During the pre-Broadway tour, the company must receive 1 calendar day off during each 3 weeks, in addition to the regular rest period of 12 hours at the end of the day (10 hours on days before matinee days, for Principal Actors). The rest period preceding the call on the day of the first paid public performance must be no less than 9 hours.

after NY opening—½ hour call

After the official New York opening in New York City, the company may not be called sooner than the one half hour call on the day following the scheduled day of rest, except in emergencies or in case of a replacement of a Star or major Featured Principal on the day of his first performance in the part.

after NY or road tour opening—chorus hourly limit

After the New York or road tour opening. Chorus rehearsals, except those necessary for emergency cast replacements, are limited to 8 hours weekly for routine rehearsals, or 12 hours weekly for understudy rehearsals or new material or numbers. In no event can the total rehearsals for the week exceed 12 hours unless overtime is paid.

after NY or road tour opening—principals' hourly limit

After the New York or road tour opening, Principal Actors' rehearsals, except rehearsals necessary for emergencies and cast replacements, are limited to 12 hours weekly; however, during the first 2 weeks after the New York or road tour opening and for emergencies or in cast replacements, rehearsals may be 5 hours per day (2 hours on matinee days).

overtime pay for rehearsals

If the Actors rehearse more than the hours stipulated, they must be paid an additional $7.50 per hour, or part thereof.

overtime pay for travel

Overtime pay for travel is $5. per hour. On a day of travel, rehearsal and travel time combined must not exceed 10 hours.

if no pre-Broadway—hourly limits after NY opening

If a show is scheduled to open without a pre-Broadway tour, but gives preview performances prior to the official opening in New York, then for a period of up to 2 consecutive weeks after the first public performance, rehearsals and performances may not exceed 10 out of 12 consecutive hours each day.

Term of Employment and Notice

The Standard Minimum Contract and the Run of the Play Contract both provide that an Actor must be guaranteed no less than 2 weeks consecutive salary plus any rehearsal expense money due. In the Standard Minimum Contract there is a probationary period during which the Actor may be dismissed, unless the Contract is signed seven or more days before the first day of rehearsal. For a Chorus member the probationary period is 3 days, and for a Principal Actor it is 5 days. Notice given on the fourth or fifth day to a Principal or to a Chorus member on the second or third day must be in writing and delivered personally and not by mail or telegram.

Guarantees—Minimum and Run of Play Contracts

The Standard Minimum Contract for Principals and Chorus both provide that the Actor will be paid a minimum of 2 weeks salary. This salary must be paid after the date of the first public performance or the opening date specified in the contract whichever first occurs.

The Standard Run of the Play Contract is distinguished from the Standard Minimum Contract in that under the Run of the Play Contract, the Actor is guaranteed a minimum of 2 weeks employment during each theatrical season. At the time the contract is entered into the Producer and Actor agree that he will be employed (if the show runs, of course) during a certain number of seasons, and the Contract sets forth the number of seasons. If the Contract is for more than 1 season, then the Producer guarantees that the

Actor will be paid a minimum of 2 weeks employment for each season contracted, unless notice is given as provided in the Contract. The notice provided for must be delivered to the Actor and to Equity not later than 5 weeks after the first public performance in New York City (which date can not be later than 15 weeks after the opening performance) or 5 weeks after the opening of the road tour (if the Contract is for a road tour) and the notice must state that the Producer does not intend to present the Play during any season following the current season. If the notice is delivered, together with payment for all of the seasons contracted after the second season, then the Producer does not have to pay the guarantee for the second season. The notice, however, must be given simultaneously to all Actors in the cast holding Run of The Play Contracts for more than 1 season or year.

If a Play continues its run, an Actor signed to a Run of the Play Contract must be paid his salary for every week during the season (s) that he is signed for, but in no event for less than 2 weeks. This is so even if the actor is replaced in the part.

The Producer and Actor may agree to a layoff during the months of July and August providing that the Producer gives at least 4 weeks written notice of such layoff to the Actor and designates a reopening date not later than September 1, or 14 days after the layoff, and also guarantees the Actor at least 2 weeks employment upon the reopening.

The advantage of a Run of the Play Contract is obvious in that the Producer can know for certain that an Actor will be with him if it is an extended run. On the other hand, the Actor can know that he will be paid for each week of the season he is signed for if the Play runs. The price that the Producer must pay is the guarantee for the minimum number of weeks in each season. If, for an example, a Producer wanted to make certain that a particular performer would be with the show if it ran for 5 years, then, if the show closed without the notice (above discussed) having been given to the Actor, then he must receive a minimum of 2 weeks salary for each of the 5 years or a minimum of 10 weeks salary. If the show closes after the notice has been given and the payment is made with the notice, the Producer could save the guarantee for the second year and would only be obligated to pay the total of 8 weeks salary; that is, 2 weeks for the first year and for each of the third, fourth, and fifth years.

It should be noted that an Actor signed on a Run of the Play Contract is entitled to be paid for the run of the Play unless his employment is terminated in accordance with some provision of the Contract.

Converting Standard Contract of Principal Actor to Run of the Play

It is possible to sign a Principal Actor to a Standard Minimum Contract and convert the contract to a Run of the Play Contract.

increased salary and written notice

If the Actor at the time he enters into the Standard Contract gives the Producer the right to convert to a Run of the Play, then at the time of the conversion, the Actor's salary on the Run of the Play Contract must be an increase of at least 10% weekly or $25. weekly, whichever is greater. In order to exercise this option and convert, the Producer must deliver personal written notice to the Actor before the fifth consecutive performance of the Actor in the Play.

no probation and five week guarantee for principal actor

The Rider which gives the Producer the option to convert

must also provide that the 5 day probationary period in the Contract is deleted, so that there is no probationary period for the Actor. Also, the rider granting the option to the Producer must provide that the Actor is guaranteed not less than 5 weeks employment, rather than the minimum 2 weeks employment that would otherwise be provided for if this rider were not added to the Standard Contract.

Chorus Six Month Run of the Play Contract

There is also provision for hiring a member of the Chorus on a 6 month Run of the Play Contract. The rider, which is added to the Contract, must provide that: (1) the probationary period of 3 days is deleted; (2) neither party may give notice of termination of the Contract before 26 weeks from the opening of the Play (26 weeks from the opening in New York for dance captains), (3) the rider must be signed by the parties before the first day of rehearsal, (4) if the member of the Chorus obtains a contract to play the part of a principal during the 6 month rider, then the Chorus member may terminate his employment upon 2 weeks notice, and (5) the rider may only be used if the Chorus member is paid at least $10. per week above the minimum, not including payment for any extras or other duties for which extra compensation is provided.

extensions of chorus six month run of play contract

If during the twenty-sixth week of the period, or any time thereafter, the Producer requests in writing that the Chorus member agrees to a further extension for an additional 6 months and the Chorus member does not consent, then the Producer has the right to discontinue the additional $10. payment. This provision also applies to subsequent 26 week periods after the first and second 26 week periods.

Conversion to Chorus Six Month Run of Play Contract

The Producer may also sign a Chorus member under a Contract which gives the Producer the option to convert to a 6 month Run of the Play Contract provided that the Producer exercises the option by giving written notice personally to the Actor before the fifth consecutive performance of the Actor in the Play. If this option is given to the Producer, then the Contract cannot provide for a probationary period and the rider must by reference delete the probationary period. The Producer must also guarantee not less than 3 weeks of consecutive employment if this option is granted.

Extra Chorus Payment

A member of the Chorus designated to swing a number in a production who is not hired solely as a swing performer must receive $5. per week in addition to his regular weekly salary. A swing performer is a Chorus member who may be called upon to perform in a number as a replacement if a Chorus member is out. The Chorus member may perform in several numbers and swing on another number if he is needed.

Number of Chorus

The Rules make specific provision as to the number of Chorus which must be retained.

No Pay For Actors' Fund

The Rules provide that an Actor must perform without compensation for 1 performance during the first 3 months of the Play's run, and for 1 performance every 12 months thereafter for the Actors' Fund Benefit. There are specific terms covering the notices, rehearsal, and procedure for an Actors' Fund Benefit.

Paid Previews Before Opening Count Toward Minimum Guarantee

If a show gives paid previews immediately preceding the opening, that is, where there are no intervening days, rehearsals, or unpaid previews, and if the Play closes within 2 weeks of the opening, then the Producer may claim the pro-rata salaries paid to the Actors for the previews as a credit and offset against the minimum guarantee provided for in the Contract of employment. The Producer need not pay rehearsal expense money if the Actor is not required to rehearse more than 4 hours on the day of a paid preview. Any sums paid to the Actor for rehearsals, whether at full salary or as rehearsal expense money, or any sum paid for unpaid previews or for paid previews not immediately preceding the opening performance, may not be credited against the minimum guarantee specified in the Contract. The point is that credit is given only for salary payments immediately preceding opening and only in the event that there are no intervening days.

If an Actor is paid rehearsal expense money in addition to payment for the preview, the Producer may have an additional day of rehearsal for each such preview for payment of only rehearsal expense money. Payment for such previews, however, may not be used as a credit against the minimum contract guarantee.

Termination Standard Minimum Contracts before or during rehearsals

If a Standard Minimum Contract is signed or entered into 7 or more days before the first day of rehearsal, then the Contract may be terminated before or during rehearsals by the Producer giving written notice to the Actor and paying him 2 weeks salary.

dismissal during probationary period

If the Contract is signed or entered into less than 7 days before the beginning of rehearsals, then either party may at any time during the probationary period, that is during the first 5 days of rehearsals of the Principal Actor (3 days for Chorus), terminate the Contract by giving written notice without liability, except payment by the Producer of rehearsal expense money and any other sums which may be due the Actor. The Actor, however, if he has been reengaged by the Producer for a part (or Chorus) which he has played the prior season or subsequent thereto, must be paid 2 weeks compensation at the time he is given the notice.

The Standard Minimum Contract may be terminated by the Producer after the appropriate probationary period and before the opening by giving written notice to the Actor and paying him a sum equal to 2 weeks compensation plus any rehearsal expense money due. The Actor may terminate the Contract during this period only upon the consent of Equity, and by giving written notice and paying to the Producer a sum equal to 2 weeks compensation plus any rehearsal expense money received by the Actor.

individual termination after opening

The Producer or the Actor may terminate the Contract at any time upon or after the date of the first public performance of the Play by giving 2 weeks written notice to the other party. If a company is closed in accordance with the notice of closing to the entire company then the company notice will supercede any individual notice then outstanding.

termination by the company after opening

The Producer may close the Play and company upon 1 week's written notice or upon payment of 1 week's contractual salary in lieu thereof, provided that he has paid the Equity Actors for all of their services rendered to the date of closing and in no event less than 2 weeks salary plus rehearsal expense money.

termination by actor after opening

If the Actor wishes to terminate the Contract after the Play has opened he must pay his own railroad fare back to New York City and reimburse the Producer for any railroad fare which the Producer will have to pay for the Actor's successor, up to an amount not exceeding the fare from New York City to a point where the successor joins the company for rehearsals or for playing. The Chorus member is liable for the fare of his successor only if the Chorus Member terminates the Contract solely for the purpose of fulfilling another engagement. In such event, the Chorus Member's successor must not be engaged at a lesser salary.

payment where actor does not work out notice

If the Actor is not allowed or required to work out any notice given to him under the Contract, he must be paid immediately and may accept other employment. If the Producer gives individual notice of termination, the Producer must pay the Actor the cost of transportation and baggage back to New York City whether he returns immediately or not; however, if at the time the notice is given the Producer has already purchased a requisite railroad ticket, he may give it to the Actor in lieu of the cash.

Termination—Run of the Play Contracts

notice of closing

The Producer must give all Actors signed to a Run of the Play Contract 1 week's individual notice in writing of the closing of the Production and company or pay 1 week's salary in lieu thereof.

Run of the Play Contracts, with certain exceptions hereafter noted, terminate on the date stipulated in the individual contract of employment without further notice. A Principal Actor engaged under a Run of the Play Contract may agree to continue with the Production after the expiration of the season (i.e., employment ending June 30) contracted for without entering into a new contract, but from and after June 30 he will be deemed to be employed under all the terms and conditions of the Standard Minimum Contract. The Parties, if they decide to extend the term of employment beyond September 1, must execute a new Contract by that date, otherwise the Contract may be terminated by either party giving 2 weeks written notice to the other party. If the Producer gives notice to the Actor at any time between June 30 and September 1, he may replace the Actor at a lesser salary only if the Actor's Run of the Play Contract was for a period longer than 5 months.

exceptions to foregoing closing provisions

There are certain exceptions to the foregoing. They include:

(1.) Termination of rehearsals as a result of fire, accident, riot, strikes, illness, or death of the Star or prominent member of the cast, act of God, or act of a public enemy. Under such circumstances the Actors must be paid rehearsal expense money up to the date of suspension of rehearsals and after the layoff has continued for 2 weeks, the Producer may pay half the contracted salary for 2 further weeks and may terminate the Contract without penalty.

(2.) Where an Actor absents himself from rehearsal for 7 days due to illness the Producer may terminate the Contract at the end of the 7 days. Equity may consent upon appeal to reduce this period.

(3.) If the Play is abandoned before opening, the Producer must pay the Actor a sum equal to the weekly compensation agreed upon multiplied by the number of weeks guaranteed, plus rehearsal payments and any other extras due, and the Contract may be terminated.

(4.) If an illness or an injury other than injury in the course of the Actor's employment prevents the Actor from performing and the illness continues or appears that it will continue for 14 days or more, Equity may at the request of the Producer modify or terminate the Actor's Contract on such terms as it considers just.

(5.) An Actor may be discharged for inability to perform due to intoxication or similar cause. There are provisions for arbitration as to whether it was for just cause.

(6.) If an Actor's part is cut out the Producer may terminate the Contract by the payment of a sum equal to 4 weeks contractual salary in addition to any other sums due for services rendered, plus 4 additional weeks salary to the extent that the Play runs more than 4 weeks after the Actor's part is cut out or the Contract terminated.

(7.) Where the Producer gives notice to an Actor who was hired for more than 1 season and notice is given not later than 5 weeks after the first public performance (no later than 15 weeks after the opening performance) or 5 weeks after the opening day of the road tour that he will not present the Play during any season following the current one, he may terminate if at the same time he pays the Actor any and all sums due him under the guarantee for each season contracted for beyond the second season.

Closing Notice

A closing notice given at or before the end of the performance on Monday night is considered to be 1 week's notice effective at the end of the following Saturday night, and notice effective at the end of the second Saturday following is deemed to be two weeks notice. If a show is playing a schedule of Tuesday through Sunday, then notice given on Tuesday is effective at the end of the following Sunday night performance as 1 week's notice and effective the Sunday after that would be considered 2 weeks notice. Except as just stated, a week's notice is considered to be 7 calendar days, and 2 weeks notice is considered to be 14 calendar days. A notice of closing must be posted for the entire notice period unless it is initialed by every member of the cast. If the notice is posted after the half-hour call (half-hour before curtain time) it must be promptly called to the attention of the cast.

Hiring "As Cast" and "Understudy As Cast"

If the part to be played by a Principal Actor is not specified, then he is only required to appear and perform in the part in which he makes his first public appearance. If a Principal Actor is employed to appear "as cast," then except in Revues, he is not required to appear and perform in any part or parts other than the part or parts he appeared in during the first 2 weeks of the run of the play. If the Principal Actor is employed to "understudy as cast," then except in revues he may not be required to appear and perform in any part or parts other than the part or parts he was assigned to understudy up to the date following the first 2 weeks after the opening of the Play in New York City, or 4 weeks after the out of town opening whichever is sooner. An Actor may not be required to understudy unless his contract specifically provides that he will understudy, and if the Actor and Producer have agreed to a specific understudy part or parts in the original contract of employment, then such provisions as are set forth in the Contract would be applicable.

Juvenile Actors

Juvenile Actors are paid the same as other Actors. A juvenile under the age of fourteen may at the time he signs his Contract agree to a 6 month Run of the Play Contract and the Contract may also provide that the Producer has an option to extend the Contract for an additional 6 month period at a 10% salary above the Actor's original Contract salary.

Extras

An "Extra" is defined as one who may not be identified as a definite character either singly or within a group who provides atmosphere and background only. An Extra may not be required to change makeup but may, however, be required to make a single costume change. Extras cannot be rehearsed for more than 2 weeks before the first public performance and may not speak except in "omnes" (in a group), may not sing, dance, understudy, and may not tour except with a pre-Broadway tryout of 8 weeks or less.

Extras are paid no less than half the minimum salary of an Actor. During a pre-Broadway tour, they must be paid $10. per day for each day they spend out of town in addition to their regular salary. Extras receive hospitalization and medical coverage. After the New York opening the Extra may be rehearsed for 2 weeks the same as Principal Actors. After the 2 weeks, Extras must be paid $7.50 for any hour or part of an hour. An Extra gets a 1 week guarantee of salary from the date of opening of the Play, 1 week notice of termination of the Contract, and there is not a probationary period provided for in the Contract.

Understudies

dramatic plays

In Dramatic Plays all parts for which Contracts are issued, except Star and Bit Players, must be covered by Understudies

extra payment for performance—principal actor

No Understudy can perform in a role which he covers without additional compensation, except that a Principal Actor understudying a Principal Actor may perform the part he understudies without additional compensation when the understudied Actor is on vacation. If, except as just stated, a Principal Actor performs in place of another Principal Actor, then if the Actor understudied received $250. or more per week, the Actor performing in his place must receive a minimum of one eighth of his own salary (in addition to his regular weekly salary), for each such performance. Unless otherwise agreed, the Understudy's total weekly salary for an understudy performance shall not exceed that of the Actor understudied.

If the Actor understudied received less than $250. per week, then the Understudy must receive a minimum of $5. (in addition to his regular weekly salary) for each performance, and his total weekly salary is not limited or affected by the salary of the Actor understudied.

chorus—extra payment under contract

If a member of the Chorus understudies a Principal, then he must be paid not less than $10. per week in addition to his weekly salary. If a member of the Chorus understudies another member of the Chorus (involving understudy rehearsals) he must be paid a minimum of not less than $5. per week in addition to his other salary.

chorus—extra payment for performance

If a Chorus performs in the place of a Principal Actor (other than as hereinafter set forth in the next paragraph for a Star billed over the title), he must be paid a minimum of at least one eighth of his own weekly salary (in addition to his regular weekly salary), for each such performance. Unless otherwise agreed upon, the Chorus' total weekly salary for understudy performances may not exceed that of the Principal Actor understudied; however, the extra payment for any understudied performance during which the Chorus also performs any ensemble work is not taken into account in determining the Chorus' total weekly salary for the purpose of this computation.

chorus understudying a star

A Chorus receiving under $200. per week understudying a Star billed over the title must be paid a minimum of $50. for each performance given in place of the Star. If the Chorus receives $200. per week or more, payment for an understudied performance must be a minimum of one eighth of the Chorus' weekly salary (in addition to his regular weekly salary).

understudies present at all performances

Understudies must be present at each performance unless the Producer consents otherwise.

time of hiring and commencement of performance as understudy

Understudies must be hired no later than 4 weeks after the first public performance of the production, but in no event later than the New York opening. If no Understudy is hired for the part within the allotted time, then when hired, the Understudy's salary for the first week of employment shall be his contractual salary, plus the salary he would have received had he been hired 4 weeks after the first public performance or at the time of the New York opening, whichever is earlier.

Understudy parts assigned to Chorus must be assigned with new Contracts or riders and with salary adjustments no later than 3 weeks after the first public performance of the production or at the time of the New York opening, whichever is earlier.

Where the Contract of a Chorus is amended so that additional compensation is agreed upon based on the assignment of the understudy work, the Producer may, within 2 weeks of the first public performance in New York, withdraw said understudy work and additional compensation and assign it to another Chorus Member. This does not apply, however, where the understudy work and compensation is part of the original Contract of employment.

An Understudy cannot be required to perform until 1 week after he is engaged. The Producer must use his best efforts to provide the Understudy with scripts and/or sides and music no later than 2 weeks after the New York opening. Understudies may be in only 1 company at a time.

Termination of Principal Actor and Replacement

If a Principal Actor's employment is terminated, a Contract for replacement must be negotiated and signed between the Producer and the Understudy or other replacement no later than 2 weeks after the Principal's last performance in the Production.

Stage Managers and Payment

There must be at least 1 Stage Manager and 1 Assistant Stage Manager on a straight Dramatic Show and at least 1 Stage Manager and 2 Assistant Stage Managers on a Musical Show. The Stage Manager must be engaged and paid the contractual salary at least 1 week before the beginning of rehearsals. The Assistant Stage Manager is paid the contractual salary from the time of the first rehearsal call. When a Stage Manager or Assistant Stage Manager is called to perform services in productions either prior to the week before rehearsals begin, or after the production is closed, he must be paid no less than one sixth of the applicable minimum weekly rate for each day. Stage Managers and Assistant Stage Managers must be members of Equity in all companies in which an Equity member is employed.

A replacement Stage Manager in a Musical must also be hired 1 week prior to the date he is to take over the production. All Stage Managers and first Assistant Stage Managers in Musicals are not permitted to act or understudy.

Lay-Offs

If the Actor has worked for 2 weeks the Manager may lay-off the Company during Holy Week and/or for no more than 7 consecutive days during the 14 day period before Christmas Day, providing that the Actor receives 2 consecutive weeks of employment after the lay-off. The Producer must give 4 weeks written notice in the event of such lay-off. During the lay-off, the Actor need not give any services except a run-through rehearsal on the day of reopening. If there is a change in cast or illness of a Star or prominent member of the company, then Equity may allow additional rehearsals. If the company is outside of New York City, then expense money equal to the minimum salary must be paid during the lay-off.

Death of Star or Illness

The Contract sets forth detailed terms and provisions in the event of the illness or death of a Star, or if there is no Star, in the event of the death or illness of the first featured Actor who is playing a leading role.

Part Cut Out of Show

If a part is cut before the end of rehearsals, an Actor on a Standard Minimum Contract dismissed before the end of rehearsal on the fifth day, must be paid an amount equal to 1 week's salary. It hardly makes sense why an Actor dismissed before the end of the fifth day of rehearsal should get an extra week's pay if the part is later cut during rehearsals, but so the Rules state.

As previously noted, if the Actor is on a Run of the Play Contract and if the part is cut before the New York opening, the Producer may terminate the Contract by payment of an amount equal to 4 weeks contractual salary in addition to all sums due for services rendered, plus 4 additional weeks salary to the extent that the Play runs more than 4 weeks after the Actor's part is cut out or terminated. In no event may an Actor on a Run of the Play Contract whose part is cut out receive less than payment for the guarantee period specified in his Contract of employment.

Producer May Terminate Contract for Absence by Actor

If an Actor absents himself from rehearsals for 7 days as a

result of illness, the Producer may terminate the Contract at the end of the seven days.

Abandonment of Play

The Rules provide that if a Play is abandoned or discontinued on or before the 5 day probationary period (3 days for the Chorus), then if the Contract has been entered into within 6 weeks of the opening date specified in the Actor's Contract, the Producer must pay the Actor a sum equal to 1 week's salary.

There seems be a discrepancy in the rules, in that if the Play is abandoned during the probationary period, the actor must be paid one week's salary. As noted under the section of this book on "Termination Standard Minimum Contracts," the Rule provides that on a termination during the probationary period, only the rehearsal expense money and any other sums due need be paid. The rule on abandonment is applicable if the contract was entered into within 6 weeks of the opening date specified in the actor's contract, and the rule on termination is applicable if the contract is entered into less than 7 days before the opening of rehearsals. Since it is possible to enter into the contract less than 7 days before the beginning of rehearsals and still be within 6 weeks of the opening date, specified in the actor's contract, there would seem to be an unresolved discrepancy in the rules.

If the Contract has not been signed or entered into within 6 weeks of the opening date set forth in the Actor's Contract, or discontinuance is after the 5 (or 3 for Chorus) days, then a sum equal to 2 weeks salary must be paid. Notice and payment must be given to the Actor not later than 3 weeks before the opening date specified in the Contract.

If a Play is abandoned before opening, then an Actor with a Run of the Play Contract must be paid an amount equal to the weekly compensation set forth in the Contract multiplied by the number of weeks guaranteed.

Billing

The Contract provides that wherever houseboards are maintained and within the limitation of the existing facilities, the names of the Principal Actors in the cast must be listed on the houseboards in front of the Theatre in letters no less than one-half inch in height. Where there is no houseboard outside the Theatre, the Producer must agree to place one prominently inside the lobby. There is also provision for removal of an Actor's name and pictures in the event that he leaves the cast and a specific provision for notification of the Producer of any breach of the billing clause. If a breach of this clause is not corrected within 7 business days, the Producer must pay a sum equal to one-eighth of the Actor's salary for the first week of the breach, two-eighths for the second week, three-eighths for the third week, etc.

Billing If Understudy Plays Part

There are specific provisions set forth for program billing in the event that an Understudy takes the place of a Principal Actor.

Clothes and Makeup

All wardrobe must be furnished for male Actors in New York City. On the road, a male Actor earning over $500. per week may be required to furnish his own wardrobe if it is conventional wear. All wigs, hats, gowns, footwear, and wardrobe must be furnished for women and must be new if they are modern and conventional wear. All costumes or clothing furnished by the Producer must be freshly cleaned when delivered, and cleaned thereafter when necessary, but at least once every month, and within 1 week before the show goes on tour. Ordinary and conventional makeup is furnished by the Actor but anything that is unusual must be furnished by the Producer. If the Actor must use body makeup the Producer must furnish a regular linen towel service for removal of the makeup.

The Chorus must be furnished with their costumes including footwear. After the probationary period the Producer must furnish 1 pair of toe shoes for each member of the Chorus who must dance on toe.

Transportation and Baggage

There are detailed Rules concerning transportation of the Actor and baggage, including specific provisions covering rail, bus, and air transportation. The Rules are very detailed concerning the times, the amount of baggage, when the parties may travel, overtime travel, and the like.

Photographs and Publicity

There are specific provisions set forth in the Rules for the taking of photographs and publicity with stated limitations upon picture calls.

Plays in Supper Clubs (Las Vegas)

There are specific provisions in the Contract covering the terms and conditions of employment in supper clubs, including minimum salaries.

Alien Actors

If a Producer wishes to import alien actors for a production, he must obtain the approval of Actors' Equity Association, which approval may be applied for in 3 different ways.

individual actor—or less than the entire cast

If a Producer wishes to import an actor or actors for a production, he must first submit the application, a copy of the script, and other pertinent information to the League of New York Theatres. If the representative of the League does not support the application, the request is denied. If the League representative supports the application, the submission together with the script and material is submitted to Equity.

Upon the receipt of the application to Equity, the representative has 5 days to consider the application and notify the League representative; however, if the application is received by Equity on Thursday afternoon or Friday, then the Equity representative has 7 days to respond. If there is disagreement between the Equity representatives reading the script, they may extend the time to respond for up to an additional 3 days in order to convene a full meeting of the Alien Committee to resolve the disagreement.

If Equity approves, the Producer is notified; and if Equity does not approve, then the League representative and the Equity representative meet to resolve the disagreement, if possible. The Producer may be invited to this meeting if either the League or the Equity representative deem it advisable.

If the League and Equity representative reach agreement, their decision is binding on both the Producer and Actors' Equity; however, if they do not agree, then a meeting is held with an impartial arbitrator not later than 5 days after the Equity and League representatives meet. If additional time (up to the additional 3 days to convene the Alien Committee) has been consumed by Actors' Equity, then this time is deducted from the 5 days.

Within 1 week after the hearing at which the Equity representative and the League representative have presented their cases, the arbitrator will render a decision binding upon both parties. The arbitrator is instructed to use as a criteria certain definitions contained in the United States Immigration and Nationality Act.

unit company

If a Producer desires to bring over a repertory company, then the application is made to Equity. Equity will approve of the application providing that it is a true repertory company. They must do at least 2 shows in repertory and the company must appear for a limited run, that is not over 20 weeks in each city in which they appear.

special character

It is possible to make an application to Actors' Equity to approve of an entire cast based on the fact that the Play is of such a unique character that by design or by the nature of the Play, the entire alien cast must be kept intact to preserve the particular quality of the Play; that it is impossible to do the Play here with local actors. Whether or not a play is of such a special character is determined solely by the Counsel of Actors' Equity which is the governing board of this group.

Theatrical Wardrobe Attendants Union, Local #764

Jurisdiction

This Agreement is applicable to every New York production and every production originating in New York and governs the Employment of Wardrobe Supervisors, Assistants, and Dressers. Each show must have a minimum wardrobe crew of one Wardrobe Supervisor, except on: (1) "One-Man Shows" and (2) on special shows where no wardrobe other than the performers' street clothes are worn and no wardrobe changes requiring the assistance of any other person are to be made.

Wardrobe Supervisors and Assistants may not perform Dressers' duties and Dressers engaged in a production may not perform the duties of Supervisors or Assistants, except in places of extreme emergency, limited to 1 performance. A performer may not assist another performer in dressing nor may the Stage Manager or his Assistants perform the duties of a Dresser.

Wardrobe, Stars, Duties, Defined

Wardrobe is considered to be all clothing, hats, shoes, etc., worn in the production, whether personally owned by the performers or purchased or rented. The term "Stars" is defined to mean performers whose names appear above the title of the show or carry the label "starring" or "also starring" before their names. The duties of Employees covered by the Contract includes maintaining, cleaning, dying, pressing, sorting, handling, distributing, hanging, packing, repacking, repairing, altering, transporting, and the general supervision of all items, costumes, wardrobes, and costume-wardrobe accessories, dressing of, and making changes for all performers. The duties also include making, executing, fitting, and remodelling of such items as well as the control, disposition, and organization of costumes and wardrobe for their efficient and artistic utilization.

Star's Dressers

Stars may personally select their own Dressers but any Dresser so selected, whether on the payroll of the Production, the Star, or both the Production and the Star, is subject to the provisions of this Agreement and must be or become a member of the Union.

Changes in the Law—May Reopen Negotiations

The Agreement provides that if the Labor Management Relations Act of 1947 as amended is further amended or repealed, or in the event that there are new rulings or legislation covering permissable Union security forms other than presently allowed, or should the NLRB issue a decision or Advisory Opinion declining to exercise jurisdiction over the League of New York Theatres or over the business of its members, then the Union shall have the option on 10 days written notice of reopening the Agreement for the limited purpose of negotiating modifications to the extent authorized by any such change in the law.

Rates of Pay—Hours of Work and Overtime

The schedule of minimum rates of pay provided in the Agreement is as follows:

	9-1-68/ 8-31-69	9-1-69/ 8-29-70
Wardrobe Supervisors	$139.00	$142.00
Assistant Supervisors	124.00	127.00
Per Diem — On Tour	10.00	10.00
Overtime Hourly Rate		
Wardrobe Supervisor	5.22	5.33
Assistant Supervisor	4.65	4.77
Seventh Day		
Wardrobe Supervisors)	One-sixth of	
Assistant Supervisors)	Weekly Salary	
Performances in Excess of Eight (8)		
Wardrobe Supervisors)	Time and half of one-	
Assistant Supervisors)	eighth of weekly salary	
Dressers:		
Per Performance	$ 10.58	$ 10.95
Per Week	84.64	87.60
Per Diem — On Tour	10.00	10.00

	9-1-68/ 8-31-69	9-1-69/ 8-29-70
Sundays and Performances in Excess of Eight (8)	15.87	16.43
Holidays (Per Performance) July 4th, Thanksgiving Day, Christmas Day, New Year's Day	15.87	16.43
Lincoln's Birthday, Washington's Birthday, Memorial Day, Labor Day, Columbus Day, Election Day, Veteran's Day	13.23	13.69
Broken time per four (4) hour call	12.08	12.52
Dressers per hour	3.02	3.13
Overtime, Sunday, and after Midnight Hourly Rate	4.53	4.70
Parking During Performance (additional)	5.29	5.48

All broken-time calls are for a minimum of four (4) hours. All daytime picture calls are for a minimum of four (4) hours except as otherwise specifically set forth.

Eight Performance—Six Day Week and Overtime

Six days constitute a regular work week and the seventh day is a rest period. Any work performed on the seventh consecutive day shall be paid for pro-rata of one-sixth of the weekly salary. When Employees are required to render services for more than 8 performances of an attraction within any regular work week, the Employee gets paid time and one half of his regular rate for each such additional performance.

Dressers

dressers' work time

Dressers are required to report 30 minutes before curtain time. If there is a change in the advertised curtain time then the Producer must notify the wardrobe personnel within the first hour of opening of the previous performance of the actual time for the next performance. Dressers are required to give their services for the payments above set forth provided that the performance does not exceed 3½ hours including the 30 minutes prior to curtain time.

dressers' hours and overtime

If the work of hanging costumes at the end of the performance runs beyond the hours of 5:30 pm or 11.30 pm with an allowance of the necessary time not to exceed 15 minutes after curtain time, but the performance time does not require an excees of 3½ hours work, then no overtime payment need be made. Where under such circumstances there is an excess of 3½ hours work excluding 15 minutes after curtain time as above referred to, all time worked in excess of 3½ hours is paid for at overtime rates. A full hour's overtime must be paid for any fractional hours worked. This does not, however, apply to opening night in New York.

dresser minimum

Any Dresser ordered to report for a performance or for

maintenance work, who reports at the specified hours, is guaranteed the minimum call as set forth in the Schedule.

dressers accompany wardrobe

Dressers are required to accompany all wardrobe removed from the Theatre for any reason whatsoever, from the time of removal until the return of the wardrobe to the Theatre. If no Dresser is available, the Wardrobe Supervisor or Assistant acts in the Dresser's place and is paid at the broken time rate set forth in the Schedule. This does not apply to wardrobe removed from the Theatre for washing, cleaning, or repairing.

dressers' holidays and vacations

Dressers are paid time and a half the performance rate if they work on July 4, Thanksgiving Day, Christmas Day, or New Year's Day. Dressers are paid time and one quarter the performance rate if they work on Lincoln's Birthday, Washington's Birthday, Memorial Day, Labor Day, Columbus Day, Election Day, or Veteran's Day.

Rehearsals

Wardrobe personnel are not paid additional during put-ons, rehearsals, and run-throughs if there is no commercial tie-up involved.

Number of Employees and Minimum Hours

After the New York opening, only the necessary number of wardrobe personnel agreed upon between the Business Manager of the Union and the Producer are required and each must receive a minimum call of 4 hours.

Closing—Wardrobe Supervisors and Assistants

When a production closes out of town, Wardrobe Supervisors and Assistants are paid from the time of closing of the show until their return to New York.

Rest Periods

All Employees who are part of the maintenance crew in the Theatre when a performance is not being given must get rest periods of 5 minutes for each hour or 20 minutes for every 4 hour period.

After Midnight

If a performance commences before midnight and runs after midnight, all Wardrobe Employees must be paid the time and a half rate for such performances. They receive waiting time at the broken time rate from the fall of the curtain on the previous (regular) evenings performance unless no regular performance was given that day.

Wardrobe Supervisors Packing for TV

Wardrobe Supervisors receive additional compensation at the rate of one-sixth of their weekly salary for the service of packing and returning the wardrobe to proper condition for use in a production when a wardrobe is sent to a television studio for use in a television show. If no Dresser is available, the Wardrobe Supervisor or Assistant will act in the Dresser's place.

TV at Theatre

If a production is televised from the Theatre during the regular performance, all Employees are paid at the prevailing television rate in addition to their regular pay.

Publicity Pictures

Wardrobe Supervisors, Assistants, and Dressers are paid an hourly rate as provided in the Contract for their services involved in the taking of all commercial or publicity pictures. This does not apply to non-commercial pictures. Commercial pictures are defined as those where the pictures are exploited in connection with an advertised product or when the Producer derives compensation for such pictures.

As a continuity of employment, pictures may be taken (on an hourly basis) 1 hour before or after a performance and in such instance all the Wardrobe personnel must be employed.

For taking of all pictures after the performance (whether commercial pictures or pictures for general publicity) those Employees involved are paid at the overtime rate in addition to their regular pay.

Working Conditions

The League agrees to use its best efforts to see that a suitable wardrobe room with a window or other means of proper ventilation is provided as well as proper sanitary conditions, toilet facilities, washbasins, etc. Personal clothing of the members of the Wardrobe crew must also be safeguarded. All sewing and other equipment furnished by the Employees must be insured against fire and theft at the Producer's expense or in lieu thereof, the Producer is required to reimburse the employees for any loss or damage to their equipment.

Equipment Furnished

The Producer agree to furnish sewing machines for proper repairs and irons and/or ironing boards and if the Employee is required to furnish any such equipment, a weekly rental as agreed upon between the Employee and the Producer is charged.

Making a Costume

If a costume is made, produced, or executed by a wardrobe Employee, whether it be a duplicate or not, the Employee is paid additional compensation in addition to the regular salary at an agreed upon sum.

Travel and Transportation

Wardrobe Employees are furnished first class transportation the same as for other members of the Stage Crew, which includes first class sleeping accomodations for travel between 8:00 P.M. and 8:00 A.M. The Producer must in addition pay the cost of, or reimburse the Wardrobe Employees for, transportation of hand luggage up to $3. each way.

Bus Travel

If bus travel is arranged, then all Wardrobe Employees must be provided with the same sleeping accomodations as the production road crew. If the bus travel, either by day or night, is more than 3 hours on days when 2 performances are given, or more than 6 hours on days when 1 performance is given, or more than 8 hours on a day when no performance is given, then each Wardrobe Employee must be paid an additional $5. per hour. All provisions applicable to bus travel by Equity Members or Stage Road Crews are also applicable to Wardrobe Employees.

Layoffs and Reductions and Dismissal for Cause and Replacement

All contract Wardrobe Employees must be given 2 weeks notice in writing by the Producer of any lay-off or dismissal, and 1 week's notice of closing. Dressers must be given 1 week's notice of lay-off, dismissal or closing. Except in the event of a closing, written notice of any lay-off or dismissal must also be given to the Union. Contract Wardrobe Employees must give the Producer 2 weeks notice in writing for resignation and Dressers must give the Producer 1 week's notice of a resignation.

No reduction in the number of Dressers is permitted after 1 week of performances in New York City unless there has been a sufficient reduction in wardrobe to warrant it.

Dismissal for Cause

Replacement of layed-off, dismissed, or resigned Wardrobe Employees is mandatory. An Employee may not be discharged without just cause, which means intoxication, dishonesty, or failure to abide by any of the terms of the Agreement between the League and the Union.

If the Producer wishes to layoff the entire company for Christmas or Holy Week, the Producer must give the wardrobe personnel at least 2 consecutive weeks of employment prior to the lay-off and 2 consecutive weeks of employment after the layoff. Wardrobe Employees on tour for any such layoff period are paid full expense money or a week's salary whichever is greater.

Termination and Renegotiation

The parties agree that at least 60 days prior to the expiration date, August 29, 1970, they will meet and confer to negotiate the terms of a new Agreement to take effect August 30, 1970.

Society of Stage Directors and Choreographers

Directors — Extra Payment for Rewriting

Nowadays Directors pick up extra money by participating

in the writing of the show. Although a Director may not get program writing credit, he may get as much as 1½ or 2% of the gross receipts for the writing, in addition to the Directing fee. The minimum Director's fee, as will be noted, is $2,000. plus 1% of the gross receipts; however, if he is a good big-name Director he is more likely to be paid between $5,000. and $8,000. and between 2½% and 4% of the gross receipts as a Directing fee. He may also receive up to 10% of the net profits of the company. In addition the Director who helps with the writing would share in the Writer's receipts from the movie sale as well as from the sale of the other subsidiaries, and this could mean big money.

Jurisdiction

The Collective Bargaining Agreement of the Society of Stage Directors and Choreographers as the name implies governs employment of Directors and Choreographers in First Class Theatrical Productions in the United States. First class productions do not include Vaudville Type Shows, Concert Type Shows, Readings, Night Clubs, Theatre Restaurants (Las Vegas, however, is considered first class where so classified by Acors' Equity as part of a road tour), Foreign Importations brought over substantially intact, Ballets, Symphonic and Musical Importations, and any production not under the jurisdiction of Actors' Equity Association. In exchange for recognition of the Society for First Class Productions, the Society has agreed that it will not attempt to seek recognition to bargain with the Producers for other than the first class presentations just noted. A theatrical production, to be covered by this Agreement, must also be presented on the speaking stage in a First Class Theatre.

The Society agrees to admit members on a non-discriminatory basis and agrees that its Constitution and By-Laws will provide that no initiation fee or similar charge will exceed $100.

Producer/Director or Producer/Choreographer

The Contract does not cover a Producer not previously a member of the Society when such Producer is acting as a Producer/Director or a Producer/Choreographer, nor will such person be induced, coerced, or otherwise required to become or remain a member of the Society. Any Producer/ Director or Producer/Choreographer who was previously a member of the Society remains a member and the Contract would be applicable.

One Waiver of Royalties Permitted

A Producer may not request that a Director or Choreographer waive any of the terms of the Agreement without the consent of the Society; however, 1 reduction of royalties of not more than 2 weeks duration may be made without the consent of the Society provided that the Agreement in writing for the reduction is signed by the Producer and the Director or Choreographer and is filed with the Society within 1 week after the reduction is agreed upon.

Twenty Year Waiver on Bargaining Certain Issues

The Society has agreed that it will waive bargaining for a period of 20 years with respect to the Director's or Choreographer's right to participate in subsidiary rights, with respect to the existing relations between Producer, Director, Choreographer, and Dramatist, and with respect to duty, authority, and control of any Production.

Renegotiable Items

On the other hand, the parties may reopen the discussion of pensions if and when the Dramatists or Scenic Designers receive pensions. If it is reopened for discussion in no event will the amount of pension contributions agreed upon be based upon royalties of more than $450. per week nor will the pension contributions or pensions, if agreed upon, exceed those received or paid by virtue of any Agreement with the Dramatists or Scenic Designers. There is provision for arbitration in connection with this. The parties may also reopen negotiations concerning the visual reproduction and transmission on film tape or the like of a production for viewing by viewers at home or in Theatres where an admission is charged.

Cost of Living Adjustment

The Agreement which became effective on August 1, 1962, provides that 1 year after its effective date and annually thereafter, minimum fees and minimum royalties shall automatically be adjusted to reflect the increase in the cost of living which may have taken place during the previous year (no mention is made of a possible decrease in the cost of living). The index used is the Consumer Price Index for the City of New York (1957 – 1959 = 100) published by the Bureau of Labor Statistics, United States Department of Labor. The index for the City of New York as of August 13, 1962, is the base index. Cost of living adjustments operate prospectively and apply only to Minimum Basic Contracts executed on or after the date of the adjustment. Cost of living adjustments must not be pyramided.

Director and Choreographer Terms

fees

The minimum fee payable to a Director of a First Class Production is not less than $2,000. and for a Choreographer is not less than $1,500. 25% of the fee in either case is paid directly to the Director or Choreographer on signing of the

Contract and is nonreturnable, and the balance of the fee is payable in 3 equal payments at the begining of the first, second, and third weeks of rehearsal, or not later than 1 week before the first performance whichever is sooner. If a production is abandoned there is no liability for fee payments after the date of abandonment; however, those fees accrued prior to the abandonment must be paid to the Director or Choreographer and may be retained by him.

royalties

In addition to the Contract Fee, the Director of a First Class Dramatic Production must be paid a royalty of not less than 1% of the gross weekly box office receipts, and the Director of a Musical must be paid a royalty of not less than one-half of 1% of the gross weekly box office receipts. The Choreographer of a First Class Musical must be paid one-third of 1% of the gross weekly box office receipts. In all instances the weekly payments must be made no later than 10 days after the week for which the weekly payments are due.

gross box office receipts defined

Gross Weekly Box Office Receipts are defined in the Agreement as the receipts from the box office less:

1. All admission taxes levied by any governmental agency on gross receipts.
2. Pension and welfare deductions exercised as a result of the New York City Tax abatement program.
3. Theatre Party Commissions and discounts, and cut rate sales.
4. Subscription fees.
5. Actors Fund Benefits.
6. Any deductions similar to the ones listed above.

In bus and truck operations where a guaranteed lump sum is paid to the producer, the lump sum less booking commissions is the basis for the computation of royalties in lieu of gross box office receipts.

option to direct future companies and payments

The Director and the Choreographer are given an option to direct all future companies presenting the Play in the United States in which the Producer is interested. If the Director or Choreographer accept the employment with the additional company, then he will receive for each Additional company one-half of the original fee. In addition a Director will receive no less than 1% of the gross weekly box office receipts for a Dramatic Production, no less than one-half of 1% of the gross weekly box office receipts for a Musical Production, and the Choreographer will receive no less than one-third of 1%. If the Director or Choreographer elects not to direct the additional company, then he will receive no fee but will receive one-half of the royalty payment that he would otherwise receive if he were directing the company, that is a Director of a Dramatic Production would receive one-half of 1% if he did not direct, a Director of a Musical would receive one-quarter of 1% if he did not direct, and a Choreographer would receive one-sixth of 1% of the company not choreographed by him. The Director or Choreographer has 10 days within which to decide whether or not he wishes to do the Additional Production.

length of employment

A maximum of 8 consecutive weeks in the case of a Drama and 10 consecutive weeks in the case of a Musical after the first public performance out of town, is the limit of the Director's or Choreographer's obligation prior to the official New York opening. If additional time is required during out-of-town tryouts, the Director or Choreographer must continue to work if he is available and uncommitted by virtue of any other professional engagement.

strike — lock-out — fire — flood — etc., and suspension rates

If a production is suspended because of strike, lock-out, fire, flood, act of public enemy, or act of God, the period of suspension is not considered part of the consecutive employment periods above referred to. When a suspension occurs prior to the date the Production opens in New York, if the Director or Choreographer is available he will continue to serve, and if unavailable and additional Directorial or Choreographer services are required, the original Director's and Choreographer's royalties are reduced as follows: (1) Production not in rehearsal—no royalties; (2) Production in rehearsal for at least 2 weeks—one-third of royalties; (3) After out-of-town opening—two-thirds of royalties.

out-of-town expenses

Directors and Choreographers are paid not less than $25. per day for out of town expenses and under certain circumstances set forth in the Contract a Producer may be required to post a bond for $350. to cover such expenses.

billing credits

The Agreement provides that the Director and Choreographer must each receive billing in all programs and houseboards. The Director's credits must appear on a separate line in an agreed size, type, and position on which no other credit will appear.

dismissal for cause

A Director or Choreographer may not be dismissed (except

where the Director or Choreographer is guity of breach of contract) without full payment as provided in the Contract.

after opening supervision

The Director and Choreographer must supervise and maintain the quality of the production after opening. Each of them must see the production at least once every 8 weeks unless prevented from doing so by other contractual obligations. If additional direction or rehearsal is necessary the Director and Choreographer must do so without additional compensation. If either the Director or Choreographer neglects to supervise and maintain the quality of the Production as set forth in the Contract, then that Director or Choreographer would forfeit one-half of his or her royalties until the work is done.

Terms Applicable Solely to Choreographer

The Choreographer's Agreement has certain provisions in it which are not applicable to a Director.

assistant

For an example, it is provided that the Choreographer may have an Assistant of his choice during the entire rehearsal period and during part or all of the out-of-town tryout period. The length of the Assistant's employment and compensation must be negotiated by the Assistant and the Producer, as the Assistant is not covered by the provisions of the Agreement between the Producer and the Society or between the League and the Society. The Choreographer may waive this requirement.

dance captain

The Choreographer has the right to designate a captain or

replacement for him among the dance company, who after the show has opened in New York, will have authority to call necessary rehearsals and rehearse understudies and replacements to maintain the quality of the dancers' performance.

approval of rehearsal pianist

The Choreographer will select or approve a dance rehearsal pianist who will be at the Choreographer's disposal for the rehearsal, road, and tour period. The duration of the dance captain's employment and compensation, and the duration of the rehearsal pianist's employment and compensation, will also be negotiated by the respective parties and the Producer as neither of them are covered by the provisions of the Collective Bargaining Agreement between the League and the Society.

The Choreographer has first call on the services of the pianist. However, when the pianist is not occupied with dance routines, the pianist is available to the rest of the company.

United Scenic Artists, Local #829B

Jurisdiction

The United Scenic Artists, Local # 829B, has 3 separate contracts applicable to a Broadway production: a Scenic Design Contract, a Lighting Design Contract, and a Theatrical Costume Designers Contract. The 3 contracts are basically identical in most of their terms with the exception of specific terms applicable to a particular Contract. If an individual designs the scenery and/or the lighting and/or the costumes he must have a separate contract for each.

Minimum Scenic Design Fees

The rates for scenic designing for either a dramatic or a

musical show, revue, opera, operetta, ballet, concert, or a theatrical production for a single full stage setting, is a minimum of $1,500.; for a second setting a minimum of $500.; for the next 4 settings, a minimum of $400. each; and for all additional settings thereafter a minimum of $250. each. The minimum for a unit set for any kind of production is $1,500. for the first phase (or scene) ; a minimum of $300. for each of the next nine phases; and a minimum of $125. each for each phase over 10.

A unit set is a set that stays in view of the audience at all times. One may bring in items or remove items from the basic set, but if the basic set remains in view it is a unit set. Each change is called a phase.

The minimum for concert readings and so called "bare stage" productions is $250. A reproduction using the original designs for a road tour or foreign use must pay a minimum of not less than one-half of the original fee. If a foreign or road reproduction uses the original scenery, and additional work is required by the Designer to make the scenery available for such road company or foreign use, then the Designer must be paid a minimum fee of not less than $75. per day. A deposit must be made with United Scenic Artists for the amount estimated by the Producer and the Designer to be the number of days required to do the work.

There are detailed provisions in the Contract covering the importation of scenic designs and scenery and the minimum rates of supervision of the various classes of importation.

Many top Scenic Designers will charge the minimum design fee set forth in the Contract, but in addition will receive a weekly royalty for the run of the play. In this way if the show is a success the Designer will do better then he would otherwise do without a royalty payment. On the other hand, the Producer will be paying for the set at a time when the Producer is making money and can afford it. The royalty payments for a top Designer will range between $100. and

$300. per week during the run of the show depending upon the Designer, whether the Play is a Musical or Dramatic, how much work is involved, and other such factors.

The Producer also generally agrees to pay the Designer for blueprint costs, art supplies and other out of pocket expenses.

Minimum Lighting Design Fees

The minimum lighting design fee for theatre is $750. For repertory the minimum fee for the first production is $1,250, and $500. for each additional production after the first production by the original Lighting Designer. If a new Lighting Designer is called in after the first production, then he is paid a minimum of $750. for each show. The same minimum charges for reproduction for the road or for foreign use are provided as are provided for the Scenic Design and services, that is, one half of the original fee and $75. per day. There are also provisions covering lighting designs for an imported show.

The weekly royalty for a Light Designer will range between $25. and $100.

Minimum Costume Design Fees

The minimum costume design fees for the Theatre are as follows: Costumes designed or selected for Stars or Featured Players are a minimum of $75. per costume.

Costumes designed or selected for Supporting Players are a minimum of $35. for the first 50 costumes and a minimum of $25. for all costumes in excess of the first 50.

Designed repeats are a minimum of $15. per repeat. A designed repeat is a repeat of an original designed costume. It is not unusual to design 1 costume for the chorus, and then have 8 or 10 or more repeats of the designed original.

Selected repeats are a minimum of $10. per repeat. A selected repeat is a repeat of a costume selected at a store for purchase. One copy is selected and 6 or 8 or any number of copies may be bought. These would be selected repeats.

Similarly, this Contract provides the same payments for reproduction for road or for foreign use, that is, one-half of the original fee and $75. per day for additional work. In addition the first 5 costumes in any production must total at least $500. unless it is a concert reading or production with less than 5 costumes, in which event the minimum fee must be negotiated. There are also provisions for supervising an imported production. A top costume designer will also most usually receive a weekly royalty payment which will range between $50. and $100.

Scenic — Lighting — and Costume Provisions in Common

dates of fee payments

In all three Contracts there is a provision that the Designer will receive one-third of the fee upon the signing of the Agreement, one-third on a date which is midway between the date of the Agreement and the date fixed for the first public performance, and the balance of one-third on the fifth office day after the first public performance. The Producer, however, must pay the full amount of the fee to the Union at the time the Contract is signed. The Union retains the money and pays it to the Designer on the dates set forth in the Agreement. In the event that a Producer files a complaint against a Designer for breach of Contract within the 5 business day limit for the payment of the last one-third, then the Union retains the last payment subject to the results of arbiration which is provided for in the Agreement.

duties and obligations

The specific requirements of each of the Designers is set forth in each contract and varies.

The Scenic Designer must either construct a working model of the settings to scale or complete sketches; supply the Contractors with color schemes or color sketches; design, select, or approve properties required for the Production, including draperies and furniture; supply specifications for the Constructing Carpenter to build and paint the sets; solicit estimates; attend the first out-of-town and the New York openings and dress rehearsals; and render the same services for road companies of the Production.

The Lighting Design Contract provides that the Lighting Designer must furnish a full equipment list and light plot drawn to scale showing type and position of all instruments necessary to accomplish the lighting; provide color plot and all necessary information required by the Contract Electrician; provide color plot showing the allocation of instruments for lighting control; supervise and plot special effects; supply specifications and solicit estimates of the same; supervise the hanging and focusing of the same; supervise the hanging and focusing of the lighting equipment and the setting up of all lighting cues; attend the first out-of-town and New York openings as well as dress rehearsals; conduct the lighting rehearsals for such performances; and to render the same services for road companies of the Production.

The Costume Designer must submit a costume plot of the Production, listing costume changes by scene for each character in the cast; complete all sketches of costumes designed for the production; supply the costume shop with complete color sketches or outline sketches with color samples attached, including drawings or necessary descriptions of detail and its application; solicit estimates from 3 different costume shops; be responsible for selection of all contemporary costumes or selection from the performers' personal wardrobe where appropriate; supervise all necessary fittings and alterations; design, select, and/or approve all costumes accessories, such as headgear, gloves, footwear, hose, purses, jewelry, umbrellas, canes, fans, bouquets, etc.; supervise and/or approve hair styling and selection of wigs, hair pieces, moustaches and beards; attend dress rehearsals and the first out-of-town opening; and render the same services for road companies of the Production.

abandonment

All three Contracts contain the provisions that if the production is abandoned, then the Designer is paid as if it were not abandoned as long as a certain specified amount of work as set forth in each contract has been completed.

transportation — out-of-town and other expenses

All agreements provide that the Designer must be furnished with first class round trip transportation whenever he is required to be outside the city of New York, and must be paid $25. per day for living expenses. In addition to the fee, the Designer must be reimbursed for out-of-pocket expenses for purchases made by him for the Production.

billing credits

The Scenic Design and Costume Design Contracts provide that the Designer is to be given billing directly under the name of the Director and that the name must appear wherever the name of the Director appears in the same size, quality, format, and boldness of type as the Director. If the Director's name is placed at the very top or bottom of the listing or given special prominence, then the Designer's name must be no less than one-third of the size of the title. Billing credit need not be given in the daily "ABC" ads. The Lighting Design Contract has the same specific provisions except that the Lighting Designer's name must appear directly under the name of the Scenic and/or Costume Designer rather than directly under the name of the Director.

no design alterations and additional payments

The Producer agrees in the Contract that he will not alter, or make substitutions for, the work created by the Designer without the Designer's approval. If additional work is needed over and above what was originally contracted for, then the Designer must be paid additional sums of money for the additional work.

time for completion

There is a provision in each contract that a Designer will be allowed a certain specified amount of time to do the design work. In the Costume Designer's Contract there is a futher specific provision that each design must bear a serial number and the name of the Production, and must be approved by signature or initial of the Producer or the Producer's representative so that it will be easy to know whether or not the Designer is entitled to additional compensation for work beyond what was originally contracted for.

additional pay for tv

Before the work of the Designer can be used for reproduction on television, the Designer must be paid an additional fee as specified in the agreement. The Designer must also be paid if his original designs are sold for use in any foreign production or for motion pictures.

strikes — fire — acts of God

There is a provision that the Designer's obligations are subject to delays due to strikes, acts of God, fire, or other causes beyond the control of the Designer, and that the Designer is not responsible for damages which result through the failure or inability of contractors, builders, painters, or other persons who are hired to carry out the execution of the plans.

title to designs

The title to all drawings, designs, and specifications remain the property of the Designer.

kick-backs forbidden

The Designer agrees that he will not accept any compensation, commission, gift, or any other remuneration or payment of any kind from any persons, firms, or corporations employed or engaged to carry out any work in connection with the Production. This is intended to prevent the Designer from receiving a kick-back for referring work to contractors.

producer limits authors use of designs

The Scenic Design Contract has a short Letter Agreement fastened to it which must be signed by the Producer. This Agreement has on many occassions elicited a good deal of dissatisfaction from Producers. The letter states in effect that the Author has in a written Agreement with the Producer agreed that he will not sell, lease, license, or authorize the use of any of the original scenery designs without the Designer's consent or the Producer's consent, and the Producer guarantees the performance of this Agreement by the Author. The Producer is liable if the Author uses the sets or designs in any foreign production even if the Producer's rights to the production have expired; however, the maximum liability of the Producer is one-half of the original fee. The letter also contains a short arbitration clause.

CHAPTER 10

CONTRACTS WITH THE PRODUCERS AND THEATRES

Association of Theatrical Press Agents and Managers, Union # 18032

Jurisdiction

This association is commonly known as ATPAM and covers the employment of Press Agents and Managers. Managers include House Managers employed by the Theatre, and Company Managers who are employed by the Production.

In fact, the Agreement specifically provides that a Contract of employment must be entered into with each Employee and that a Press Agent, a House Manager, and a Company Manager must be employed at all times that a Production is playing within the Union's jurisdiction.

The Agreement states that the jurisdiction of the Union is intended to include not only Stage Productions, but Variety and Vaudeville Attractions, Summer Theatre, Burlesque, Road Show Picture Presentations, Theatrical Entertainment, Opera Musical Presentations, Concerts, Ballets, Carnivals, Circus, Sport Expositions, and similar exhibitions and events.

The jurisdiction is not confined to the New York Metropolitan Area.

Wage Rates

The minimum weekly wage scale for the period commencing Labor Day 1968 to Saturday night preceding Labor Day 1969 is as follows:

House Managers (All Cities)	$213.50
House Managers (Musicals)	$213.50
Company Managers (New York)	$213.50
Company Managers (Musicals, NY)	$218.00
Press Agents (New York)	$289.50
Company Managers (Dramatic Tour)	$277.00
Company Managers (Musical Tour)	$329.50
Press Agent (Tour)	$336.00
Second Press Agent (Tour)	$243.50
Press Agent (Second Show same Producer)	$248.00

Doubling Prohibited

An Employee may not double. For example, one Employee many not be both the House Manager and Company Manager.

Work Week

The work week consists of 6 working days from Monday to Saturday inclusive with not more than 8 performances during the 6 days. For each additional performance during a week the House Manager and Company Manager must receive an additional one-eighth of their respective weekly salaries. If a production is performed 7 days a week in New York City (defined in the Contract as the 5 boroughs of the Greater City of New York) then the Company and House Manager must be paid for the seventh day on a per diem basis based on the actual salary received.

Time of Salary Payments

Salaries payable to Managers and Press Agents must be paid no later than 6 P.M. on Friday of the week in which the services have been rendered, and expense statements must be paid at the same time if the statements are rendered sufficiently in advance for the payment to be made.

The Employer must pay all transportation charges including lower pullman booths on overnight travel by train, and by scheduled first class flights on major air-lines. Non-scheduled flights are not permitted.

Summary Dismissal

An Employee may be summarily dismissed for intoxication on duty or dishonesty in the discharge of his employment.

Production of Radio — Industrial — TV — or Movies from Theatre

If a radio, TV, or motion picture performance of substantially the entire production originates in the Theatre, then the House Manager and the Company Manager must receive 1 week's pay in addition to their regular salary. A House Manager also receives an extra day's pay for each day an Industrial Show is performed in the Theatre. A Company Manager and Press Agent receive an additional one-sixth of their respective weekly salaries if a recording is made of the Production.

Closing Run of Less Than Four Weeks

An Employer may close a play and terminate the employment of all members of the Union engaged for the play or the Theatre without any notice to the Employees if the Play runs for 4 weeks or less. They must however be paid the minimums; a Company Manager for a Musical must be employed for at least 5 weeks prior to the Monday of the week in which the first public performance takes place (4 weeks for a dramatic production) and a House Manager must be employed at least 1 week prior to the day in which the first public performance takes place and for at least 2 weeks. This does not effect the tenure of the House Manager who is, as stated, entitled to tenure after 1 week's employment.

Closing Run of Over Four Weeks

If the Play has run more than 4 weeks, then the Employer must give 1 week's notice of closing. If the Production closes on a Saturday night then the Company Manager and House Manager must be paid at least 1 day's additional pay for the purpose of finishing the detail work in connection with the closing of the show. If either the Company or House Manager is called upon to render more than 1 day's service, he must be paid for each additional day an amount equal to one-sixth of his weekly salary.

Fire — Strike — Riot — Etc.

If the Show cannot be performed because of fire, accident, strike, riot, the public enemy, act of God, the illness of the Star or a Principal or Featured Performer, or if the Employee cannot perform on account of illness or other valid reason, then the Employee is paid only up to the date of the closing of the attraction if such be the case or to the date of the Employee's incapacitation.

Termination of Employment — Notice — Company Manager or Press Agent

If an Employer wishes to terminate the employment of a Company Manager or Press Agent prior to the closing of a show, he must give the company Manager or Press Agent at least 2 weeks notice in writing if he has been employed for 12 weeks or less, and must give 4 weeks notice in writing if the employment has been for more than 12 weeks. A Company Manager or Press Agent who wishes to terminate his employment must give the Employer at least 2 weeks notice in writing.

Midnight and Extra Performances — Pay and Commercial TV

House Staff Employees and Company Managers must also receive additional pay in the amount of one-sixth of the regular weekly salary for midnight performances. Extra performances are also covered in the Agreement. These is also provision that House and Company Managers must be paid for pay TV and Commercial TV.

Managers — Specific Terms

minimum term of employment — company manager

During the period from September 1, 1968, to August 31, 1969, a Company Manager for a musical production must be employed at least 5 weeks (4 weeks for a Dramatic Production) prior to the Monday of the week in which the first public performance (paid or otherwise) takes place. He may be employed for a period less than 2 weeks only in an emergency.

minimum term of employment — house manager

A House Manager must be employed at least 1 week prior to the day in which the first public performance takes place. If the box office of the Theatre opens for ticket sales at any time prior to the commencement of the House Manager's employment, then the House Manager must receive 1 additional day's pay. The House Manager must be on service at all times when the Theatre is open to the public. A House Manager must receive at least 2 weeks salary, even if the production closes within the first week of its engagement. If a House Manager is hired, he must continuously remain until the attraction is postponed or abandoned, and until he is given proper notice in accordance with the Agreement.

limited engagement — company manager

If a limited engagement in New York City is booked and played as a road tour after the original engagement in New York City, then the Company Manager must be paid his contracted salary as a Company Manager on tour throughout the New York engagement, rather than his salary as part of a New York engagement.

sunday — extra pay — house and company managers

House Managers and Company Managers are entitled to receive additional compensation for Sunday performances at the rate of one-sixth of the regular weekly salary for 1 performance and one-fourth of the regular weekly salary for 2 performances. These additional payments are not made if Sunday is part of the regular 6 day week.

House Staff Employees

house staff defined

House Staff means the House Manager and House Press Agent, if there is a House Press Agent. A House Manager must be employed but a House Press Agent is optional.

seasonal employment

House Staff Employees are hired for a season (unless the

lease, if the premises are leased, terminates before the end of the season) which runs from Labor Day to the Saturday night preceding the following Labor Day. Although the hiring is seasonal subject to other specific contract provisions, a House Staff Employee is not paid during a period that the theatre is dark. A House Staff Employee under contract for seasonal employment may accept other employment while his Theatre is dark, provided that his new engagement does not interfere or conflict with his Contract for seasonal employment.

dismissal during first week

A House Manager employed for the first time may be dismissed by an Employer during the first week without the consent of the Union, but after the first week the House Manager has tenure and cannot be dismissed, except in accordance with the terms of the Agreement.

automatic renewal

A House Staff Employee is automatically engaged for the following season unless he is otherwise notified in writing not later than May 31 of the current season.

severance pay

A House Manager is entitled to receive 4 weeks severance pay if he has up to 3 years of employment with the same management or same theatre, and 6 weeks severance pay if over 3 years. 10 weeks work in any season is considered a year of employment. The employee cannot receive credit for more than 1 year during any season. There is no severance pay if the Employee is discharged for just cause.

ownership change — severance pay

If the ownership or the control of the Theatre changes and

the House Staff is not continued, then the Employee must be paid severance pay equivalent to 4 weeks salary. The Employer agrees, however, that he will exercise every reasonable effort to continue the same House Manager on the job for the balance of his Contract. Notice of any sale or rental of the Theatre must be given to the Union.

theatre owner guarantees house manager and staff

The Contract of employment for a House Manager must be guaranteed by the Theatre Owner or Operator, and if it is a four-wall rental of the Theatre, then the House Staff must be guaranteed payment by the Theatre Owner as well as the Lessee.

Press Agents

minimum term of employment

A Press Agent must be employed 3 weeks prior to the Monday in which the first paid public performance is given when the attraction opens cold in New York City. If the attraction opens out of New York City on a pre-Broadway tour, a Press Agent must be employed at least 4 weeks prior to the first paid public performance.

If an attraction goes on tour after a New York City engagement the Employer must employ a Press Agent at least 4 weeks prior to the day of the first public performance on tour. This does not relieve the Producer of the obligation to employ a Press Agent until the end of the New York engagement.

part time

As with a company manager, a Press Agent may be hired for a period less than 2 weeks only in an emergency. If the

Employer engages a Press Agent on a part time basis prior to the times above set forth, then the Press Agent must be paid 1 week's salary for part time work during the fourth and fifth weeks before the week in which the opening occurs in New York City, and 1 week's salary for part time work in the course of the sixth and seventh weeks before the week in which the opening occurs in New York City, and 1 week's salary for part time work in the course of the eighth, ninth, tenth, and eleventh weeks, or any of them, before the week in which the opening occurs in New York City. A Press Agent may not be discharged unless he has received the equivalent of 2 weeks full salary for such part time work. The part time arrangements are applicable only in New York City and, of course, are not applicable if the Press Agent is required to devote full time during any of the weeks. Oddly enough the Agreement provides that the Union is the sole judge as to whether or not the employment is part time or full time.

opening postponed — abandonment

If the opening is postponed or abandoned the Union and the Employer will make arrangements for compensation to the Press Agent during the period that he does not render services but the Press Agent must have received at least 2 weeks full salary before the week in which the attraction was scheduled to have opened.

after opening closing

If the Press Agent does not have a Run of the Play Contract, and the Producer wishes to close the show, he may terminate the Press Agent's employment during the first week after the opening of the Play and pay him for each day's compensation at one-sixth of the regular weekly salary on the condition that the Play actually closes on the Saturday following the notice to the Press Agent. If notice is given before noon, the Press Agent need only be paid up to and including the day preceding the notice. If notice is given after noon he must be paid up to and including the day that the notice is given to him. If the Play continues beyond the Saturday, then the Press Agent resumes work and receives a salary for the period of the layoff.

temporary closing

If a production is temporarily closed and reopens in the same city within 4 weeks, then the same Press Agent must be employed at least 1 week prior to the reopening. If the closing is longer than 4 weeks then the same Press Agent must be hired at least 3 weeks prior to the Monday of the week in which the first paid public performance is given, or 4 weeks prior to the first paid performance (the number depending upon whether the show is opening cold in New York City or out-of-town pre-Broadway) the same as above stated for a new production.

exclusive services

The Employer and Press Agent may mutually agree that the Press Agent's services are exclusive. An Associate Press Agent's services are limited to engagements within the City of New York City or pre-Broadway tours. No Press Agent on tour after the New York engagement, or after 6 weeks of a pre-Broadway tour, may handle more than 1 attraction, nor may a Press Agent handle more than 1 Production on pre-Broadway tour at the same time.

Advertising Agency

After the Press Agent is hired, the Producer will have to

give consideration to the selection of an Advertising Agency. The Advertising Agency, as distinguished from the Press Agent, handles all of the paid advertising; the Agency works in conjunction with the Press Agent. The Agency does not cost the Producer any additional money for placing the advertising, as an Advertising Agency is paid a percentage of the billing by the periodical or newspaper in which the advertising is placed. The Agency is of course paid for artwork.

The Advertising Agency will help with all of the artwork and the ad layouts, will work up the logo, will advise where and when and how much to advertise, and will do this for the Producer together with the advice of the Press Agent, who is in fact in charge of the entire advertising campaign.

Actually one Agency handles most of the Broadway advertising. There are 1 or 2 other small Agencies which account for the balance, but the one Agency has more or less a monopoly on the theatre business.

Associated Musicians of Greater New York, Local #802 American Federation of Musicians

Hiring of Musicians

All Musicians are hired by the Theatre, that is, they are signed by the Theatre even though the payment of the Musicians may be shared by the Theatre and Producer as discussed in the chapter on the Theatre License Agreement. A Contractor selects and hires the Musicians and signs the Contract with the Theatre. Very often the Composer or Conductor has someone that he would like in the Orchestra, so this will influence the actual selection.

When a Musical is travelling on the road, they usually carry 5 or 6 Musicians with them. They are paid by the Production while on the road and then go on the Theatre payroll when the show comes in to New York.

Jurisdiction

The League of New York Theatres has entered into a Collective Bargaining Agreement with the Musicians Union which sets forth the minimum rates of pay as well as other provisions of employment.

Contract Houses and Penalty Houses

Each Theatre Owner or Operator at the beginning of the season decides whether or not to enter into a Contract with the Union for the ensuing year. If a Contract is not signed then it is not necessary to hire any musicians unless they are needed for the Show. If they are needed, however, then the musicians appearing in the non-contracted House (a Penalty House) must be paid more than they would be paid if the Theatre were a Contracted House.

If the Theatre is a Contracted House then a certain number of musicians must be hired, whether you need them for the Show or not. The number depends upon the size of the Theatre and whether the Play is a Musical or a Dramatic Production. The Contract with a Contracted House constitutes an Agreement with the Union to employ a certain number of musicians for every show in the Theatre during the term of the Contract.

The Theatre and the Producer will share the cost of the Musicians, as discussed in the section covering the Theatre License Agreement.

Minimum Number of Musicians — Musical

The minimum number of Musicians required in a Musical Show depends upon the number of seats. If the Theatre has between 1,000 and 1,100 seats, the Orchestra must consist of a minimum of 16 musicians. If the Theatre has over 1,100 seats the Orchestra must consist of a minimum of 25 musicians. If the Theatre has less than 1,000 seats the number of musicians is fixed by the Union's executive board. Every Musical Show must have an Assistant Conductor.

Minimum Number of Musicians — Dramatic

A Dramatic Show is considered the same as a Musical Show if it includes music as an integral part of the Play. If, however, the music in a drama does not exceed 25 minutes and there is no overture, entre-acte, and exit music, then a minimum of 4 Musicians must be employed at the dramatic scale, whether it is a Contracted or a Non-Contracted House. This is applicable even if some pit music is used as well as some background music if the aggregate does not exceed twenty-five minutes. There are certain exceptions listed in the contract.

Minimum Number — Ballet — Grand Opera — Vaudeville — Etc.

On the other hand, if the music consists of the accompaniment to a ballet, grand opera, vaudeville, singing in excess of an aggregate of 16 measures per performance, or regular or interpretative dancing instrumentally accompanied, then the Musicians must be paid the musical scale (whether in a Contracted or Non-Contracted House) and not 4 but a minimum of 6 must be used.

Mechanical Devices

If a mechanical musical device or reproduction is used to displace Musicians, then a minimum of 4 Musicians must be employed in the Theatre and the Producer must notify the

Union in advance if any mechanical music or musical reproduction will be used.

Wage Rates

The minimum weekly wages to be paid are as follows:

in New York City

Contracted Houses	Musical	$200.00 per week
Contracted Houses	Dramatic	148.50 per week
Non-Contracted Houses	Musical	247.50 per week
Non-Contracted Houses	Dramatic	192.50 per week

Additional performances shall be paid pro-rata.

out-of-town, break-in

For a week's work	$275.00 per week
For one (1) performance on one (1) day	$44.50
For two (2) performances on one (1) day	$74.25

Musicians taken out-of-town for the full period to break-in a musical shall receive pay between the end of the break-in and the New York opening, but regular rehearsal pay in lieu of performance (not overtime) will be credited.

work outside pit

Orchestra members who are required to play in view of the audience and anywhere outside the pit shall receive in addition to their regular weekly salary the sum of $35.00 per week.

week's work defined

A week's work shall consist of eight (8) performances or less, six (6) days out of seven (7) consecutive days.

contractor paid extra

The Contractor shall receive fifty (50%) percent additional, and the Conductor shall receive seventy-five (75%) percent additional over and above the appropriate applicable rate set forth above.

assistant conductor paid extra

The Assistant Conductor shall receive $39.60 per week additional over and above the appropriate applicable rate set forth above. Any amount over the scale to be paid to a person appointed to this position shall be negotiated. This arrangement is to apply to present contracts where the musician proposed to be designated or already so designated is receiving over the scale.

librarians paid extra

Librarians shall be paid $31.52 per week.

Rehearsal Rates

2½ hours or less up to 6:30 P.M.

For rehearsals terminating not later than 6:30 P.M., the rates shall be as follows for two and one-half (2½) hours or less:

For Musicians $13.75 Contractor $20.62 Conductor $24.03

overtime

Overtime for rehearsals referred to above shall be paid for at the following rates for each thirty (30) minutes or less of such overtime:

For Musicians $2.75 Contractor $4.07 Conductor $4.84

for 1 hour after night performance

A one (1) hour rehearsal may be called immediately after a night performance, for which the following rates shall be paid for one (1) hour or less terminating after midnight. The above one hour rehearsal after the show may start after a ten (10) minute break with the usual five (5) minute intermission during the rehearsal thereafter.

Per Musicians $9.90 Contractor $14.85 Conductor $17.33

for 1 hour before evening performance

For a one (1) hour rehearsal before an evening performance, the following rates shall be paid:

Per Musician $5.50 Contractor $8.25 Conductor $9.63

for 1 hour on 2 performance day or after matinee

For a one (1) hour rehearsal on a two performance day before or after a matinee performance, the following rates shall be paid:

Per Musicians $8.25 Contractor $12.38 Conductor $14.45

after midnight

Rehearsals starting at or after midnight for one hour or less shall be paid for at the following rates with overtime in fifteen (15) minute segments:

Per Musicians $9.90 Contractor $14.85 Conductor $17.33

during break-in period

During break-in period of a show a four hour rehearsal may be substituted in lieu of a performance. When such a rehearsal occurs in the afternoon to be followed by an evening service it shall terminate no later than 6:30 P.M. The evening service following shall then begin no sooner than 8:00 P.M., allowing one and one-half (1½) hours for dinner. Such services shall be either rehearsal or performance but not a combination of both.

rehearsal pianists

Rehearsal for all shows preparatory to opening and not in conjunction with orchestra shall be paid for at the following rates for a six (6) day, forty (40) hour week, exclusive of Sundays:

Per pianist $175.00

Overtime prior to midnight, for each fifteen (15) minutes or fraction thereof — $1.72.

Rehearsals on Sunday, for six (6) hours or less shall be paid for at the rate of $41.30.

No more than eight (8) hours playing shall be permitted within a period of twelve (12) hours in any one (1) day, which must terminate not later than midnight.

For rehearsal pianists employed by the day shall be paid at the following rates:

Day Rate

Three (3) hours or less terminating not later than 7:00 P.M., shall be $18.00.

Overtime on day call for one-half hour or less segments shall be $3.00.

Night Rate

Night rehearsals, four (4) hours or less terminating not later than midnight, shall be $28.00.

Overtime continuing before midnight for one-half (½) hour or less shall be $3.50.

Overtime continuing after midnight for each fifteen (15) minutes segment shall be $2.63.

Audition Pianist

Two (2) hours or less	$26.00
Overtime (per hour or fraction thereof)	13.00

doubling rates

No member of an Orchestra or Stage Band can perform on more than 1 instrument unless he receives additional compensation. If he plays an additional unrelated instrument he must be paid an additional $35. per week, and if he plays 2 unrelated additional instruments he must receive an additional further sum of $17.50 per week. Doubling charges need not be paid if he is required to play certain instruments that are set forth in the contract as being very similar. That is, for example, a Musician may play more than one member of the saxophone family, or the basoon and contrabasoon, or the tuba and souzaphone, etc., at no additional charge.

Notice of Closing

Musicians must be given at least 1 weeks notice of the closing of the Show unless members of other Unions, such as Actors' Equity or Stage Hands, must get more than 1 week's notice in which case the Musicians must get the same notice.

Temporary Lay-off

The show may be temporarily closed and the musicians laid off temporarily, only for certain conditions set forth in the Contract. If the Star's Contract permits a vacation then a layoff for up to 2 weeks is permitted during any 1 year, provided that 25 weeks have accrued for each week of layoff. If the show is to be closed down temporarily because of poor business, a layoff of up to, but not exceeding, 8 weeks may be made during the months of June, July, and August, but only if the consent of the Union is obtained, which consent will not be unreasonably withheld. The Musicians must be given 2 weeks notice of layoff if a show is closed for poor business, and they may leave the engagement. If the show does reopen after such a layoff, the Musicians must be guaranteed at least 2 weeks employment.

Dressing Rooms

The Musicians must be furnished with convenient dressing rooms, rest rooms, lockers, and sanitary wash rooms.

Musicians Cannot Invest in Show

The Agreement specifically provides that Employers who are Producers will not engage any Musicians who invest in the Producer's Show.

Pay TV

In the event that there is a closed circuit or pay television production during the period commencing with the tryout period and ending 1 year after the end of the New York run, the Employer must offer employment for said production to the Orchestra who played the Original Show.

Original Cast Album

If an original cast album is made, the Musicians that have been employed for the run of the show and extra performing Musicians must be the ones who record the album.

Schedule Changes

Show schedule changes must be sent to the Union, as well as notification 4 weeks in advance of an Actors' Fund Performance.

CHAPTER 11

OUT-OF-TOWN PRE-BROADWAY

Purpose—Audience Response

Up until recently, almost every show would go out of town for a pre-Broadway run prior to the Broadway opening. The purpose of an out of town try-out is to get audience response so that the show can be fixed before it is subjected to the grueling attention of the Broadway critics. Taking a show out of town is an expensive operation, so consequently someone was eventually bound to come up with the idea that it isn't really necessary.

It Depends on the Play

In fact there are some Plays that definitely should be tried out out of town, and others where it would make little difference. If a Play does not have a pre-Broadway try-out then the Play will probably preview on Broadway for a longer period of time so that the Broadway preview audience response may be utilized to fix anything that needs fixing, to the extent that it can be fixed in the available time.

Dramatic Differs from Musical

A Dramatic Show probably should not go out of town unless there is a star in the Show, a Star with out-of-town drawing power. The Dramatic Show without a Star on a pre-Broadway tour is likely to have difficulty finding that Audience from which a response is to be measured.

A Musical, without a Star, likewise should not go out of town on a pre-Broadway tour unless there is a Subscription Audience waiting to see the show when it arrives. If the Theatre wants the show, then the Theatre will make arrangements for you to take advantage of the Subscription Patrons which some Theatres have. This could mean guaranteed box office receipts of $50,000. to $60,000. a week. An example is the Fisher Theatre in Detroit, or the Mechanic in Baltimore, or the O'Keefe in Toronto, which do have Subscription Patrons.

A Show, Dramatic or Musical with a Star, or a Musical with a Subscription Ticket Sale, should most usually plan on a pre-Broadway Tour.

How Long on the Road — And Previews

Most usually a straight Dramatic Show will stay on the road for from 4 to 6 weeks before coming into Broadway and a Musical will generally stay out for between 6 and 10 weeks. After the Show comes into New York, it may preview for a few days, a week, or if it is in trouble and needs a lots of fixing, then for several weeks, if the money holds out. The very least is a run through and Dress Rehearsal prior to the official Opening.

If the show does not go out of town, then it may preview for between 1 week and 3 weeks. If it does not go out of town, it is likely that there is not an excess amount of money, so it will in most instances be difficult to preview for more than a week or 2, as it costs money. Do not count on making money during the previews. It can happen, but only if you have that big box-office drawing Star, the Play is written by a currently hot famous Author, or some other such unusual situation.

Sets And Props Moved By Truck Or Train

Although the cast and crew may be flown between stops, the sets and props are almost always moved overland. If it is a big hop, it is possible that the sets and props will also be flown, but this is not usual on most moves. It is not usual to risk the chance of bad weather in transporting the sets, for a certain amount of time is required to set up after arrival. Overland one knows that it will require a certain number of hours from the time you are out of the Theatre, and one can figure that the last truck will leave at about 8 o'clock in the morning following the last evening performance. There is no assurance if the sets are flown that they will arrive in time to be installed and ready to go for the next scheduled performance.

Where to Go Pre-Broadway

Most knowledgable Producers like to play New Haven because it is the cheapest to get on out of town with perhaps one exception—Wilmington, which might in some instances be cheaper, but has many other disadvantages. Even though New Haven is the cheapest to put on, don't count on making money there, for in all probability you won't. The prices that one can charge in New Haven are limited and you will in all probability not play there for more than a week or a week and a half. Traveling and setting up is costly, so ideally one would hope to stay in a Theatre long enough to pay for the moving, the take in and the take out.

Boston is a very desirable out of town try-out city. Boston has major critics (several of whom are well respected in the Trade) and most Shows can hope for mixed reviews from the

Boston critics at the very least, even if the show is less than good. Of course a good show will come off with unanimous raves. Boston generally means some business even if the show is less than good, if it is short of a disaster.

Philadelphia used to be considered very good for a straight Dramatic Show. For some reason, not completely know or understood, Philly is considered less desirable than it used to be.

Desirable Musical Houses

The most desirable Musical Houses are the very large houses, The weekly operating expenses for a Musical are so great that unless the show is in a large Theatre there is little chance of making money. The O'Keefe Theatre in Toronto and the Fisher in Detroit are ideal since they are immense and can easily gross over $100,000. a week if you come in with a hot property.

Moving a Show — Deck Complicates Move

Moving a show is an expensive, complicated procedure. The main complication arises from the fact that the last thing out of the Theatre has to be the first thing into the next Theatre. The floor is the complicating factor. The last truck to arrive with the floor, or deck as it is called, must be the first to go into the new House. What generally happens is that you can sometimes unload some of the other things and fly them while the deck is being put down.

A deck is a platform (usually 8 inches deep) which contains all of the turntables and winches. There are some shows which do not require a deck; however, almost all Musicals, and many Dramatic shows do require a deck.

Some Shows Own Two Decks

Sometimes a successful Road Company will own two decks

so that there is always one ready to be installed into the next Theatre. While the deck is being disassembled at midnight in one city, it is at the same time being installed in the Theatre at the next stop.

Out-of-Town — Union Requirements

The Union requirements are different in each Theatre out of town. One pays more for the cast and there is a per diem expense payment which must be made to the cast and crew.

Out-of-Town Advertising

Out-of-town, a show advertises in all of the major dailies as it costs relatively little. All of the out-of-town advertising for a large Musical during a 3 week stay in a city might amount to a total of $3,000.

New York Advertising

In New York City at the present time, the only really important newspaper for Theatre advertising is the New York *Times*. Some small amount is sometimes spent on the New York *Post* because it is an afternoon paper, and also because it has an audience which responds to a particular kind of show in some instances.

Out-of-Town — When Fold — When Get Help — Etc.

A show will never close out-of-town unless the Producer runs out of money and has to close, or in that most rare instance where a Producer with loads of money decides that the show is so bad, has no chance, and for his reputation's sake, he must deliver the coup de grace. There are too many Show Biz tales of the out-of-town flops that went on to become the greats of Theatre History, so the Producers keep the shows alive and bring them in to New York for the opening night reviews if at all possible.

Musicians — On the Road

Usually a Musical will carry 5 or 6 Musicians and pick up enough others on the road to make 25 or 26 in all. The Union does not really care whether the Production carries the musicians with them or hires them on the road; however, since some of the out-of-town Houses have Contracts with the local Musicians Union to hire a certain number of musicians, it is wise to leave room for the hiring of that number to fulfill the requirements. Then, too, it is more costly to carry the musicians with the Production, and usually unnecessary, especially when very competent musicians may be employed in all of the towns booked into. There are usually between 25 and 30 musicians on most Musicals.

Out-of-Town Advance Man

The Advance Man on a Show that goes out of town is the Press Agent. If the Show is on a road tour, the Advance Man never sees the company since he is always a week or two ahead of them. His job is to make sure that as many people as possible learn of the show's coming. To accomplish this, he sets up press interviews for the Stars and does whatever else that he can to obtain publicity.

On a pre-Broadway tour, the Advance Man will go out of town 2 or 3 weeks ahead of time, but will usually only stay out for a day or 2 in each town. He may come back for any important interviews and will come back for opening night. In his absence, the Press Agent will ask the Company Manager to act as the clearing house for the local newspaper and radio people. This may be difficult in some instances for it is not always easy for the Company Manager to go to a Star, who may at the time feel harrassed and overworked, and ask her to get up an hour early to see a newspaper reporter that he or she has never heard of and that one cannot know the possible results of.

Out-of-Town License Agreement

The out-of-town license agreement is discussed in detail after the discussion of the Broadway license agreement. If one has an understanding of the Broadway license agreement later discussed in great detail, it is easier to understand the out-of-town license agreement.

CHAPTER 12

BROADWAY AND OUT-OF-TOWN THEATRE LICENSES

Theatre Arrangement

The Theatre should be arranged for as soon as possible after one is certain that the Production will proceed. If there is a Theatre jam-up, it is possible for a show to wait around for 1 or 2 months for a Theatre to open up. This could be expensive.

Broadway Theatre License Agreement

License — Not Lease

The Rental Agreement for the use of a Broadway Theatre is usually a License Agreement, rather than a Lease. There are some technical differences between a Lease and a License Agreement, which for our purposes it is not necssary to explore. The Theatre is generally in a strong bargaining position and for this reason the License Agreement is usually heavily weighted in favor of the Theatre Owner or Operator.

No Standard License Agreement

There is no Standard License Agreement; however, there

is an Agreement that is used by many theatres. Even the Theatres not using that particular Agreement have an Agreement which contains most of the same terms, albeit sometimes in slightly different language.

Date of Occupancy

The Theatre Agreement will state that the Theatre Owner agrees to furnish the Theatre from a certain specified date, which is the proposed opening date of the show. It is not unusual for the Producer to have the Theatre in advance of the opening date for the purpose of running paid previews. Under some circumstances, if a Broadway theatre is dark, it might also be used for rehearsals. This is not usual, however, since it is more economical for the Producer to hire a rehearsal studio. In all events, it will be necessary to get into the House at least a few days before the first paid preview to do a dress rehearsal.

What Theatre Furnishes

The Theatre Agreement provides that the Theatre will furnish the Theatre, house programs, ushers, porters, matrons, doormen, ticket takers, the treasurer and assistant treasurer, a house manager, and a specified number of stage hands. The stage hands furnished include a head property man, a head carpenter, and a head electrician, but do not include the company crew or production men working for the Producer.

What Producer Furnishes

The Producer agrees to present the Play and to furnish the scenery, costumes, electrical and sound equipment, literary and musical material, advertising and press, and all other properties, materials, and services not furnished by the Theatre.

Star Named and Term of Occupancy

The Agreement will sometimes provide that the Producer agrees to present the Play with a Star who is named in the Agreement, and hires the Theater for not less than 12 months, unless the Show closes sooner, or the License Agreement is terminated in accordance with the terms of the Agreement.

The Producer also agrees to display to the Theatre Owner or Operator copies of the Agreements with the Star and agrees that he will not alter or modify these contracts without the consent of the Theatre.

Percentage Payment for Theatre

It must be remembered that the Theatre Owner is paid a guaranteed payment against a percentage of the box office receipts.

Theatre Guarantee

The guaranteed payment is usually computed as the amount necessary to cover the Theatre Owner's expenses so that if the Theatre Owner is going to make any money it must be because he has a show in his Theatre that is selling tickets and earning money at the box office. It is for this reason that the Theatre Owner, having an interest in the Play, wants to know who the Star will be, and wants to make certain that the Producer will present the Play with that particular Star. The range of weekly guarantees on License Agreements in the City of New York is from $4,500. to $15,000. The 15,000. guarantee would be for a musical and this was raised from a recent maximum guarantee of $10,000.

License Fee — Percentage of Gross

The license fee (which would be rental if it were in fact

a Lease rather than a License Agreement) is usually 30% of the gross receipts. The percentage arrangements will vary depending largely on how badly the Theatre Owner or Operator wants a particular show in his Theatre. The Agreement may provide that the Theatre is to be paid 30% of the gross receipts up until a certain amount during each week, and 25% of all gross receipts over that specified amount. For a Dramatic Show it might be provided that the Theatre will receive 30% until the gross receipts are $25,000. or $30,000. during any week, and 25% above that specified amount.

Sometimes a Theatre Owner will give the Producer a bonus if a show grosses in excess of a certain specified amount. For an example; the Theatre might allow the Producer of a Musical a $1,000. bonus if the show grosses in excess of $70,000. Another way of providing this kind of incentive is to make arrangements that the Theatre will be paid 25% of the first $20,000. of gross receipts, 30% of all of the gross receipts over $20,000. up to $70,000., and 25% of all gross receipts over $70,000.

Gross Receipts Defined

Gross receipts are computed as the receipts from the sale of tickets less admissions and other taxes and broker's fees, commissions, and discounts, if any payable upon such receipts, and less any amounts required to be paid by the Theatre or the Producer for pension and/or welfare benefits when the source of the payments are funds representing a reduction or elimination of admissions taxes by any governmental entity. This would cover the 5% New York City Amusement Tax which was discontinued, and the proceeds of which were turned over to certain Unions to cover payments toward the pension and welfare funds. Losses because of non-payment of checks or non-collection of bank orders reduce the gross receipts to the extent of the loss.

Charge for Air Conditioning

The Agreement has a provision that the Producer will pay a fixed amount whenever the air conditioning system is in operation. The additional amount will usually range between $50. and $100. per performance.

Stop Clause

Since the Theatre Owner or Operator relies upon the gross box office receipts for the licensing fee, there is also a provision in almost all License Agreements to the effect that if the gross box office receipts are less than a specified amount (this amount is very often referred in the License Agreement as the "stop clause sum") for 2 weeks then the Producer or the Theatre may terminate the Agreement. The stop clause in some contracts specifies 2 weeks, and in some contracts 2 "consecutive" weeks. A stop clause protects both the Theatre and the Producer in that if the gross receipts of a Show fall below the stop clause amount for 2 consecutive (or non-consecutive, depending upon the contract) weeks then either the Theatre or the Producer can get out of the obligations of the Agreement.

Stop Clause Amount Computation

The stop clause is computed roughly on the basis of what the weekly gross receipts must be for the Producer to break even. The amount is sometimes left blank when the License Agreement is entered into and later decided upon when the show comes into New York and the parties are in a better position to fix the amount. The stop clause sum usually ranges between $18,000. and $50,000. (although some Musicals may finally end up requiring considerably more than $50,000. each week to break even).

Break Even

What a show requires to break even depens upon a lot of factors. If it is a Dramatic Show, other than a show starring a single performer, then the show may break even at between $18,000. and $40,000. of gross weekly box office receipts. If it is a Single Performer show then it might possibly break even for as little as $12,000. If the Show is a Musical then it will break even at something between $35,000. and $70,000. ($70,000. is unusually high) of gross box office receipts.

Neither the Producer or the Theatre may purchase tickets for the purpose of increasing the gross weekly receipts above the stop clause sum.

Stop Clause Termination Procedure

In order to terminate in accordance with the stop clause, one party must give the other party written notice no later than the Monday night following the 2 weeks in which the box office receipts were not in the amount of the "stop clause sum." If the notice is given, then the run ends at the close of the evening performance on the next succeeding Saturday.

The Agreement may be terminated at the end of any 2 weeks during which weeks the receipts fall below the stop clause sum, even if the Agreement could have been sooner terminated at the end of any prior week, but was not. If the opening performance occurs after the beginning of a week so that less than 8 performances are given before the end of the week, then that part of a week is considered a week for the purposes of the stop clause determination, and the stop clause sum is reduced by one-eighth for every performance less than 8 given that week.

Theatre Security Deposit

The Producer must make a deposit with the Theatre as

security for the payment of the minimum weekly guarantee and the other obligations under the Agreement. The deposit will generally range roughly between 1 and 2 times the weekly guarantee. Thus the deposit will probably be between $6,000. and $30,000. Some Theatre Agreements also have a provision that the Theatre in its discretion may demand an additional deposit from the Producer if the Theatre estimates that the expenses which will be incurred by the Producer, for which the Theatre may be responsible, will be in excess of what was originally anticipated. This may seem like a harsh term and should be deleted from the Agreement whenever possible, but one ought not be surprised if it's there.

Increase in Stop Clause Sum and Guarantee

There is another provision in the Agreement which seems grossly unfair, but is nevertheless often there and should be expected. The Agreement may state that the amount fixed as the stop clause sum and the minimum weekly guarantee were based on the potential gross receipts of the Theatre at capacity for the play which was previously presented at the Theatre. If at any subsequent time the potential receipts, at capacity, are increased, then the stop clause sum and the minimum weekly guarantee are to be increased by multiplying each of them by a factor, the denominator which consists of the present gross receipts at capacity, and the numerator which consists of the gross receipts at capacity as so increased.

There is often a further provision to the effect that notwithstanding anything else in the Agreement to the contrary, the stop clause sum will in no event be less than 50% of the potential gross receipts at capacity, and the minimum weekly guarantee will be no less than one-eighth of the potential gross receipts at capacity. This provision is very often deleted from the form Agreement, and the specific dollar amount fixed for each of these items is applicable.

Sharing Expenses

The Theatre Owner shares the receipts with the Producer and shares as well certain expenses of the production. The expenses are shared each week in the same proportion that the box office receipts are divided for that week.

compute each week separately

This may vary from week to week for any given show. If, for an example, the receipts are shared with the Theatre receiving 30% of the first $30,000. of gross receipts and 25% of all receipts over $30,000. and the show grosses over $30,000 for a week, then the receipts for that week and the expenses shared will be computed as a percentage larger than 25% but smaller than 30%. Each week is separately computed. The Theatre might receive receipts and share expenses based on 29.1% one week and based on 28.7% the next week, depending upon how much over $30,000. that week's receipts are.

share only amounts actually spent

The expenses are only shared by the Theatre to the extent that that amount is actually spent for the item. The Producer may be required to show proof a certain amount was spent. If a Theatre shares on $2,500. newspaper advertising each week, but only $1,800. is spent during a week, then that is the amount that is shared.

It should also be understood that when it is said that the Theatre shares on $2,000. of an item, it means that if $2,000. is spent on that item during that week, then the Theatre would be responsible for the same percentage of $2,000. that the Theatre receives from the receipts. It does not mean that the Theatre is responsible for up to $2,000. but rather for the particular percentage of $2,000., if $2,000. is spent.

may limit theatre share of items

Most generally the Agreement sets forth the items which are shared and may place certain dollar or other limits to the maximum amount that the Theatre would have to pay.

maximum advertising limit

For an example, the Agreement will provide that the Theatre and Producer would share advertising expenses and will usually refer separately to newspaper, outdoor, and preliminary (prior to opening) advertising.

newspaper limit

The newspaper advertising would only be shared up to a fixed specific amount, which may be up to the amount of $1,500., $2,000., $2,500., or $3,000. per week. Anything above that stated amount is not shared but is the sole responsibility of the Producer.

outdoor advertising limit

Up to $500. for outdoor advertising each week is sometimes shared.

Sometimes the outdoor and newspaper advertising are combined, and the Agreement will say that the Theatre will share on both outdoor and newspaper advertising up to a specific amount each week, such as $2,000. or $2,500.

preliminary advertising limit

Preliminary advertising (prior to opening) is shared up to a specific amount. The amount may vary between $6,500. and

$30,000. and is usually at a rate which is divided over the first 8 or 10 or 20 or 30 weeks of the run.

The pre-production amount shared and the number of weeks it is spread over is completely arbitrary. A Theatre may share on $15,000. spread over 20 weeks, or on $30,000. spread over 30 weeks. The amount and the number of weeks depend on the bargaining strength of the parties, how badly the Theatre wants the show, whether it is a Musical or a Dramatic Show, and other such factors. Bear in mind that the Producer, as stated, must spend the money. If he has only spent $23,000. on pre-production advertising, then that is all that the Theatre would share on, even though the License Agreement may state that the Theatre will share on $30,000. A Dramatic Play would more likely share on $7,500. spread over 15 or 20 weeks.

theatre tries to spread payments

The Theatre will try to spread the payments over the longest period possible so that if the show closes the Theatre will part with less money, for if the Play does not run that number of weeks then the Theatre is only liable for payment during the weeks that it does run.

eight performance week

These expenses for advertising are based on an 8 performance week, and if less than 8 performances are given during any week, the amount shared is reduced by one-eighth for each performance less than 8.

joint control of advertising

The Agreement also may provide that the advertising is under the joint control of the Producer and the Theatre; however, the Producer's Attorney will often succeed in striking this from the Agreement so that the Producer may control his own advertising.

share cost of signs after three weeks

The Agreement usually provides that if the Play runs for 3 weeks, the Theatre and Producer share the cost of painting the houseboards on the front of the Theatre prior to the opening, painting them out after the last performance, as well as the cost of putting up the electric sign prior to opening and taking it down after the last performance. If the Play is not presented for 3 weeks then the Producer alone must assume these costs. The Theatre usually has the right to approve of the advertising on the outside of the theatre and to designate the place where it will be located.

producer may urge additional sharing

It is not unusual for a Producer to appeal to the Theatre after opening to help with additional advertising. If a show looks like it is in trouble but has a chance, the Producer may want to put an additional $30,000. into publicizing the show, and of course would like the Theatre to share as much of this as possible. The Theatre might give the Production a credit toward the advertising, but never cash. It might be that the Theatre will share another $500. per week for 10 weeks. This is more likely if the Theatre does not have another show with promise waiting to get into the Theatre, and it is not early in September when there are a large batch of plays trying to get in before Christmas. The Theatre Owner, of course, is looking for the smash hit in his house, and wants early in the season to find it, if possible.

paid previews shared — other extras cost producer

Paid preview performances are to be treated like any other

regular performance as far as the sharing of expenses. All expenses and charges, including wages of Theatre Employees, upon invitation preview performances (as distinguished from paid preview performances) are paid for solely by the Producer. Any excess costs and expenses for Sunday, holiday, and/or holiday eve performances in excess of those for a weekday performance are paid for by the Producer.

ticket costs shared

The Theatre will supply the tickets, and the expense of all tickets that are actually used for paid performances is shared. All other tickets not used, such as tickets ordered for the period after the close of the Play and for cancelled performances are solely the Producer's obligation and expense.

some taxes shared

The parties share taxes imposed on the Theatre by any governmental authority such as but not limited to a tax based on the gross receipts or a flat tax based on performances but not sales, use or occupancy tax which must be paid solely by the Producer.

preliminary box office help shared

It is sometimes provided that the Preliminary box offiice expense is shared for the Treasurer, First Assistant Treasurer, and also for the Portrer for the 5 days prior to the first paid performance of the Play. All other preliminary box office expenses must be paid by the Producer.

additional box office help shared

Additional box office personnel other than the Treasurer, and First Assistant Treasurer, if the Theatre deems the services advisable, is a shared expense. The Form Agreement ought to be changed to require approval by both the Producer and the Theatre so that it is not simply the Theatre's discretion whether additional box office personnel is hired. Since the Producer would be obligated to pay the largest share of this expense, he should have some say.

mail order costs shared

The parties share the cost of wages for additional employees in addition to the regular box office staff to service mail orders and ticket sales. The cost of stamps, envelopes, and other expenses in connection with mail orders is also shared.

contracts differ on box office sharing

Some Agreements may provide that the Producer pays for all box office help up until 2 weeks before the opening, which means the first paid preview. With a big show, it may be necessary to open the box office 4 weeks before the opening and very often 10 weeks is needed to handle the mail orders on a show that has a big Star. The Producer pays for all of that. 2 weeks before opening, the Theatre will furnish 2 Treasurers, share on 2 others, and anything other than that the Producer must pay for.

As with many of the other Agreement provisions, the terms are dependent, as has been noted, upon the bargaining power of the parties. Whether the box office personnel is shared starting 5 days prior to opening, or 10 days prior to opening, and the number that is shared is dependent upon all of the factors that determine the results of negotiations like this.

sharing of musicians

The parties will make some arrangement for the sharing of musicians. How many is a negotiable item. It is not unusual for the Theatre and Producer to share 4 musicians for a Dramatic Play in a House that has a contract with the American Federation of Musicians which provides that that is the minimum number required.

For a Musical, the terms also vary. It is not unusual to share on 10 to 12 musicians. Sometimes the Theatre will furnish 10 at the Theatre's expense and the parties will share 10. In other instances, the Theatre may agree to share on 12 musicians and the Producer may have to pay the total cost of 13 more.

retroactive wages — pension and welfare shared

The parties also share any retroactive wages paid to employees whose wages are shared, and pension and welfare benefits for any employee whose salary is shared.

theatre shares only for amount worked — not amount paid

There is a specific clause to the effect that if in any week there are less than 8 performances, but because of the Union Regulations the Producer must pay the Employees for 8 performances, then the Theatre must only contribute to the wages for those Employees during the period actually worked by them and not the additional amount payable to them because of the obligation of the Union Contract.

Take In and Take Out — Similar to Sharing

The Agreement provides that if the Play runs for 3 consecutive weeks or longer at the Theatre, the Theatre will allow the Producer a fixed amount to take the production into the Theatre, put it up and hang it, and a fixed amount for the removal of the production. This may be set forth as a fixed dollar amount or as an hourly allowance for payment of the employees to do the work. It is usually on an hourly basis since it would be more nearly related to the actual payment, especially if a show ran for 5 years and the cost to take it out had materially changed. It may be provided that the Producer will be allowed up to 275 hours to take the show in and up to 275 hours to take it out. Simply stated, this means that if more than 275 man hours are used (not including Department Heads) to take the show in, then the Producer would pay for all over 275, and if less than 275 man hours are needed, the Theatre would reimburse the Producer for the full cost.

Must Vacate Theatre Within Fixed Time

If the Producer does not remove the production from the Theatre within a fixed time (the Agreement will say 12 hours but this may be changed to 24 or 48 hours) after the closing performance, then the Theatre may dispose of the sets and props or store them at the Producer's expense.

Producer Pays Extra for Star's Temporary Absence

If a Star or Featured Player is temporarily prevented from appearing in a performance because of illness or otherwise, then the amount of the salary for that person for the period of the non-performance may be deemed a receipt payable by the Producer to the box office and divisible according to the provisions under which the gross receipts are divided. Such an amount "may be" deemed a receipt to be treated in this fashion, for the Agreement contains such a provision. Sometimes the provision may be stricken from the Agreement at the time of the execution, but even if it isn't, this is one of the "Owner's Provisions" that the Owner may enforce, but often does not enforce.

Producer Pays Extra for Star's Termination or Non-Appearance

The Agreement further provides that if the employment of the Star or Featured Players, named in the Agreement, is terminated, then in addition to any other damages the Theatre may increase its share of the receipts by an additional 5%. If a performance is suspended as a result of the Star or Featured Player's non-appearance, then the Agreement provides that the Producer must pay the Theatre an amount equal to the Theatre's share of the gross receipts at capacity. These provisions are somewhat harsh and are sometimes stricken from the Agreement before signing. Even if the provisions remain, the Theatre may elect not to enforce them. This sometimes does happen.

Theatre May Terminate Agreement If Star Leaves

The Theatre may also terminate the Agreement upon 48 hours notice to the Producer if the Star or Featured Player does terminate. If this part of the Agreement cannot be deleted, one should at least attempt to make it applicable solely to a Star.

Producer Pays If Opening Delayed

If the Producer fails to open the Play on the date set forth in the Agreement, it is provided that the Producer must pay the Theatre all of its expenses, including salaries of the Theatre personnel during the delay, and must also pay a fixed dollar amount for each week that the opening is delayed. The payment is pro-rated for less than an 8 performance week. It is not unusual that the weekly penalty (the fixed dollar amount added to the expenses) should be in the amount of $1,000., $1,500., $2,500., or $3,500. depending upon the Theatre's bargaining power. In lieu of the expenses and the additional dollar amount, the Theatre may receive the sum which is set forth as the minimum weekly guarantee, or the pro rata share if the delay is less than a week, based on 8 performances.

Theatre Sometimes Waives Late Opening Payment

The penalty for a late opening is sometimes waived by the Theatre if there is a good relationship between the Producer and the Theatre, and if the opening is delayed only from 1 to 3 weeks. Long delays will usually result in a forfeiture of the weekly guarantee amount for the period of the delay especially if the Producer wants the Theatre to hold the House for him. Postponements are very difficult for the Theatre Owner, for the period that the show is postponed is generally the time that theatre parties are booked, so that in addition to the loss of revenue, it can mean great inconvenience.

Theatre May Terminate If Opening Is Delayed

If the play is not presented during the 2 weeks after the scheduled opening date, the Theatre may terminate the Agreement by giving written notice to the Producer. If the Agreement is thus terminated, the Theatre (at its election) may either receive payment for expenses plus the fixed dollar amount (the penalty amount previously referred to) for the period from the opening date until delivery of the notice of cancellation, or in the alternative may receive twice the weekly minimum guarantee.

Guarantee Doubled for Early Closing

If the Play closes within 2 weeks after the opening date, the weekly guarantee is twice the amount of the minimum weekly guarantee as set forth in the Agreement. This provision is also sometimes stricken from the contract by mutual agreement at the time that the negotiations take place.

Producer's Insurance

There are specific provisions in the Agreement to the effect that a Producer must carry certain insurance and he agrees to make payment for all social security, unemployment insurance, and disability benefits which the Producer is obligated to pay for his Employees.

Concessions are Theatre's

The Theatre has the exclusive right to operate or contract with others for the operation of concessions of all kinds. Some License Agreements permit the Producer to sell souvenir books through the Theatre's concessionaire if the Producer pays to the concessionaire a commission of not less than 10% of the gross sales.

No Radio — TV — or Other Theatre Production

The Producer makes certain other commitments which he must abide by. He agrees, for an example, that he will not permit the Play to be done on radio, television, or in any other Theatre during the term of the Agreement with this Theatre, and for a period of 8 weeks after the end of the run. There is an exception noted that radio or television broadcasts not exceeding 15 minutes may be made for publicity purposes. The Producer also agrees that if a Star or Featured Player appears on television, the Producer will use his best efforts to get credit for the Play at the Theatre.

Producer Responsible for Theatre Alterations — Compliance with Laws — Etc.

In addition, the Producer agrees that he will not make any

changes or alterations in the Theatre, that he will present the Play in accordance with all existing laws, that he will pay for breakage and damage, that he will not violate the copyright laws or infringe upon any literary rights of other persons, that all scenery, costumes, and other props will be fireproofed, that any improvements required by the Star or other persons shall be the Producer's sole expense but that any alterations or furnishings placed in the Theatre (which can only be done with the Theatre's consent) become the property of the Theatre, that if the Producer receives a payment in consideration of his permitting the Star to terminate the Contract, then the Theatre will receive 50% of any such peyment, and that the Producer will restore the Theatre to its original condition if any changes have been made.

Theatre May Terminate If Fire — Act of God — Etc.

If the Theatre is rendered unsuitable due to fire, national or local calamity or emergency, act of God, strike, labor dispute or other unforeseen contingency, the Theatre is not responsible to the Producer and the Theatre may terminate the agreement upon 24 hours notice to the Producer.

Producer Will Not Interfere with Union Agreements

The Producer agrees that he will not do anything contrary to or inconsistent with any of the collective bargaining agreements between the Theatre and the Unions, nor will he interfere with the contract with Playbill, Inc.

Theatre Controls Box Office

Although the sale of tickets is under the joint control of the Theatre and the Producer, the Agreement provides that the Theatre has sole and exclusive control of the supervision of the box office and its personnel, and all gross receipts are under the control of the Theatre until a settlement is made. The Theatre License issued by the Department of Licenses requires that its employees be in charge of the funds. The tickets are ordered only by the Theatre, and the Producer agrees that he will not order, distribute, or issue tickets without the Theatre's prior consent.

Theatre House Seats and Free Seats

The Agreement will provide that the Theatre is entitled to purchase a certain number of house seats for opening night and a different number for each performance after opening night. In addition to the house seats which it may purchase, it may also provide that the Theatre is entitled to a certain number of free tickets. If the Play is a dramatic production, the Agreement may provide that the Theatre is entitled to purchase between 60 and 70 orchestra tickets for opening night and if it is a Musical, between 80 and 90. For all other performances, the Theatre may be entitled to purchase between 30 and 40 house seats which may be reduced to between 10 and 15 if there is a full theatre party on any specific night. The Theatre will try to get between 20 and 35 tickets for each performance, including opening night, free of charge. Try to limit or avoid this.

Press Seat Limitation

The number of press seats for opening and second night is under the joint control of the parties and the number is set forth. Opening night and second night will probably have between 160 and 200 free press seats.

Theatre May Terminate If Producer Has Not Funds

The Agreement contains two provisions which are eminently unfair to Producers and should, if possible, be changed or deleted. One provision is to the effect that the Theatre relies upon the representation that the Producer has sufficient funds to finance the Show and if the Theatre, after the Agreement is signed, determines *in its sole discretion* that the funds are not available to the Producer for this purpose, then the Theatre may upon 7 days notice terminate the Agreement and return the security deposit to the Producer less any expenses incurred by the Theatre. The Theatre ought to decide before it enters into the Agreement whether or not it wants a particular production and ought not be permitted to cancel the Agreement, if in its sole discretion it decides that the Producer may not have enough money.

Theatre May Terminate If Producer Breaches or Law Suit Likely

The other provision which seems unfair is to the effect that the Theatre, in addition to its remedies at law or in equity, may terminate the Agreement upon 48 hours notice if the Producer breaches any of the terms of the Agreement, or if the Theatre (again in the Theatre's sole discretion) determines that the showing of the Play will subject the Theatre to actions for damages, fines, penalties, revocation of license, copyright infringement, or any other legal action or proceeding. It's perfectly obvious that the way this clause is worded may be an out for the Theatre upon any grounds. Any *threatened* action against the Theatre, no matter how small, could be used by the Theatre as the excuse for terminating the Agreement.

Play Must Continue in Theatre

The Contract specifically provides that the Producer must continue the Play in the Theatre unless this Agreement is terminated, and that even an interim closing of the Play for a holiday, Star's vacation, or otherwise without the Theatre's consent, constitutes a breach of the Agreement by the Producer.

Physical Limitations

The Agreement contains specific provisions with respect to certain physical requirements. The Producer agrees that not more than 1,200 pounds will be placed every 12 inches on the headblock beam, that the spot line cables, platforms, etc., will be constructed and used in a certain manner, etc., and if the Producer does not comply with these requirements the Theatre may do so at the Producer's expense.

Theatre May Use Injunction

If the Producer does not comply with any terms of the Agreement, the Theatre is entitled to enforce its rights by injunction, and the Producer must pay the Theatre's reasonable attorney's fees and disbursements.

Changes and Approvals Must Be in Writing

This Agreement states that it cannot be changed or terminated orally, and contains the entire agreement between the parties. All approvals required by the Theatre are not granted unless they are in writing.

Limitation on Assignment

The Producer may not assign or transfer the License Agreement except that he may assign it to a Corporation controlled by the Producer or a Limited Partnership (of which the Producer is a General Partner) organized by the Producer to produce the Play. In the event of such assignment, the Producer, of course, continues primarily liable for all his obligations and an executed copy of the assignment must be delivered to the Theatre. If the Theatre is sold, or if the Theatre lease is transferred, the license may be assigned by the Theatre and in such event the original Theatre owner or operator would be relieved of any further responsibility or liability under the Agreement.

Theatre May File Form 1099

The Agreement further provides that the Producer authorizes the Theatre to prepare and file a joint form 1099 information return on behalf of the Producer and Theatre with respect to all payments by the Theatre and the Producer to Theatre Party Agents as compensation for services rendered by them .

Out-of-Town License Agreement

Sharing of Gross Receipts

The out-of-town Theatre License Agreement is very similar to the Broadway License Agreement. It is most usual that the Producer pay 30% of the gross weekly receipts to the Theatre, and there may be an arrangement that over a certain amount the Theatre will receive only 25%. For an example, it may be provided that the Theatre receives 30% of the first $20,000. of gross weekly receipts and 25% of all over that amount.

Guarantee and Deposit

The amount of the weekly guarantee and the amount of the security deposit vary with the size of the House, whether or not it is a musical or a non-musical coming into the Theatre, and other factors. The weekly guarantee will vary between $6,000. and $15,000. and the security deposit is usually the amount of the 1 week guarantee.

No Stop Clause Usually

There is no reason to have a stop clause, since in most instances the Play tries out out of town only for a very limited engagement.

Sharing of Expenses

There are provisions similar to the Broadway Agreement on the sharing of expenses in the same proportion that the parties share the receipts.

sharing advertising

Advertising may be shared up to a stated amount which might be up to an amount between $1,000. and $2,500.

sharing take in and take out

The Theatre allows the Producer a stated number of hours of stage hands to be used for the take in and take out.

The allowance to the Producer will probably range between 200 and 300 hours. There is also generally a limitation on the number of stage hands furnished at the Theatre's expense which will usually be between 5 and 10 for a Dramatic Production and between 15 and 20 for a Musical.

promotion shared

The parties share (at the agreed percentage—the same as receipts) the cost of postage, stationary, and labor to promote the local subscription list in an amount usually fixed as something between $1,200. and $2,000.

sharing on musicians

If the Play is a straight Dramatic Play, then the parties

agree to share the cost of the Theatre's regular House orchestra. If it is a Musical, the Theatre will share on all of the musicians or will in the alternative furnish and pay for a certain number of musicians and share on the balance. It is not unusual to provide that the Theatre will furnish ten musicians and the Theatre and Producer will share an additional 10 or 12 musicians.

theatre party costs shared

There are provisions that Theatre Party costs will be shared.

Air Conditioning Charge

The Agreement will most usually provide that there is an added charge for the air conditioning system which will probably range between $75. and $100. per performance.

Equipment Must Comply with Laws

The electrical equipment brought into the Theatre by the Producer must comply with all local statutes and laws.

P.A. System Furnished but Not Operator

The Producer may use the public address system in the Theatre at no additional charge; however, it is most usual for the Producer to pay for the Operator who operates the P.A. system .

Souvenir Book Sales

The License Agreement sets forth the maximum that may be charged for souvenir books, usually a dollar or a dollar and a half, and also provides that the Theatre must be paid either a 10% or 20% commission, which is paid to the House

Concessionaire. All other concessions are reserved for the Theatre.

Penalty to Producer if Star Out

In the out-of-town License Agreement, there is also a penalty provision in the event that the Star or Featured Player leaves the show or cannot perform. It is not unusual to provide that the Theatre will receive its actual out of pocket operating expenses plus an additional $2,000. or $2,500. or in the alternative the 30% of the gross box office receipts, whichever is greater. Like the Broadway License Agreement, if a Star or Featured Play is temporarily ill or out of the show, the salary saved during the week or weeks is deemed a receipt and divisible as a box office receipt according to the terms on division of receipts set forth in the Agreement.

Theatre Furnishes Treasurer and Assistant

The Theatre will furnish a Treasurer and Assistant Treasurer, but if it is necessary to engage a second Assistant Treasurer in the box office, the salary of the second Assistant is shared by the parties in the same percentage that they share the receipts. Any additional box office help required is paid for solely by the Producer.

Theatre Use Before Opening

Some out of town License Agreements will provide that for a stated period prior to opening, a fixed licensing fee is paid. This may be between $1,000. and $1,500. per week. When a fixed sum is paid for the Theatre prior to opening, the Producer must usually also pay for the cost of electricity during that period. Bear in mind that the Theatre must (or ought to, at any rate) be used for rehearsals for a few days prior to the opening.

Theatre Designates Newspaper for Advertising — Insurance — Fireproofing Sets — and Miscellaneous

It is not unusual to provide that the Theatre may designate the newspapers in which the advertising appears. The Theatre maintains jurisdiction of the sale of the tickets at all times. The Producer agrees that he will carry liability and compensation insurance during the time that the Play is at the Theatre. Scenery and paraphenalia must be fireproofed. An out-of-town lease also contains certain limitations on the appearance of the company in other clubs, restaurants, or other places patronized by the public. If the show closes for further rehearsals, or due to sickness or inability of the Principal Performer, there is a provision that the Producer must pay a fixed amount each week that it is closed.

CHAPTER 13

PRE-OPENING – DURING RUN – AFTER OPENING

Pre-Opening

Star and Director — Raising Money

With but one or two exceptions, having a particular Star or Director helps very little in raising money for a Production. The one or two exceptions are those very rare persons whose names have become household words and who cannot possibly do anything that does not make money, even if it is something somewhat less than good.

Record Company Financing

Record Companies have in the past invested large sums of money in Musicals, in exchange for the right to do the Origina Cast Album. A Record Company's investment interest varies from time to time, depending on the recent luck they may or may not have experienced. Very often a Producer is in a position to make a pre-production record deal for an Original Cast Album if he wants to, but if it does not include an investment in the show as part of the deal, the Producer will usually not accept it, but will wait until after opening to arrange for the Cast Album. If the Play is a smash hit, then the Production makes a better deal, and if the Production is a flop, the Album rights are of little value irrespective of when the deal is made.

Insurance

Most Broadway Producers will find it advisable to have the following insurance coverage:

Workman's Compensation (this coverage is mandatory).

Disability Insurance (mandatory in New York).

A Theatrical Floater Policy. This is an all-risk policy (with some minor exceptions) covering costumes, electrical equipment, sets, and basically all the other personal property of the show except buildings and improvements.

Business Interruption Coverage. This is coverage for an indirect profit loss caused by loss of the theatre, loss of sets, or such similar happening.

Personal Effects Insurance (required by Actors' Equity Association). This is an Inland Marine Form Policy which covers the actors and stagehands' jewelry, clothing, furs, and personal property.

Liability Insurance insuring injuries to the public and the cast and crew. The coverage includes bodily injury and property damage.

Non-Apperance Coverage for a Star. If the Star does not appear for one reason or another, the Producer may suffer a large loss. This insurance coverage may range between $200,000. and half a million dollars.

Of course there are many other special kinds of insurance to cover special kinds of things, and special kinds of events.

The Theatres will, in most instances, have the following insurance coverage:

Workmen's Compensation for all theatre personnel.

Fire and Allied Peril coverage on the building.

Fire and Allied Peril coverage on the contents of the building.

Boiler & Machinery Insurance covering the heating and air-conditioning equipment.

Business Interruption (rental insurance) to compensate for the Theatre being dark because of fire or other peril.

Broad Form Money and Securities Coverage Inside and Outside which would cover box office hold-up and payroll hold-up.

Fidelity Bond.

There is a large variety of miscellaneous insurance policies which a theatre owner may have to cover glass, signs, marquees, and numerous other parts of the theatre.

In most cases there is a very small market for this kind of insurance, and, in some instances, it is not easy to place the insurance.

Bonds Required

Before the show goes into production, the producer can expect to have to furnish certain bonds and guarantees which have been previously discussed in different places throughout this book. The following will be required:

Actors' Equity Association — Two (2) week's salary.

A.T.P.A.M. — Two (2) weeks salary.

Stage Hands — Payable to I.A.T.S.E. for Local No. 1, one (1) week's salary.

American Federation of Musicians — One (1) week's salary.

American Federation of Musicians, Arrangers & Copyists Bond — Varies in amount, usually between $2,500. and 5,000.

Wardrobe Attendants, Local No. 764 — One (1) week's salary.

United Scenic Artists — Payment for the entire set, costume and lighting design must be made in advance to the union.

The Theatre — A deposit usually in the amount of one (1) or two (2) weeks of the guaranteed rental.

The union guarantees are for the minimum salaries provided for in New York City.

Independent Booking Office, Out-of-Town Booking

The Independent Booking Office came into existence as a result of the efforts of the New York theatres to expedite and coordinate out-of-town bookings. It functions as a non-profit corporation and handles the arrangements for all pre-Broadway bookings and all first class or national tours. It does not handle second class tours or bus and truck tours. In the event that the out-of-town theatre does not have its own license agreement, the Independent Booking Office form is filled in and used.

The fee of the Independent Booking Office is $150. per playing week which is shared equally with the producer paying $75. and the theatre owner paying $75. For part of a week, the fee is pro-rated based on a 6 day week, so that each party pays $12.50 per day.

Play Doctor

payment

Rarely does a Production call someone in to rewrite a show as it rarely works with two Authors, so most doctoring comes from Directors, or persons acting as Directors. Generally what is needed is a point of view about the script, and this comes from the Director and not from rewriting. If a top Director is called in to Doctor a Show it can cost as much as $1,000. per day for his services. Expensive yes, but if it means saving the show, it is money very well spent. Most usually the Doctor Directors will be paid $2,000. or $3,000. as a fee, plus a percentage or two of the gross receipts. Directors have also done doctoring for different considerations. On one occasion the Doctor was given a well know European sports car for the job. It happens to have been a used car at that. Other gifts are sometimes settled on.

billing

The billing credits are often a hassle when there is a Director replacement. Often the new Director does not want his name on the billing, and often the original Director agrees with him, and doesn't want the new Director's name on the billing. If the new Director wants billing and the original Director will not permit the removal of his name, then the Producer has just one more problem to deal with and to settle. But then this is a Producer's role.

Advertising

Most usually the first big ad for a show is run during the 2nd or 3rd week of rehearsal; however, if the show has a big Star, the first big ad might be as early as 4 or 5 months before the scheduled opening.

Advance Sale

The Treasurer handles the money and is personally responsible if there is a shortage, or if the show closes and there are insufficient funds to make refunds for the Advance Sale. Tickets would be printed in advance for as far in advance as needed. On a Dramatic Show it is very unlikely that tickets would be printed farther in advance than 10 weeks (sometimes 6 weeks, or something between 6 and 10) unless the show has a lot of Theatre Parties signed. A Musical Show would likely start with tickets for 12 weeks in advance, unless there is indication of a huge advance sale and a long run.

A large advance sale by itself is not enough to provide a Producer with a great feeling of security. What is important is how far the advance sale is spread out. Even a million dollar advance on a big Musical might not by itself spell success. In a Theatre grossing $100,000. that would mean that the equivalent of 10 weeks tickets are sold in advance. If the equivalent of 10 weeks tickets is spread over 30 weeks or more, and there is little sale at the window, the show would be in big trouble, million dollar advance sale notwithstanding.

Ticket Sale Deductions

There are no amusement or other taxes on the sale of Theatre tickets. The only deduction is the 5% that used to be for the New York City Amusement tax which is now used for the Union Pension and Welfare Plans and is shared by the Unions in accordance with the arbitration award of Burton Turkus, dated April 23, 1963.

Ticket Brokers

The box office personnel deal with the Ticket Brokers. By and large Ticket Brokers can do very little to make or break a show, since they more or less cater to the demand for tickets rather than being a very moving force in creating the demand.

Theatre Parties

In a Shubert House, the Theatre takes care of the Theatre Party arrangements. In other Houses, the General Manager or the Producer arranges an audition for the Theatre Party Agents. It is then necessary to find out what dates each may want and shuffle things around so that they are all fairly happy.

A Theatre Party Contract will specify the name of the Star and if that Star does not appear in the show, then the Party may be cancelled and the money must be refunded.

Scene Changes — Automated

The changing of sets and moving of scenery and props may now be automated. It costs between $40,000. and $60,000. to automate a show. Recently there was a major squabble between a Producer and the Union, because automating the show meant replacement of between 8 and 10 men. The Producer won and the men were dropped after the change-over took place.

If the show looks like a borderline possibility, then it would be foolish to invest the money to automate the scene changes. If the show appears to be a sure thing early in the run, or if it looks promising after coming into New York, then this could be a good investment. The show must run some time to amortize the initial cost before the installation makes sense.

If the set changing is automated before the show opens on Broadway, then it precludes the union disagreement since it does not mean replacing the men as the men are never hired to do the job the machine does. For this reason, it is recommended that if the Producer has reasonable probability for assuming the play will be a success, then pre-Broadway automation would represent a good investment. Some Producers may not wish to take the risk ahead of opening and do not want to face the union battle after opening, so the show goes unautomated.

Someone has to tell the machine what to do, so it does not completely eliminate manpower. What happens is that a Stage Hand at the proper time pushes a button on the machine and then things happen automatically. Sets and props move in and out, things fly, and curtains move from the directions given by the card.

Automating appears to be a good investment for a Show that has the possibility of a decent run.

Computerizing a Box-Office

There is a minor revolution taking place in the sale of theatre tickets. There are people involved in the revolution who are convinced that it is somewhat more than minor. I am referring to the sale of tickets with the help of computers.

The advantages of computerized ticket sales are many. The theatre can eliminate the printing, storage, and auditing of pre-printed tickets. Sales may be made at remote locations, expanding the market so that persons unable to get to the box office to purchase a ticket may purchase a ticket locally. In addition, the computer method permits complete control and immediate accountings.

At the push of a button, it is possible to know what is the total advance sales for a particular show. It is also possible to determine the total advance sale for a particular show for any particular performance.

The concept is a basically simple one; however, the machinery necessary to accomplish this end is less than simple.

The way the computerized sale of tickets works is that the seating arrangement of a theatre is programmed into a machine at the central office with the programming covering the number of performances in advance that there is a demand for ticket sales. The machine keeps a complete inventory, and whenever a ticket is sold for a particular performance, the inventory is accordingly decreased.

There will be terminals connected with the central office machine, which terminals will be located in supermarkets, department stores, hotels, and other outlets where people congregate. It is anticipated that terminals will be in all the major cities of the United States and also in Europe. A customer wishing to purchase a ticket for a show on a specific date asks the terminal operator for the ticket and the operator inquires of the machine by pushing a series of buttons what is the best location available for that particular performance. Immediately, the terminal machine checks with the central office machine and responds with an answer. The best seating location will vary in each theatre and what is thought to be the order of preference will have also been programmed into the machine. If a customer wishes to purchase the best available seats, another button is pushed to order the seats. The tickets are printed on the spot by another part of the machine and delivered to the purchaser, and the central office machine decreases the inventory for that performance and stores the information of the sale for later accountings.

The terminal machine is capable of requesting a particular location such as center seats, seats on the aisle, seats close to the stage, etc., to accommodate a purchaser's particular whim or necessity. It is believed that the availability of tickets in the suburbs and various parts of the country will account for more ticket sales and will more than compensate for the cost of computerization.

The terminal machine located in the box office will be the only machine that can order and sell a specific seat in a specific location on a specific date. This gives the box office personnel absolute control. "House Seats" are excluded from the inventory covered by the other terminal machines, and are controlled solely by the box office personnel through the terminal machine in the box office.

The Treasurers Union has accepted the sale of tickets by computer. The machines are simple to operate and can be learned with a minimum of effort. In addition, the machine can virtually eliminate any dishonest practices surrounding ticket sales.

There are two companies presently vying for the business of computerizing box offices. The two companies in the business are Ticket Reservation Systems, Inc., also known as TRS, which presently has contracts for several Broadway houses, and Computicket which informs me that they will be operating on Broadway but at the present time have no Broadway contracts.

The technical difference I have been able to determine is that TRS functions on a teletype and Computicket on a cathode ray type of scope. What this difference means I am not certain, as each system has different conflicting claims.

TRS charges the theatre $150. per month rental for the equipment at the theatre, and charges 2¢ per seat per performance. A theatre of 1,000 seats would pay at the rate of 2¢ per seat per performance — $20. per performance. In addition, a charge is made of 25¢ for each ticket sold at sources other than the box office.

Computicket, Inc., bases its charges on a percentage of the receipts rather than a per ticket charge. Each company claims its cost to be less.

The machines have provision for the box office reserving a block of tickets so that they will not be sold. In this way, the box office personnel can insure their having the tickets for sale at the box-office. Of course if tickets are not sold that otherwise would have been sold, the box office personnel will have erred in holding the tickets aside from sale.

It is desirable to save 25¢ per ticket, but not if it means not selling a large group of tickets that otherwise would have been sold.

During Run

Range of Production Costs

The range of cost of a Dramatic Show is between $75,000.

(an extremely low, highly unlikely, but possible figure) and $300,000. (which would be on the high side), and a Musical between $350,000. and $700,000. ($500,000. to $600,000. is usual).

Potential Weekly Gross and Weekly Net

One can plan on a Dramatic Show grossing between $45,000. and $70,000. at capacity, depending upon the size of the Theatre, and a Musical at capacity grossing between $70,000. and $100,000. A Dramatic Production will likely break even when it grosses between $20,000. and $30,000. and a Musical at between $45,000. and $65,000. A Musical might later in the run break even at $35,000. with certain cuts, which would include Star's salaries, but at the time that this would happen the show would no longer gross anywhere near capacity.

Time Necessary To Recoup

If a Dramatic Show is doing sold out business, it is not unusual for it to break even and recoup the total investment in 7 weeks. A show grossing $50,000. per week could have a $15,000. profit each week and recoup a $100,000. investment in 7 weeks. These are not unusual amounts.

A movie sale can, of course, speed the recoupment considerably since as has been noted the Production will share 40% of such receipts.

A Musical will in all probability take longer to recoup since it will cost much more to mount, and although the potential weekly profits may be greater, they are usually not enough to make up for the increased cost of producing a Musical. Also a tough week for a Musical (and there are sometimes tough weeks intersperced with the good if it is something less than a sold out show) can be very costly.

After Opening

Reviews — What To Do

The morning after the Opening there is customarily a meeting in the office of the Advertising Agency to plan the expenditure of money for advertising. The Producer, the Press Agent, the General or Company Manager, and sometimes the Attorney are present. If the show gets raves the job is an easy one. If the show gets unanimous pans, although painful, the job is once again an easy one. The difficult area is when a Play gets mixed reviews and there is a chance that it could make it, but its hard to tell how good that chance is and therefore difficult to know how much money to spend to try to keep it alive.

New York Advertising

In New York City at this time, the only really important newspaper for Theatre advertising is the New York Times. Some small amount is sometimes spent on the New York Post because it is an afternoon paper, and also because it has an audience which responds to a particular kind of show in some instances.

When To Close

It is not an easy decision to close a show if there is the possibility of business developing at a later date. One has to weigh the amount of the advance sale and the number and size of the Theatre parties, against the current box office sales and try to come up with some kind of divination of what the future holds. It isn't always easy. Most usually when a show starts downhill there is very little chance of its making it, and often ego, or what have you, motivates keeping it open.

National Company

If a Show is a big hit in New York, then there is no problem at all with a National Company since the show will probably get guarantees of a certain amount everywhere it goes. A smash hit can know before it leaves New York that it will gross $80,000. to $90,000. in Detroit, and so forth.

Generally the Production must be simplified technically, that is the scenery and props, so that it may be moved in and out of towns with some degree of speed. The staging is most generally a duplication of the Broadway Production. Most usually the Stage Manager puts the show together and then the original Director comes in for the last week of rehearsals and takes it out of town through the opening night.

Most often the show will have a dress rehearsal with the Broadway set before it leaves New York, with an invited audience, for the first performance out of town is generally with a paid audience.

As with the pre-Broadway tour, the Independent Booking Office sets up the bookings and is paid, as with the pre-Broadway bookings, $75. each week by the Producer and another $75. by the Theatre.

Producer

A Producer ought to do what the name implies, "Produce." Strangely enough Show Biz happens to appeal to a wide assortment of people. Sometimes people go into the business for the wrong reasons. Playboys should restrict their activities to other than Theatre. Sharpies who want to cash-in-quick should stick to the racetrack. One ought not practice being a dilettante while producing. Producing means making a lot of difficult decisions and carrying them out. Painful as it may be, it sometimes means firing your favorite

Star, or even your favorite person if he happens to be the Director and is not right for the show.

A Producer has to be in a position to select wisely, raise money, hire, fire, influence people, convince people that they should or should not do something, mediate disputes, encourage and assist people to work together and to get along together, buy wisely, sell sharply, hold hands and soothe heads, comfort the sick, assist the needy, and to be all things to all people. In a word, to "Produce."

APPENDIX

There are reproduced here some forms which are typical of the kind of agreements used in the production of a Broadway show. There is no reproduction of standard printed forms which may be obtained from the various unions or the League of New York Theatres.

The Dramatists Guild form of Minimum Basic Production Contract is a printed form and is not reproduced here. It has been discussed in detail. Paragraph TENTH of this contract is not part of the printed form and is usually prepared by the attorney for the author or for the producer.

If a provision in Paragraph TENTH replaces or amends a part of the printed form, then the printed form will have stamped or typed near the particular paragraph a reference which reads "See paragraph TENTH."

There is here set forth a typical example of Paragraph TENTH which would be part of the Minimum Basic Production Contract for a straight play such as "Blossom Out," which is the hypothetical example for which certain agreements are here set forth.

After Paragraph TENTH, there is set forth a co-production agreement typical of the kind used for this kind of show, a copy of the estimated production budget and a copy of the estimated weekly operating budget, an SEC offering circular for an offering under Regulation A and a Limited Partnership Agreement.

There is also set forth a copy of a typical production budget for a musical and an estimated weekly budget for this same show. There is also set forth a copy of an Offering Circular for a full SEC registration. The co-production agreement and the Limited Partnership Agreement set forth for the straight play would be adapted with minor changes for a musical and hence they are not reproduced here.

DRAMATISTS GUILD, INC., MINIMUM BASIC PRODUCTION CONTRACT TENTH: ADDITIONAL CLAUSES

To the extent that any provision of the Additional Clauses contained in this Paragraph TENTH conflicts with any printed portion of this Contract (which includes the Schedule of Additional Production Terms), such provision of these Additional Clauses shall prevail:

A. The initial performance referred to in Paragraph SECOND hereof shall be the first paid first-class public performance of the Play hereunder. (*Note*: Some author's representatives insist upon this provision to supplement Paragraph SECOND of the contract which provides that the show must be presented on or before a certain date or all rights revert to the author. From the author's point of view, the important addition of this paragraph is that the presentation must be a *paid* first-class public performance.)

B. Simultaneously herewith Producer is paying the Author the sum of Two Thousand ($2,000) Dollars, non-returnable, in lieu of the payments specified in Paragraph THIRD (a) hereof. Such Two Thousand ($2,000) Dollar payment shall entitle Producer to maintain his right to produce the Play for a period of one (1) year from the date hereof.

C. For each performance of the Play, the Producer shall cause four (4) adjoining house seats in the first six (6) rows of the center section of the orchestra (except that on theatre party and benefit performances said house seats shall be reduced to two [2]) to be held available at the box office for the Author or the Author's designees, to purchase at the box office price. Such tickets shall be held until 6 P.M. of the day prior to the scheduled performance for evening performances, and 12 Noon of the day prior to the scheduled performance for matinees, unless the Producer's office or the box office of the Theatre shall be informed prior to such time that the tickets will be picked up later and that the Author guarantees payment therefore, in which case such tickets will continue to be held for purchase by the Author or his designees, up to the time of performance, In addition, the Author or Author's designees, shall have the right to purchase at the box office price ten (10) pairs of seats in the center section of the orchestra for the official New York City opening of the Play.

D. The Producer shall be entitled to proceeds under Paragraph EIGHTH hereof only if the Producer is entitled to proceeds under Paragraph SEVENTH (*Note*: It will be remembered that in the text of the book, in discussing the rights which the producer may acquire, under the title "Interest Outside United States, Canada and England," attention was called to the fact that the contract nowhere specifically provides that the producer's interest in the author's share from such productions is dependent upon the play running for any length of time. This additional clause is intended to remedy the apparent oversight so that the producer acquires this additional interest only when the play runs for the Right Acquisition Time.)

E. If the Play is produced in Great Britain by the Producer in association with a British manager or on lease from the Producer to British manager, by reason of which association or lease the Producer receives an advance against royalties or profits, or a lump sum as royalties or in lieu of a portion of royalties, the Author shall receive fifty (50%) percent of such advance or lump sum, as an advance against the Author's percentage compensation with respect to such British production. Such advance to the Author, if greater than the payments to which the Author may be entitled under Paragraph FOURTH (a) hereof, shall be inclusive thereof. (*Note*: Paragraph FOURTH (a) provides that, if the play runs the Rights Acquisition Time, the producer may, without any advance royalty, present a production in the British Isles at any time up to six months after the date of the New York opening. This initial period may be extended an additional six months upon payment of $500. and an additional six months after that upon payment of a second $500.)

F. (i) when the Author accompanies the Play on its pre-Broadway tour and/or (ii) when the Author takes a trip at any time at the Producer's request in connection with the Play and/or (iii) when the Author is not a resident of New York and comes to New York for the rehearsal of the Play in connection with the Play or (iv) when the Author accompanies the Play on its post-Broadway tour, the Producer shall furnish Author's economy jet transportation and traveling expenses on each such tour, trip or travel, including return to the Author's residence if the Author is not a resident of New York and shall pay the Author Thirty ($30.00) Dollars a day (including travel days) toward the Author's living expenses throughout each such tour, trip or stay in New York. Unless requested by the Producer to stay in New York, the Author shall not be paid such living expenses after opening night. In the event of any first-class production of the Play in London and/or the British Isles by the Producer (alone, together or in association with, or on a lease basis to, a British producer), the Author shall have the right to attend rehearsals, try-outs and the opening of the Play in London and/or in the British Isles. The Producer shall pay the Author's air economy round-trip transportation from New York (or if the Author is not a resident of New York, from his residence in the United States) to London, plus the sum of Thirty ($30.00) Dollars a day in Pounds Sterling (including travel days) during said rehearsal, try-outs and opening plus first-class round-trip transportation from London in connection with try-outs within the British Isles. Unless requested by the Producer to stay in London or the British Isles, the Author shall not be paid such living expenses after opening night.

G. All the Author's rights with respect to changes in the Play and approvals of cast and director shall similarly apply to any British production hereunder as well as productions in the United States and Canada.

H. Prior to the final close of the Play under this Contract, or prior to one (1) month after the New York opening, whichever is earlier, the Producer shall deliver to A, B, and

C, literary agents, as the Author's property, a neat and legible "stage manager's script" in customary form, including lighting and property plots and all other details and information customarily contained in a "stage manager's script."

I. The Author represents and warrants that the Author's right to use the title of the Play has not been affected by any act or omission on the Author's part and that to the best of his knowledge and belief, the Author has the right to use said title as the title of the Play. As between the Author and the Producer the title of the Play and any changes therein shall be the property of the Author. No changes in the title of the Play shall be made without the approval of the Author.

J. The Author shall receive billing as sole Author of the Play in any and all advertising and publicity issued by, authorized by or under the control of the Producer, including but not limited to all theatre programs, houseboards, billboards, displays, posters, circulars, announcements, advertisements, paid newspaper advertising under the control of the Producer and whenever and wherever the title of the Play appears. The Author shall also be accorded billing wherever the Producer's name appears with the title of the Play. The foregoing notwithstanding, the Producer need not accord the Author credit in so-called "ABC" and "teaser" ads, where only the title of the Play, the name of the theatre and the names of the stars appear. The Author's billing shall be on a separate line upon which no other matter appears and shall immediately follow the title of the Play. The name of the Author shall be at least one-half (½) of the size of the type used for the title of the Play. No persons other than the stars, the director and the Producer shall be accorded billing as large as that accorded the Author. No persons other than the stars or Director shall receive billing larger or more prominent than that accorded the Author. Such Director's credit may not be larger or more prominent than that accorded the Author without the Author's approval. Such approval will not be unreasonably withheld. Only the names of the stars and the Producer may precede the Author's name. Notwithstanding anything contained above, the Producer shall not be required to give the Author billing credit in any special display advertising where no credits are given other than to the title of the Play and the name of the theatre.

K. The Author represents and warrants that to the best of his knowledge and belief the Play is wholly original with him and the Play and the use of the contents thereof in connection with the Play will not violate, conflict with or infringe upon any rights whatsoever of any person, firm or corporation, and he has the right to enter into this Contract and the full warrant and authority to grant the rights granted by him herein. Nothing herein contained shall be deemed to alter the rights and obligations of the parties under Section 41 of the Schedule of Additional Production Terms. (*Note*: Section 41 of the Schedule of Additional Production Terms makes provision for the defense of a suit in the event of the claim by a third party of libel, infringement or interference with the rights of any third party.)

L. "Gross weekly box-office receipts" shall be computed in the manner set forth in Article III, Section 9, of the Schedule of Additional Production Terms annexed hereto; provided, however, that in making such computation there shall be deducted: (a) any Federal admission taxes or any similar taxes which may be imposed on admissions; (b) any commissions paid in connection with theatre parties or benefits; (c) those sums equivalent to the former 5% New York City Amusement Tax, the net proceeds of which are now set aside in Pension and Welfare Funds of the theatrical unions and ultimately paid to said Funds. (*Note*: Section 9 of the Schedule of Additional Production Terms is as follows: "Section 9. Basis of Computation. Where percentage weekly compensation is based upon gross weekly box office receipts, the percentage shall be computed upon receipts from all sources whatsoever, including any and all sums over and above regular box office prices of tickets received by the Producer, or by anyone in his employ, from speculators, ticket agencies, ticket brokers or other persons, and any other additional sums whatsoever received from the production of the Play. Should the Play be performed by more than one company, percentage compensation accruing from each company shall be computed and paid separately.")

M. In addition to the box office and any other statements sent to the Dramatists Guild pursuant to this Contract, the Producer shall at the same time send duplicates of such statements to A, B, and C, literary agents.

N. Author hereby irrevocably appoints A, B, and C, 000 Sunset Boulevard, New York, N. Y., as his sole and exclusive Agent with respect to the Play and authorizes and directs the Producer to make all payments due or to become due to the Author hereunder to and in the name of said Agent (except for those payments which are specifically required to be made in the name of the Guild by this Contract) and to accept the receipt of said Agent as full evidence and satisfaction of such payments. In consideration of the services rendered and to be rendered by such Agent, the Author hereby agrees that said Agent is entitled to receive and retain as its commission ten (10%) percent of all such proceeds (including but not limited to the Author's share of proceeds derived from any and all subsidiary and additional rights whether or not the Producer participates therein) except that, with respect to proceeds derived from amateur performances, said Agent's commission shall be twenty (20%) percent. With respect to any proceeds from the sale of motion picture rights, it is expressly understood that there shall be deducted from the aforementioned ten (10%) percent, the Author's pro-rata share of the three and one-half (3-½%) percent fee payable to the Negotiator.

Producer hereby agrees that said Agent is entitled to receive and retain as its commission ten (10%) percent of the Producer's share of all proceeds from the sale, lease, license or other disposition of any and all subsidiary and additional rights in and to the Play, except that with respect to amateur performances, said Agent's commission shall be twenty

(20%) percent. With respect to any proceeds from the sale of motion picture rights, it is expressly understood that there shall be deducted from the aforementioned proportionate share of ten (10%) percent the Producer's share of three and one-half (3-½%) percent fee payable to the Negotiator.

The foregoing shall not be construed to give the Agent any commission computed upon any share of monies or other proceeds derived by the Producer from any first class production of the Play produced by the Producer in the United States or produced in London and/or the British Isles by the Producer, alone or in association with a British producer, or produced by a British producer under a lease of rights from Producer hereunder.

O. The Schedule of Additional Production Terms is part of this Contract whether or not a copy of same is attached.

P. The Producers shall have the right to assign this contract to any partnership in which either one of the Producers is a general partner or to a corporation in which either one of the Producers has the controlling interest, or of which either of them is the directing head or to a joint venture in which either one is one of the joint venturers, or to a joint venture in which a partnership in which either is a general partner is one of the joint venturers, or to a joint venture in which a corporation in which either has the controlling interest or of which either is the directing head is a joint venturer; all subject to Section 49 of the Schedule of Additional Production Terms. (*Note*: Section 49 of the Schedule of Additional Production Terms provides that there may not be an assignment of the contract without approval in writing of the author and of the Guild. The provisions of Section 49 that certain assignments may be made without approvals if the producer is a signatory to the Producing Manager's Contract is no longer applicable since producers no longer enter into this contract with the Guild.)

Q. The Producer may extend the option to produce the Play herein granted, for an additional six months, upon the payment to the Author of Two Hundred ($200.00) Dollars for each month of the extension which payment must be made prior to the month for which the option is to be extended. This extension of the option is conditioned upon the Producer having entered into a contract on or before the 15th day of September, 1969, with a star, to appear in the show during the six month period that the option is extended, and the star's unavailability for appearance until the period covered by the six month extension of the option. The additional option payments herein provided for shall be deemed to be advances against royalties payable pursuant to the provisions of this agreement, in the same manner that the Two Thousand ($2,000) Dollar option payment is to be deemed an advance against percentage royalty payments.

R. If the Author accompanies the Play on the post-Broadway tour, the Producer shall only be responsible for payment to the Author of his living expenses as herein provided in Paragraph Tenth F of this agreement for a period of two weeks.

S. When a production date is scheduled and the Author is informed of said date by the Producer, the Author agrees to use his best efforts to make himself available in New York City one month ahead of the scheduled rehearsal date to do the necessary rewrites on the Play. The Author will be paid Thirty ($30.00) Dollars per day for living expenses, and will be furnished with economy jet round-trip transportation.

T. The Author agrees to use his best efforts to require that the Producers receive visual billing with respect to all motion pictures, or live or filmed television productions based on the Play substantially as follows: "Originally produced on the stage by Harry Harrison, Robert Roberts and D. & F. Productions, Inc."

U. In the event that the Play is presented out-of-town prior to the New York opening, then the royalty payments provided in Paragraph THIRD (c) of this agreement shall not exceed the sum of Seven Hundred and Fifty ($750.00) Dollars in any one of the first four weeks of such out-of-town performances prior to the New York opening, as therein provided in said Paragraph THIRD (c) and in addition such payment shall not exceed Seven Hundred and Fifty ($750.00) Dollars during the first week of preview performances in New York prior to the official opening. In the event that the Play does not try-out out-of-town prior to the New York opening, then the royalty payments provided in Paragraph THIRD (c) shall not exceed Seven Hundred and Fifty ($750.00) Dollars in any one of the first two weeks of preview performances in New York prior to the official opening. If any of the weeks herein referred to in this Paragraph is not a full calendar week, then the maximum for such shorter week shall be pro-rated.

CO-PRODUCTION AGREEMENT

AGREEMENT made as of this 16th day of October, 1968, between Henry Harrison residing at 000 Central Park South, New York, N.Y. 10019 (sometimes hereinafter referred to as Harrison), Robert Roberts, residing at 00 Madison Avenue, New York, N.Y. 10017 (sometimes hereinafter referred to as Roberts), and D & F Productions Inc., a New York Corporation with offices at 000 Lexington Avenue, New York, N.Y. 10017 (sometimes hereinafter referred to as D & F).

FIRST: The parties hereto do hereby form a joint venture to be conducted under the firm name of THE BLOSSOM OUT JOINT VENTURE (sometimes hereinafter referred to as the "Joint Venture"), for the purpose of producing and presenting the play presently entitled "Blossom Out" (sometimes hereinafter referred to as the "Play") by Zachary Zoe (sometimes hereinafter referred to as the "Author").

SECOND: Harrison and Roberts have heretofore entered into a Minimum Basic Production Contract of the Dramatists Guild, Inc., with the Author, dated as of September 15, 1968, granting them a right to produce the Play pursuant to the terms of said Contract. An executed copy of said contract has been examined by the officers of D & F and they do acknowledge that they are familiar with the contents of said contract. Harrison and Roberts do hereby assign to the Joint Venture the aforesaid Minimum Basic Production Contract entered into as of the 15th day of September, 1968, with Zachary Zoe, subject however to Harrison and Roberts receiving written approval from the Author and the Dramatists Guild, Inc., in accordance with Section 49 of the Schedule of Additional Production Terms of said Minimum Basic Production Contract. In the event that approval is received from the Author and the Dramatists Guild, Inc., and the assignment becomes effective, then the Joint Venture does hereby assume all of the obligations of said Minimum Basic Production Contract heretofore referred to. All future agreements entered into in connection with the production of the Play, after this agreement becomes effective, shall be entered into by the Joint Venture.

THIRD: The parties do hereby agree that as soon as the minimum amount of money necessary to produce the Play as agreed upon by the parties to this agreement has been raised, that they will expeditiously form a Limited Partnership under the laws of the State of New York (hereinafter sometimes referred to as the "Limited Partnership") which Limited Partnership shall produce said Play. The Limited Partnership will be known as "The Blossom Out Company." The Limited Partnership Agreement shall incorporate those terms as hereinafter set forth applicable to the Limited Partnership as determined by Pro and Pro, Counsel for the Joint Venture and the Limited Partnership, who shall prepare the Limited Partnership Agreement.

(a) The parties to this agreement shall be the general partners of the Limited Partnership and the parties contributing the capital to the Limited Partnership will be the limited partners thereof.

(b) The capital of the Limited Partnership will be in the amount of $160,000. Each of the Joint Venturers agrees to exert his best efforts to the job of financing the production.

(c) The limited partners shall receive fifty (50%) percent

of the net profits of the Limited Partnership and the general partners shall receive the remaining fifty (50%) percent of the said net profits. Before net profits are shared by the Limited partners with the general partners, the limited partners shall first recoup the total amount of their investment.

If any star(s) or other artistic person is entitled to receive any part of the net profits, the same shall be deemed to be an expense and deducted before computing the net profits to be divided between the general and limited partners.

The net profits of the general partners shall be divided among them as more fully set forth in paragraph FIFTEENTH of this agreement. The debts and obligations and net losses of the partnership shall be shared in the same proportion that the parties share in the net profits of the company.

FOURTH: All contracts and checks on behalf of the Joint Venture and the Limited Partnership shall be valid if signed by any two of the following: Harrison, Roberts, Joe Joe (hereinafter referred to as "Joe") and Loren Loe (hereinafter referred to as "Loe"). The exception of the foregoing is that any contracts which are customarily signed by the general manager of a production, if approved by three of the parties to this Agreement need only be signed by one of them as said general manager.

FIFTH: The parties acknowledge that Harrison and Roberts have advanced certain sums of money to date in connection with the acquisition of the option agreement and other incidental expenses. The parties further acknowledge that the Joint Venture has acquired the sum of $16,000. from Mr. William Woe to be used as front money for the preproduction expenses. There is no obligation on the part of D & F to reimburse Harrison and Roberts for the expenses which they have heretofore incurred in connection with the property, however they are specifically authorized to make reimbursement to themselves for such reasonable out-of-pocket expenses from the front money on hand. All future pre-production expenses in connection with the property shall be made from the front money or reimbursed to the Joint Venturer who expends his personal funds for such purpose. To the extent that the front money may be insufficient to cover any pre-production expenses, it is intended that all expenses of the Joint Venture shall be shared with Harrison and Roberts each responsible for one-quarter and D & F Productions, Inc., being responsible for one-half of said expenses.

The Limited Partnership Agreement shall provide that after the partnership is formed each of the Joint Venturers shall be reimbursed from the Limited Partnership funds for reasonable out-of-pocket expenditures made by each in connection with the production of the play to the extent that they have not been reimbursed.

SIXTH: All artistic decisions, business decisions, and decisions of any kind or nature made by the Joint Venture or by the Limited Partnership shall be arrived at after consultation among all of the parties to this Agreement; however, the decision of the majority, of Harrison, Roberts, Joe and Loe, shall be binding. Each of the above people shall have one vote and in the event of a tie vote, then the Author, Zachary Zoe shall cast the deciding vote which under such circumstances shall be final and binding upon the parties.

SEVENTH: It is agreed that Pro and Pro, 000 Park Avenue, New York, N.Y. 10017, shall be the attorneys for the Joint Venture and for the Limited Partnership, and Hay, May and Ray, 000 Fifth Avenue, New York, N.Y. shall be the accountants for the Joint Venture and for the Limited Partnership. The attorneys and accountants each agree that they will charge the same fee respectively that they charge all other similar theatrical productions for similar services rendered.

EIGHTH: Wherever producer's credit is given, Harrison's name shall appear first followed by Roberts, Joe and Loe in that order. The billing credits given to the parties shall be as specifically set forth in paragraph FIFTEENTH of this agreement.

NINTH: Each of the parties to this Agreement shall devote as much time as is reasonably necessary for the production and presentation of the Play; it being understood and agreed that each party may be engaged in outside activities whether or not of a competing nature so long as he devotes sufficient time to the Joint Venture and to the Limited Partnership, and to the proper running of the business of producing and presenting the Play.

Rehearsals for the Play shall commence on such date as the parties agree upon subject however to the terms of the Minimum Basic Production Contract.

TENTH: Upon formation of the Limited Partnership, all contracts entered into by the Joint Venture in connection with the production of the Play shall be assigned to the Limited Partnership.

ELEVENTH: The Joint Venture shall terminate upon the happening of the first of the following:

(a) The formation of the Limited Partnership;

(b) The date the Joint Venture loses its rights under the Minimum Basic Production Contract; if the Limited Partnership shall not have been formed prior thereto;

(c) The death, insanity or retirement of any of the individual Joint Venturers or the dissolution of the corporate Joint Venturer.

TWELFTH: Any and all disputes, differences or controversies arising out of, under or in connection with this Agreement, or the breach or alleged breach thereof, shall be submitted to arbitration, to be held in New York City under the rules and regulations of the American Arbitration Association then obtaining, and each of the parties hereto agrees to be bound by the determination of the majority of the arbitrators. Judgment on the award rendered may be entered in the highest court of the forum, state or federal, having jurisdiction.

Any party demanding the arbitration may, if he so elects, demand a quick arbitration. In such event, the following procedure shall apply: the party demanding the arbitration shall, in his said demand, specify that the arbitration desired is a "quick arbitration." In such event, the respondents shall within two business days after receipt of the demand for arbitration, file their answers to the arbitration demand. Within three business days after demand for arbitration is filed, the American Arbitration Association shall designate a single arbitrator to conduct the arbitration. The arbitration shall proceed with due dispatch and the arbitrator shall make known his decision, which decision shall be made within forty-eight (48) hours after he shall have been appointed. The cost of the arbitration shall be borne as the arbitrator may direct.

THIRTEENTH: This contract shall be interpreted under the laws of the State of New York.

FOURTEENTH: Unless otherwise notified by certified or registered mail, the addresses of the parties for the purpose of giving notice shall be as follows:

Henry Harrison	000 Central Park South New York, N.Y. 10019
Robert Roberts	00 Madison Avenue New York, N.Y. 10017
D & F Productions, Inc.	000 Lexington Avenue New York, N.Y. 10017

A copy of all such notices shall be sent to Donald Pro, Esq., Pro and Pro, 000 Park Avenue, New York, N. Y. 10017, the attorneys for the joint venture and the limited partnership.

FIFTEENTH: It is understood and agreed that D & F is responsible for raising a certain amount of the production budget.

D & F shall have the right to raise Eighty Thousand ($80,000.00) Dollars, and in the event that it does raise the sum of Eighty Thousand ($80,000.00) Dollars it will be entitled to one-half (½) of the producer's share of the net profits of the producing company and Joe and Loe will receive co-production billing credit. If they do receive co-production billing credit their names will follow Harrison and Roberts and will be of the same size, prominence and boldness of type.

If D & F does not raise Eighty Thousand ($80,000.00) Dollars of the production budget but raises Sixty-Four Thousand ($64,000.00) Dollars of said budget, it will receive fifteen (15%) percent of the net profits of the producing company payable to them from the producer's share of said net profits, and will receive billing credits as follows: "Henry Harrison and Robert Roberts with Joe Joe and Loren Loe." If D & F raises an amount greater than Sixty Four Thousand ($64,000.00) Dollars but less than Eighty Thousand ($80,000.00) Dollars, it will receive the pro-rata difference between fifteen (15%) percent of the net profit and twenty-five (25%) percent of the net profits.

If D & F does not raise Sixty Four Thousand ($64,000.00) Dollars of the production budget but raises Fifty Thousand Two Hundred ($50,200.00) Dollars of said budget, it will receive twelve (12%) percent of the net profits of the producing company payable to it from the producer's share of said net profits, and will receive billing credits as follows: "Henry Harrison and Robert Roberts in association with Joe Joe and Loren Loe". If D & F raises an amount greater than Fifty Thousand Two Hundred ($50,200.00) Dollars but less than Sixty Four Thousand ($64,000.00) Dollars, it will receive the pro-rata difference between twelve (12%) percent of the net profits of the producing company and fifteen (15%) percent of the net profits of the producing company.

In the event that D & F does not raise at least Fifty Thousand Two Hundred ($50,200.00) Dollars toward the production budget by April 15, 1969, or six (6) weeks prior to the commencement of rehearsals, whichever is later, Joe and Loe will receive billing credit somewhere on the title page, the size, location and copy at the sole discretion of Harrison and Roberts jointly and D & F shall receive a percentage amount which bears the same ratio to the amount contributed by them as twelve (12%) percent bears to Fifty Thousand Two Hundred ($50,200.00) Dollars.

The producer's share of the net profits payable to D & F shall be computed only after the deduction, if any, of any share of the producer's net profits which it is deemed advisable and necessary to assign to artistic or production personnel, it being intended that for example if it is necessary to assign a percentage of the producer's net profits to the star or director that Harrison and Roberts jointly and D & F will share in the percentages hereinabove set forth after the payment to said star or director. In other words any contribution from the producer's share of the net profits shall be in the same proportion that the parties share in the producer's net profits.

Any payments to D & F for the producer's share of the net profits shall be made to them at the same time and under the same terms and conditions that payments are made to Harrison and Robert's from the producer's share of the net profits.

The parties agree that under no circumstances will they commence rehearsal unless they actually have raised eighty (80%) percent of the production budget as agreed upon by Harrison and Roberts.

IN WITNESS WHEREOF, the parties hereto have herein set their hands and seals as of the day and year first above written.

ACCEPTED AND
APPROVED:

....
HENRY HARRISON

....
JOE JOE

....
ROBERT ROBERTS

D & F PRODUCTIONS, INC.

....
LOREN LOE

by..
President

ESTIMATED PRODUCTION BUDGET
DRAMATIC SHOW
"BLOSSOM OUT"

PHYSICAL PRODUCTION		
Scenery & Props	20,000.	
Costumes	15,000.	
Electrics (Rental & Purchase)	2,000.	
Sound	500.	37,500.
FEES		
Director	3,500.	
Set Designer	2,500.	
Lighting Designer	1,250.	
Costume Designer	2,500.	9,750.
REHEARSAL SALARIES		
Cast	15,600.	
Stage Managers	2,550.	
Company Manager	750.	
Crew	2,650.	
Wardrobe	350.	
Production Secretary	625.	22,525.
REHEARSAL EXPENSES		
Theatre or Hall	1,500.	
Scripts	500.	
Casting	1,000.	
Misc. & Dep't Expenses	1,750.	4,750.
ADVERTISING & PUBLICITY		
Press Agent – Salary & Expenses	1,500.	
Newspapers	10,000.	
Photos & Signs	1,500.	
Printing	750.	13,750.
OTHER		
Office	2,100.	
Legal	3,500.	

Audit	750.		
General Manager	2,500.		
Payroll Taxes	1,800.		
Health & Welfare	2,240.		
Insurance	1,500.		
Hauling	1,750.		
Take in, Hang & Rehearse	4,500.		
Transportation	1,000.		
Preliminary Box Office Expenses	1,000.		
Living Expenses	1,500.		
Pre-Production & Misc.	2,045.		
Music	4,140.	30,325.	
TOTAL ESTIMATED PRODUCTION COSTS			118,600.
BONDS & DEPOSITS			
Theatre	6,000.		
Actors' Equity Association	21,000.		
I. A. T. S. E.	1,500.		
A. T. P. A. M.	1,100.		29,600.
RESERVE			11,800.
TOTAL CAPITALIZATION			160,000.

ESTIMATED WEEKLY OPERATING BUDGET DRAMATIC SHOW "BLOSSOM OUT"

SALARIES				
Cast & Understudies	10,000.			
Stage Managers	550.			
Crew	875.			
General & Company Managers	450.			
Press Agent	300.			
Wardrobe	450.	12,625.		
ADVERTISING				
Newspapers – Share	2,000.			
Press Agent Expenses	75.	2,075.		
OTHER				
Office	350.			
Legal	100.			
Audit	100.			
Payroll Taxes	1,000.			
Insurance	100.			
Departmental Expenses	400.			
Rentals	250.			
Box Office Expenses	250.			
League Dues	50.			
Health Insurance & Vacation	50.			
Misc.	150.	2,800.		
TOTAL FIXED EXPENSES			17,500.	
GROSS	25,000.	30,000.	35,000.	40,000.
HOUSE SHARE	7,250.	8,500.	9,750.	11,000.
COMPANY SHARE*	17,750.	21,500.	25,250.	29,000.
FIXED EXPENSES	17,500.	17,500.	17,500.	17,500.
ROYALTY				
Author	2,500.	3,000.	3,500.	4,000.
Director	500.	600.	700.	800.
Designers	140.	140.	140.	140.
Music	50.	50.	50.	50.

Producers	250.	300.	350.	400.
Star	—	—	500.	1,000.
TOTAL EXPENSES	20,940.	21,590.	22,740.	23,890.
PROFIT OR (LOSS)	(3,190.)	(90.)	2,510.	5,110.

GROSS	45,000.	50,000.	55,000.	60,000.
HOUSE SHARE	12,250.	13,500.	14,750.	16,000.
COMPANY SHARE*	32,750.	36,500.	40,250.	44,000.
FIXED EXPENSES	17,500.	17,500.	17,500.	17,500.
ROYALTY				
Author	4,500.	5,000.	5,500.	6,000.
Director	900.	1,000.	1,100.	1,200.
Designers	140.	140.	140.	140.
Music	50.	50.	50.	50.
Producers	450.	500.	550.	600.
Star	1,500.	2,000.	2,500.	3,000.
TOTAL EXPENSES	25,040.	26,190.	27,340.	28,490.
PROFIT OR (LOSS)	7,710.	10,310.	12,910.	15,510.

* The net profit or loss is computed by totaling the fixed expenses and the royalty payments and subtracting it from the company share of the gross receipts.

SEC OFFERING CIRCULAR UNDER REGULATION A

OFFERING CIRCULAR DATED MARCH 11, 1969
$160,000 in Limited Partnership Interests
in
THE BLOSSOM OUT COMPANY
A limited partnership to be formed to finance
the play
"BLOSSOM OUT"
(Tentative Title)

THESE SECURITIES ARE OFFERED PURSUANT TO AN EXEMPTION FROM REGISTRATION WITH THE UNITED STATES SECURITIES AND EXCHANGE COMMISSION. THE COMMISSION DOES NOT PASS

UPON THE MERITS OF ANY SECURITIES NOR DOES IT PASS UPON THE ACCURACY OR COMPLETENESS OF ANY OFFERING CIRCULAR OR OTHER SELLING LITERATURE.

THE OFFERING

Henry Harrison, Robert Roberts, and D & F Productions, Inc., intend to produce the Play "Blossom Out." They offer Limited Partnership interests in a Partnership to be formed for that purpose, and they will be the General Partners. They will make no financial contribution but will receive fifty (50%) percent of any net profits. Limited Partners will make the entire financial contribution for which they will receive fifty (50%) percent of any net profits. If there are no net profits, Limited Partners will bear the entire risk of loss to the extent of their respective contributions. Any losses in excess of that amount will be borne by the General Partners. Partners' share in net profits, if any, will be computed only after payment to others of as much as an estimated fifty-four (54%) percent of the gross box office receipts and deduction of all other expenses from the balance of the gross receipts.

There is no minimum fixed amount that each individual Limited Partner must contribute. A contribution of Three Thousand Two Hundred (3,200.00) Dollars entitles a Limited Partner to a One (1%) percent share of any net profits. A Maximum of One Hundred Sixty Thousand ($160,000.00) Dollars will be raised. The Partnership will be formed when One Hundred Sixty Thousand ($160,000.00) Dollars has been raised, or any amount between One Hundred Thirty Thousand ($130,000.00) Dollars and One Hundred Sixty Thousand ($160,000.00) Dollars, with which the Producers believe they can present the play.

The rights and obligations of the General and Limited Partners are set forth in the Limited Partnership Agreement. This must be signed by all subscribers to Limited Partnership interests and may be obtained from the Producers c/o Henry Harrison, 000 Central Park South, New York, or

Donald Pro, partner of the firm of Pro and Pro, Attorneys for the production, at 000 Park Ave., New York, New York, telephone No. YT 0-0000.

TABLE OF CONTENTS

Page

The Risk to Investors ....
Subscriptions ....
Overcall ....
The Producers ....
The Play ....
The Author ....
The Director ....
The Cast ....
The Theatre ....
Scenic Designer ....
Compensation of General Partners ....
Use of Proceeds ....
Estimated Weekly Budget ....
Net Profits ....
Return of Contributions—Share of Profits ....
Production and Subsidiary Rights ....
Other Financing ....
Financial Statements ....

THE RISK TO INVESTORS

(1) The sole business of the Partnership will be the production of the Play. In such a venture the risk of a loss is especially high in contrast with the prospects for any profits. These securities should not be purchased unless the Investor is prepared for the possibility of total loss.

(2) Of the Plays produced for the New York Stage in the 1967/68 season, 80% resulted in loss to Investors.

(3) On the basis of estimated expenses, the Play would have to run for a minimum of 11 weeks (88 performances) on Broadway, to a full capacity house, even to return to Limited Partners their initial contribution. More than 64% of

the Plays produced for the New York Stage in the 1967/68 season failed to run this long. Of those that did, a mere handful played to capacity audiences.

SUBSCRIPTIONS

Offers to subscribe to Limited Partnership interests are subject to acceptance by the Producers. Contributions must be paid in cash at the time of signing the Limited Partnership Agreement, and will be held in trust by Donald Pro, one of the partners of Pro and Pro, attorneys for the Production, in a special account with the Tenth National City Bank and may not be used until One Hundred Sixty Thousand ($160,000.00) Dollars has been raised (or such lesser sum in no event below One Hundred Thirty Thousand [$130,000.00] Dollars which the General Partners regard as sufficient to present the Play) and then only for Partnership purposes. After the Partnership is formed, the funds will thereafter be held by the Producers in a special bank account in trust until such funds are actually employed for pre-production, Production, or Running Expenses of the Production or returned to the Investors. The Partnership will not be formed and all contributions will be returned in full if One Hundred Sixty Thousand ($160,000) Dollars has not been received (or such lesser sum in no event below One Hundred Thirty Thousand [$130,000.00] Dollars which the General Partners regard as sufficient to present the Play) by November 15, 1969, on which date Production rights expire unless the Author wishes to extend them, except to the extent contributions have been expended by consent of individual subscribers who have also waived their right of refund.

An individual subscriber may agree in writing to the use of his contribution prior to formation of the Partnership, or waive his absolute right of full refund in event of an insufficency of funds on abandonment prior to formation of the Partnership. The Producers will be liable to subscribers who agree to immediate use but do not waive full refunds of their contribution. A subscriber who agrees to earlier use may, under certain circumstances, be personally liable as a General Partner for Production debts incurred prior to the date of the formation of the Partnership. Investors should note that there is no advantage to entering into these agreements. In fact there is a distinct disadvantage since persons who do so risk loss of their entire investment even if the Partnership is never formed.

The Producers reserve the right to pay to any individual investor an additional participation in net profits for any reason whatsoever provided such participation is payable solely from the Producer's share and does not affect the percentage of net profits payable to the subscribers.

OVERCALL

There will be no overcall. If additional funds are needed, the General Partners may advance their own funds or obtain necessary funds in a manner that will not reduce the percentage interest of the original Limited Partners in the net profits of the Partnership. Such advance, if made, would be repaid prior to the original Limited contributions.

THE PRODUCERS

The Play will be produced by Henry Harrison, Robert Roberts and D & F Productions, Inc. who are also Promoters and will be the General Partners of the Partnership, with exclusive control of the Production of the Play.

(*Note*: There is here set forth a brief biography of each of the producers. Also included is a chart setting forth the plays previously produced by the producers, and listing the names of the plays, the opening and closing dates, the number of performances, and the gain or loss per dollar invested.)

THE PLAY

(*Note*: There is here set forth a short description of the play.)

THE AUTHORS

(*Note*: There is here set forth a brief biography on the author. It must also state whether or not the author has authored a play which has been produced on Broadway. The author's royalty is also hereinto set forth.)

THE DIRECTOR

Ken Keene has agreed to direct the play. He will receive Three Thousand Five Hundred ($3500.00) Dollars as a fee plus two (2%) percent of the gross weekly box office receipts until the production has recouped the pre-production and production expenses. After recoupment Mr. Keene will be paid two and one half (2-½%) percent of the gross weekly box affice receipts.

(*Note*: There is here set forth the credits of the director.)

THE CAST

To date none of the cast has been selected. Negotiations are presently going on with several interested persons and it is anticipated that a star or stars will be engaged for the Production who, in addition to the weekly fee, will be paid approximately ten (10%) percent of the gross box office receipts.

THE THEATRE

No contract has yet been entered into for a theatre. However it is estimated that the New York Theatre into which the Play will be booked will have a box office capacity of approximately Sixty Thousand ($60,000.00) Dollars per week and that the theatre's share of the gross weekly box office receipts will be thirty (30%) percent of all receipts. The theatre booking customarily provides for a deposit aggregating approximately Six Thousand ($6,000.00) Dollars.

SCENIC DESIGNER

To date no scenic designer has been engaged. It is not anticipated that a percentage of the gross weekly box office receipts will be paid to the scenic designer.

COMPENSATION OF GENERAL PARTNERS

In addition to their Fifty (50%) percent share of any net profits, Henry Harrison, Robert Roberts and D & F Productions, Inc., will receive the following compensation and advantages whether or not the Partnership returns a net profit:

As a Producers' management fee – One (1%) percent of the gross weekly receipts.

For furnishing the office space and secretarial services, the General Partners will receive Three Hundred Fifty ($350.00) Dollars per week for each company presenting the Play. The office charge shall commence two weeks before the commencement of rehearsals and end one week after the close of each company presenting the Play. The offices will be located c/o Henry Harrison, 0000 Broadway, New York, New York, and will not be used exclusively for the Partnership. To the extent that charges received from the Partnership by the General Partners for office space or other items furnished by them exceed their own cost, they will receive additional compensation.

In the event that a Producer finds it necessary to perform any services of a third person, the Producer may, if he so desires, receive reasonable compensation in the amount that the third person would have received for such services, for example in the event that a Producer should find it necessary to act as Stage Manager.

They will receive no compensation, other than stated above, for any services, equipment or facilities customarily rendered or furnished by a General Partner, Producer or Author of a theatrical venture; nor will they receive concessions of cash, property or anything of value from persons rendering services or supplying goods to the Production.

The producers or a company controlled by them may purchase British Production and subsidiary rights for their own behalf. If this right is exercised, the Partnership would still receive the percentage due it; however, individual Limited Partners would have no legal standing to assert that the price or terms of sale were not the best available. The Producers have undertaken that such a sale will only be on fair and reasonable terms.

USE OF PROCEEDS

The present estimated allocation of proceeds is as follows:

1. PHYSICAL PRODUCTION		
Scenery & Props	$20,000.00	
Costumes	15,000.00	
Electrics (Rental & Purchase)	2,000.00	
Sound	500.00	$ 37,500.00
2. REHEARSAL SALARIES		
Cast	15,600.00	
Stage Managers	2,550.00	
Company Manager	750.00	
Crew	2,650.00	
Wardrobe	350.00	
Production Secretary	625.00	22,525.00
3. REHEARSAL EXPENSES		
Theatre or Hall	1,500.00	
Scripts	500.00	
Casting	1,000.00	
Miscellaneous & Department Expenses	1,750.00	4,750.00
4. FEES		
Director	3,500.00	
Set Designer	2,500.00	
Lighting Designer	1,250.00	
Costume Designer	2,500.00	9,750.00
5. ADVERTISING AND PUBLICITY		
Press Agent – Salary and Expenses	1,500.00	
Newspapers	10,000.00	
Photos and Signs	1,500.00	
Printing	750.00	13,750.00
6. OTHER		
Office	2,100.00	
Legal	3,500.00*	
Audit	750.00	
General Manager	2,500.00	

Payroll Taxes	1,800.00	
Health and Welfare	2,240.00	
Insurance	1,500.00	
Hauling	1,750.00	
Take In, Hang and Rehearse	4,500.00	
Transportation	1,000.00	
Preliminary Box Office Expenses	1,000.00	
Living Expenses	1,500.00	
Preproduction and Miscellaneous	2,045.00	
Music	4,140.00	30,325.00
TOTAL ESTIMATED PRODUCTION COSTS:		$118,600.00

* Includes expenses of this offering at $1,500.00.

7. BONDS AND DEPOSITS		
Theatre	6,000.00	
Actors' Equity Association	21,000.00	
I.A.T.S.E.	1,500.00	
A.T.P.A.M.	1,100.00	29,600.00
RESERVE:	11,800.00	11,800.00
TOTAL CAPITALIZATION		$160,000.00

ESTIMATED WEEKLY BUDGET

The weekly budget for the Play, once it opens in New York, is estimated at approximately Forty Four Thousand Four Hundred Ninety ($44,490.00) Dollars at capacity. Based on a theatre capacity of Sixty Thousand ($60,000.00) Dollars, taking into consideration payments to artists, author, theatre, stars and others out of gross receipts, the Play would have to run a minimum of Eleven (11) weeks (Eighty Eight [88] Performances) at full capacity merely to return to Limited Partners their original investment. Of course there can be no assurance that the Play will run for that length of time or that it will have audiences of any specified size for any length of time. Furthermore, additional production, running or other expenses may be incurred which would increase the budget and consequently the period of time to recover invested capital.

NET PROFITS

"Net Profits" consist of the excess of gross receipts over all "Production," "Running" and "Other" Expenses, as those terms are defined in the Limited Partnership Agreement.

As of the date of this Offering Circular, running expenses may be expected to include payments to the Author, Director, Producers and Theatre, amounting to Forty-four (44%) percent of gross weekly box office receipts. In addition it may be necessary to pay ten (10%) percent of the gross weekly box office receipts to a star or stars. The effect of this is to reduce the Limited Partners share to Fifty (50%) percent of the net profits attributable to roughly Forty-six (46%) percent of gross box office receipts. However, before there can be net profits other "Running," Production" and "Other" Expenses must be paid out of the remaining Forty-six (46%) percent of gross box office receipts. It is not anticipated that anyone else will be engaged at a percentage of gross receipts or net profits.

RETURN OF CONTRIBUTIONS—SHARE OF PROFITS

The Limited Partners as a group will receive fifty (50%) percent of any net profits, each in the proportion his contribution bears to the total Limited Contributions. Any net profits will be distributed only after the Broadway opening after all contributions have been repaid and when such distributions will still leave the Partnership with a Thirty Thousand ($30,000.00) Dollars reserve (plus any amounts which the Producers wish to accumulate for the formation of additional companies to present the Play).

Before net profits are earned, all losses will be borne by the Limited Partners to the extent of their respective contributions. After net profits are earned, the General and Limited Partners will bear losses to the extent of the net profits in proportion to their respective interests. If the Partnership liabilities exceed its assets, all Partners will be required to return pro-rata any net profits distributed to them and if a shortage remains, any repaid contributions as well.

SUBSIDIARY AND PRODUCTION RIGHTS

Under the production contract with the Author, the Producer has the right to produce and present the Play in the United States and Canada, and upon a run of at least twenty one (21) performances in New York City, to participate in subsidiary rights including motion picture and television. When the Partnership is formed the Producers will transfer their interest in the production and subsidiary rights to the Partnership. The Author has retained the right to dispose of subsidiary rights as he may choose subject to the terms of the Production contract. The Partnership's interest in any sale of these rights decreases from Forty (40%) percent during the first ten years after the close of the last first-class run of the Play, to nothing after eighteen (18) years after the Play closes.

OTHER FINANCING

Except as described above, no person has advanced anything of value toward the Production of the Play.

FINANCIAL STATEMENTS

The ultimate issuer of these securities will be the partnership to be formed. Accordingly, no financial statements are available. Limited Partners will be furnished with all financial statements required by New York law, which will include after formation of the partnership, monthly unaudited statements of operations, annual statements which may or may not be audited and also six-month statements personally verified by the producer. In cases where a long enough period elapses after the initial expenditure of investor's funds, financial statements may have to be furnished even before formation of the partnership. If the producer furnishes an unaudited annual statement, limited partners will not have the benefit of an audit of the Producers' accounts by an independent certified public accountant and will rely wholly upon the producer's figures for the determination of their share in any net profits.

LIMITED PARTNERSHIP AGREEMENT

AGREEMENT made in New York City, New York, as of the 15th day of March, 1969, between Henry Harrison, Robert Roberts and D & F Productions, Inc., hereinafter referred to as the General Partners, and the parties who shall execute this Agreement as Limited Partners for the purpose of organizing The Blossom Out Company, a Limited Partnership in connection with the Production of the Stage Play now entitled "Blossom Out."

FIRST: The Firm name of the Partnership shall be The Blossom Out Company and the address of the Partnership shall be c/o Henry Harrison, 000 Central Park South, New York, New York. The Attorneys for the Partnership are Pro and Pro, 000 Park Avenue, New York, New York 10017.

SECOND: Wherever used in this Agreement the following terms shall have the following meanings:

(a) The term "The Play" shall mean the Play "Blossom Out," written by Zachary Zoe.

(b) The term "Contributions of Limited Partners" shall mean the amounts which the Limited Partners shall have set forth opposite their signatures, including any amounts which may be paid by giving obligations pursuant to Paragraph EIGHTH hereof, or which may be or may have been, paid in advance as provided for in said Paragraph EIGHTH.

(c) The term "Aggregate Limited Contributions" shall mean the aggregate of the contributions required to be made by the Limited Partners.

(d) The term "sinking fund" shall mean the sum of Thirty Thousand ($30,000.00) Dollars.

(e) The term "estimated Production requirements" shall mean an amount of cash which together with any bonds or guarantees furnished, totals One Hundred Sixty Thousand ($160,000.00) Dollars.

(f) The term "cash office charge" shall mean the sum of Three Hundred Fifty ($350.00) Dollars.

(g) The term "Net Profits" shall be deemed to mean the excess of "Gross Receipts" over all "Production Expenses", "Running Expenses," and "Other Expenses."

(h) The term "gross receipts" shall be deemed to mean all sums derived by the Partnership from any source whatsoever from the exploitation or turning to account of its rights in the Play, including all proceeds derived by the Partnership from the liquidation of the physical Production of the Play at the conclusion of the run thereof and from return of bonds and other recoverable items included in "Production expenses".

(i) The term "Production Expenses" shall include fees of Director, Designers, cost of sets, curtains, drapes, costumes, properties, furnishings, electrical equipment, premiums for bonds and insurance, cash deposits with Actors' Equity Association or other similar organizations by which, according to customs or usual practices of theatrical business, such deposits may be required to be made, advances to Authors, rehearsal charges and expenses, transportation charges, cash office charge, reasonable legal and auditing expenses, advance publicity, theatre costs and expenses, and all other expenses and losses of whatever kind (other than expenditures precluded hereunder) actually incurred in connection with the Production preliminary to the opening of the Play in New York, New York, including any summer stock and out-of-town losses. The General Partners have heretofore incurred or paid, and, prior to the inception of the Partnership, will incur or pay, certain production expenses as herein set forth, and the amount thereof, and no more, shall be included in the Production Expenses of the Partnership, and (but only if the Aggregate Limited Contributions in full shall have been paid in) the General Partners shall be reimbursed for the expenses so paid by them individually, including those set forth in Paragraph SIXTH hereof.

(j) The term "Running Expenses" shall be deemed to mean all expenses, charges and disbursements of whatsoever kind actually incurred as running expenses of the Play, including without limitation of the generality of the foregoing, royalties and/or other compensation to or for Authors, Business and General Managers, Director, Orchestra, Cast, stage help, transportation, cash office charge, advertising, rentals, miscellaneous supplies, reasonable legal and auditing expenses, theatre operating expenses, and all other expenses and losses of whatever kind actually incurred in connection with the operation of the Play and taxes of whatsoever kind and nature other than taxes on the incomes of the respective Limited and General Partners. Said Running Expenses shall include payments made in the form of percentages of gross receipts as well as participations in profits to or for any of the aforementioned persons, services, or rights.

(k) The term "Other Expenses" shall be deemed to mean all expenses of whatsoever kind or nature other than those referred to in " (i) " and " (j) " hereof actually and reasonably incurred in connection with the operation of the business of the Partnership, including, but without limiting the foregoing, commissions paid to Agents, monies paid or payable in connection with claims for plagiarism, libel, negligence, etc.

(l) The term "Expenses" shall be deemed to include contingent expenses and liabilities, as well as unmatured expenses and liabilities, and until the final determination thereof, the General Partners shall have the absolute right to fix, as the amount thereof, such sums as they, in their sole discretion, deem advisable.

(m) The term "Author" shall be deemed to mean the Author, Adapter and/or Owner of the Play, as the case may be, and shall be deemed to be used in the singular or plural, as the identity of the person or persons may require.

(n) In the event that only one person shall sign as General Partner, then the phrase "General Partners" shall be construed to mean the singular.

(o) All pronouns and any variations thereof shall be deemed to refer to the masculine, feminine, neuter, singular or plural, as the identity of the person or persons, firm or firms, corporation or corporation may require.

THIRD: The General Partners represent, warrant and/or agree:

(a) That they have duly acquired the first-class Production rights of the Play by Contract under terms no more favorable to the Author than the minimum terms provided for in the Minimum Basic Production Contract of the Dramatists Guild, Inc. (except as otherwise set forth in the Special Arrangements of this Agreement), and the limitations, restrictions, conditions and contingencies of the General Partners' right to produce the Play and in all subsidiary rights in the Play is as set forth in said Minimum Basic Production Contract, a copy of which is on file at the Office of the Attorneys for the Partnership, and is available for inspection by the Limited Partners.

(b) That in their opinion, the total cost of opening a first-class Production of the Play in New York City, including all theatre deposits and all cash deposits (or the amount of obligations given in lieu thereof) required by Actors' Equity Association or similar organizations, and including all Production expenses and the cost of an out-of-town try-out run (but only in the event that an out-of-town try-out run is anticipated) will not exceed the sum hereinabove set forth as the estimated Production requirements.

FOURTH: The parties hereto hereby form a Limited Partnership, pursuant to the provisions of the Partnership Law of the State of New York, for the purpose of managing and producing the Play, and for the purpose of exploiting and turning to account the rights at any time held by the Partnership in connection therewith, and for no other purpose.

FIFTH: The General Partners shall be the persons who shall execute this Agreement as General Partners. All of the other parties (and, in addition, those persons who shall execute this Agreement as General Partners, provided they also contribute as Limited Partners) shall be Limited Partners. If the General Partners enter into Agreements with others pursuant to which such other persons undertake obligations or privileges as General Partners with the General Partners herein specified, the Limited Partners hereby consent to such Agreement provided the General Partners herein specified are not released from any obligations hereunder.

SIXTH: The only sums expended by the General Partners, as of the date of this Agreement, in connection with the Play, and for which they are to be reimbursed hereunder, are such sums as the General Partners have theretofore reasonably incurred or spent and such sums as they may hereafter reasonably spend or incur, including but not limited to advances to the Author.

SEVENTH: The General Partners hereby agree to contribute to the Partnership, by due and proper assignment, all of the rights in the Play held by them, including those acquired or to be acquired under the aforesaid Production Contract with the Author, and further agree that all other rights acquired or which may be acquired relating to the Play, and all services rendered or to be rendered in connection therewith, shall belong to and be held in the name of the Partnership. To the extent that any rights are now held or are acquired prior to the beginning of the term of the Partnership, the General Partners agree to execute due and proper assignments to the Partnership.

EIGHTH: Each of the Limited Partners shall contribute to the capital of the Partnership, at the time hereinafter stated, the sum set forth as his contribution opposite his signature hereto; and such sums may be used for the payment of production, running and other expenses as defined herein.

(a) If a Limited Partner shall give, or cause to be given, to Actors' Equity Association or any other similar organization an obligation acceptable to it in lieu of any cash deposits otherwise required from the Partnership by such Association or other organization, and if he shall have stated in substance on the page of this Agreement bearing his signature that he will so give or cause to be given such obligation, and the face amount thereof so given or to be given, and the organization to which given or to be given, then the amount specified in such acceptable obligation, when given, shall be deemed equivalent to the making by such Limited Partner of a cash contribution to the Partnership of that amount. In the event that the Play shall close before the repayment in full of the principal amount of the Limited Partners' contributions, and all or any part of such obligation shall have been satisfied by action of the Partnership, then immediately after such action each Limited Partner who shall have furnished such an obligation shall pay to the Partnership, in cash, the full principal amount originally stated in such obligation (less any amounts which he may already have been called upon to pay, and actually shall have paid, thereunder), and such cash payment to the Partnership (plus any such amounts theretofore paid as referred to in the immediately preceding parentheses) shall thereupon and thereafter represent the capital contribution to the Partnership by such Limited Partner to the extent formerly represented by said amount originally stated in said obligation.

(b) The General Partners may also arrange for the deposit of bonds required by Actors' Equity Association or any other union or organization without, however, reducing the percentage of net profits payable to the Limited Partners. Such arrangements may provide for obtaining such bonds from persons who may or may not be Limited Partners upon terms which require that prior to the return of Limited Partners' contributions, or the payment of any net profits, all funds otherwise available for such purposes shall be set aside and paid over to Actors' Equity Association or any other such union or organization in substitution for and in discharge of the bonds furnished by such others.

(c) Any prospective Limited Partner may, at the time of executing this Agreement, pay to the General Partners all or part of his agreed contribution, and may authorize the General Partners to expend all or part thereof for any proper purpose of the Partnership. In such event, the General Partners shall, upon or before the filing of the Certificate of Limited Partnership hereinafter mentioned, assign to the Partnership all of the benefits derived from the expenditure of said funds for such purposes, and pay any balance of the sum so advanced to them into the Special Bank Account hereinafter provided for, and, when the Partnership shall have received, in cash, the balance, if any, of the agreed contribution of such Limited Partner, the Partnership shall thereupon be deemed to have received, in cash, the full agreed contribution of such Limited Partner. In the event that the Partnership shall not come into being, the General Partners shall return the full sum so paid to them, without interest, to such prospective Limited Partner, unless otherwise agreed in writing between them and him at the time such contribution is paid to the General Partners. In no event shall any other Limited Partner be in any way liable in connection with any such transaction.

(d) If so provided in the Special Arrangements hereof, each Limited Partner agrees, on demand of the General Partners in writing, to make an additional contribution in cash equal to such percentage of his original contribution as is set forth in said Special Arrangements. Each such contribution shall be paid promptly after receipt by each Limited Partner from the General Partners of a written notice requesting such payment. In the event of the failure of a Limited Partner to pay the additional contribution when due, the General Partners may bring an action or proceeding against such Limited Partner for the amount of his unpaid additional contribution plus all disbursements, costs and expenses (including reasonable counsel fees) of bringing and maintaining such action or proceeding.

NINTH: The capital contribution of each Limited Partner shall be payable upon written demand of the General Partners.

All such payments shall be kept in a Special Bank Account

to be opened by the General Partners under such name as they deem appropriate and shall not be used for any purpose of the Partnership until the aggregate Limited contributions in full shall have been so paid in except as may be specifically authorized in writing by the Limited Partner making such contribution.

TENTH: After the aggregate Limited contributions shall have been paid in, any additional persons who desire to become Limited Partners may do so, but such additional persons shall not be entitled to any compensation with respect to their contributions as Limited Partners, or to any share in the net profits of the Partnership, except such as they may become entitled to by special agreement with the General Partners, and then only upon condition that such compensation or share shall be payable from the General Partners' own share of the net profits.

ELEVENTH: The General Partners, at their option, may advance or cause to be advanced to the Partnership funds in a form and/or manner other than as contributions of Limited Partners to the capital hereof. In addition thereto, if the Partnership funds shall be insufficient or otherwise not available to pay any of its running expenses or other expenses, the General Partners may also advance or cause to be advanced, funds for this purpose in a form and/or manner other than as contributions of Limited Partners. All such advances shall be entitled to be repaid in full prior to the return of any of the contributions of the Limited Partners hereunder. In no event, however, shall the Partnership incur any expenses in connection with such advances nor shall the percentage of the net profits payable to the Limited Partners be affected thereby.

The aggregate Limited Contributions (including overcall, if any), in the discretion of the General Partners, may be used to pay running and other expenses as well as Production expenses.

TWELFTH: The Partnership shall commence on the day upon which, pursuant to the New York Partnership Law, the Certificate of Limited Partnership is duly filed in the Office of the Clerk of New York County, and shall continue until terminated as in this Agreement provided. Such Certificate shall be filed and the notice of Limited Partnership duly published immediately after (but in no event prior to) the date on which the aggregate Limited Contributions shall have been actually paid in.

THIRTEENTH: Anything herein to the contrary notwithstanding, the General Partners shall have the right (whenever in their discretion they shall deem it necessary) to abandon the Production at any time prior to its New York opening for any reasonable reason whatsoever. In the event of such abandonment, the Production shall be forthwith liquidated and all funds then held in the Special Bank Account or Accounts, and all "gross receipts" shall be distributed to the same persons and in the same manner as set forth in this Agreement.

FOURTEENTH: The Production of the Play shall be announced as the General Partners may determine.

FIFTEENTH: Subject to the other provisions of this Agreement, the Partnership shall continue until all rights of the Partnership in the Play shall have terminated. Upon said termination the General Partners shall liquidate the affairs of the Partnership as hereinafter provided for.

SIXTEENTH: The net profits that may accrue from the business of the Partnership shall be distributed to, and divided among, the General and Limited Partners in the following proportions:

The Limited Partners shall each receive that proportion of fifty (50%) percent of the net profits which his contribution bears to the aggregate Limited contributions, excluding, however, from such Limited Partners all persons who may be entitled to compensation with respect to their contributions as Limited Partners so made by such persons. The other Limited Partners, if any, shall receive such proportion of the other fifty (50%) percent of the net profits as the General Partners may have agreed to pay them from the General Partners' share of net profits, and the General Partners shall receive the remaining net profits, to be divided between them as they shall agree.

If the estimated Production requirements shall be less than the amount specified in Paragraph SECOND, then, in lieu of returning any part of the capital contribution made by any Limited Partner, the aggregate Limited contributions required to be made hereunder shall be accordingly reduced to such lesser sum, and the percentages of net profits specified herein shall be accordingly increased, so that each Limited Partner shall receive that proportion of fifty (50%) percent of the net profits which the contribution made by the Limited Partner bears to such reduced aggregate Limited contributions, excluding, however, from such Limited Partners all persons who may be entitled to compensation with respect to their contributions as Limited Partners only from the share of the General Partners in such net profits, and excluding from such aggregate Limited contributions the contributions as Limited Partners so made by such persons.

SEVENTEENTH: Until net profits shall have been earned, losses suffered and incurred by the Partnership, up to but not exceeding the aggregate Limited contributions and additional contributions, referred to in Paragraph EIGHTH hereof, shall be borne entirely by the Limited Partners in proportion to their respective contributions. After net profits shall have been earned, then, to the extent of such net profits, the General Partners and Limited Partners shall share such losses pro rata in the same percentages as they are entitled to share in net profits pursuant to the provisions of Paragraph SIXTEENTH hereof.

No Limited Partner (other than a Partner who is both a Limited and a General Partner) shall be personally liable for any debts, obligations or loss of the Partnership in any event, except from the capital contributed by him hereunder, but the provisions of this Paragraph SEVENTEENTH shall not affect such obligations of the Limited Partners as are set forth in Paragraph EIGHTEENTH hereof to return capital contributions or profits actually received by them.

EIGHTEENTH: (a) The Contributions of the Limited Partners shall be returned to them at the following times:

At such times (after the opening of the Play in New York City) as the Partnership has a cash reserve not less than the sinking fund (plus a reasonable amount for initial expenses in the event that the original company is sent on tour, and plus an amount for any additional company or companies organized to present the play referred to in paragraph THIRTIETH of the agreement) after the payment or reasonable provision for payment of all debts, liabilities, taxes and contingent liabilities, all cash received from time to time by the Partnership in excess of said cash reserve shall be paid monthly to the Limited Partners until their total contributions shall have been thereby fully repaid. Each Limited Partner shall receive that proportion of each monthly excess of cash as the total of his contribution bears to the aggregate amount of all contributions made by all Limited Partners. Except as provided in Paragraph TENTH, no distinctions shall be made under this Subparagraph between original Limited Partners and additional Limited Partners. (In the event that any Limited Partners, as herein provided in Paragraph EIGHTH (a), shall have given an obligation to the Actors' Equity Association or similar organization, then, at the time of each such payment aforesaid, the Partnership shall set aside the amount which would have been payable to such Limited Partner had he made a contribution in cash equal to the face amount of such obligation until there shall be accumulated a sum sufficient to release the liability of such Limited Partner, and the Partnership shall thereafter hold such Limited Partner harmless from any liability under such obligation. If, upon the termination of the Production, the amount so accumulated shall not have been used, it shall revert to the funds in the Special Bank Account or Accounts for distribution as in this Agreement provided.)

(b) The time and manner of distribution of the net profits of the Partnership shall be as follows:

Such part of the net profits of the Partnership as can be paid in cash and still leave the Partnership with a cash reserve not less than the sinking fund (plus a reasonable amount for initial expenses in the event that the original Company is sent of tour) after the payment, or reasonable provision for the payment, of all debts, liabilities, taxes and contingent liabilities, and after making the payments provided for in subdivision "(a)" of this Paragraph EIGHTEENTH, shall be paid monthly to the Limited and General Partners (in accordance with the percentage provisions hereinbefore set forth in Paragraph SIXTEENTH). Monthly distribution of profits hereunder to the Limited Partners and General Partners shall be deemed to be an advance payment on account of the distributive shares which each of such Limited and General Partners is entitled to receive at the end of the fiscal year of the Partnership, and such payments on account shall be subject to all of the terms and conditions hereof.

(c) Solely for the purpose of determining whether or not any contributions are to be repaid or net profits are to be distributed to the Limited and/or General Partners under the provisions of this Paragraph EIGHTEENTH (but not for any other purpose) the monthly financial report prepared by the accountants for the Partnership shall be utilized;

(d) Upon the closing of all Companies presenting the Play under the management of the Partnership, and the abandonment of further intention of Producing the Play, the assets of the Partnership shall be liquidated as promptly as possible and the cash proceeds shall be applied as follows, and in the following order or priority:

(1) To the payment of all debts, taxes, obligations and liabilities of the Partnership, and the necessary expenses of liquidation. Where there is a contingent debt, obligation or liability, a reserve shall be set up to meet it, and if and when said contingency shall cease to exist, the moneys, if any, in said reserve shall be distributed as herein provided for in this Paragraph EIGHTEENTH.

(2) To the repayment of the capital contributed by the Limited Partners (if any shall then remain unpaid), the said Partners sharing each such repayment proportionately to their respective contributions.

(3) The surplus, if any, of the said assets then remaining shall be divided among all the Partners in the proportion they share in the net profits.

In liquidating the assets of the Partnership, all physical assets of a saleable value, belonging to the Partnership, shall be sold at public or private sale, as the General Partners may deem advisable. No assets other than physical ones need be sold. It is agreed that any Limited and/or General Partner may purchase said physical assets at such sale.

At any time after the completion of the run of all Companies presenting a first-class Production under the management of the Partnership, the General Partners shall have the right to sell or otherwise dispose of the Production Rights and the Partnership's interest in the subsidiary rights other than the Motion Picture Rights. The Limited and/or General Partners may be purchasers upon any such sale provided the amount paid by them as purchasers shall be a fair and reasonable one. The signatories hereto agree that the then President of the League of New York Theatres may pass upon the fairness and reasonableness of the amount the proposed purchaser shall offer to pay at any such proposed sale, and his judgment shall be final and binding upon all parties.

(e) If any sum by way of repayment of contribution or distribution of profits shall have been paid prior or subsequent to the termination date of the Partnership, and at any time subsequent to such repayment there shall be any unpaid debts, taxes, liabilities, or obligations of the Partnership, and the Partnership shall not have sufficient assets to meet them, then each Limited and each General Partner shall be obligated to repay to the Partnership up to the amount of capital so returned to him and profits so distributed to him as the General Partners may need for such purpose and may demand. In such event the Limited Partners and General Partners shall first repay any profits theretofore distributed to them, respectively, and if such distributed profits shall be insufficient, the Limited Partners shall return contributions of capital which may have been repaid to them, such return by the Limited Partners, respectively, to be made in proportion to the amounts of contributions of capital which may have been so repaid to them, respectively. All such repayments by Limited Partners shall be repaid promptly after receipt by each Limited Partner from the General Partners of a written notice requesting such repayment.

The obligations herein set forth in this Subparagraph shall be in lieu of the obligations imposed under Sections 105 and 106 of the Partnership Law of the State of New York insofar as said obligations are imposed by said Sections and in addition thereto insofar as they are not imposed by said Sections.

NINETEENTH: The General Partners agree that upon the commencement of the Partnership they will, in the name of the Partnership, open, and will thereafter maintain, in New York City, a Special Bank Account or Accounts, in which shall be deposited all of the capital of the Partnership, and all of the gross receipts as hereinbefore defined, and no other funds. The funds in said Special Bank Account or Accounts shall be used solely for the business of the Partnership.

TWENTIETH: At all times from the inception of financial transactions during the continuance of the Partnership, the General Partners shall keep or cause to be kept full and faithful books of account in which shall be entered fully and accurately each transaction of the Partnership. All of said books of account shall be at all times open to the inspection and examination of the Limited Partners, or their representatives. The General Partners shall likewise have available for the examination and inspection of the Limited Partners or their representatives, at any time, box office statements received from the theatre (or theatres, as the case may be) at which the Play produced by the Partnership shall be shown. The General Partners agree to deliver to the Limited Partners, not later than sixty (60) days after the opening of the Play in New York City, a complete statement of Production expenses and a monthly unaudited statement of operations, and such other financial statements as may be required by the New York Theatrical Syndication and Financing Act and the Regulations promulgated thereunder. The General Partners further agree to deliver to the Limited Partners all information necessary to enable the Limited Partners to prepare their Federal and State Income Tax Returns.

TWENTY-FIRST: The General Partners agree to render, in connection with the Play, services customarily and usually rendered by theatrical Producers, and to devote as much time thereto as may be necessary, it being agreed, however, that subject to faithful performance by the General Partners of this obligation, they may engage in other business, including other theatrical productions. They agree to furnish, from the date of this Agreement, office facilities including local telephone, stationery, secretarial and like facilities (but not including a press department) for which they shall receive the cash office charge beginning two weeks prior to the first rehearsal and continuing through the week after the close of the Play. In the event the charges received from the Partnership by the Producers for office space or other items furnished by them exceed their own cost, they will receive an additional compensation above the cash office charge herein provided for. In the event that there is more than one company, the cash office charge shall be payable for each additional company for the period beginning two weeks prior to the first rehearsal of such additional company and continuing until one week after its close. Payments made hereunder shall be deemed to be, and shall be charged as, Running Expenses and/or Production Expenses of the Partnership.

The General Partners (subject to the rights of the Play's Author) shall have complete control, in their discretion, both of Production of the Play and the exploitation of all rights therein, including, without limiting the generality of the foregoing, changes in script, choice of cast, Directors and

Designers, properties, sets, prices of tickets, time of opening and closing the New York City Company or any other company, and organizing and arranging for additional companies.

TWENTY-SECOND: No assignment of a Limited Partner's interest may be made without the written approval of the General Partner.

TWENTY-THIRD: The Partnership shall terminated upon the death, insanity or retirement of any individual General Partner, or the dissolution of a Corporate General Partner.

If a Limited Partner shall die, his Executors or Administrators, or if he shall become insane, his Commitee or other representative shall have the same rights that the Limited Partner would have had if he had not died or become insane and the share of such Limited Partner in the assets of the Partnership shall, until the termination of the Partnership, be subject to all the terms, provisions and conditions of this Agreement as if such Limited Partner had not died or become insane.

TWENTY-FOURTH: Unless otherwise specified in writing, the address of each party hereto for all purposes shall be that set forth next to the signature of that party at the end of this Agreement.

TWENTY-FIFTH: Unless agreed to in writing by all of the parties hereto, the Limited Partners shall have no right to demand and receive property other than cash in return for their contributions.

TWENTY-SIXTH: Any dispute arising under, out of, in connection with, or in relation to this Agreement, or the making or validity thereof, or its interpretation, or any breach thereof, shall be determined and settled by arbitration in New York City, pursuant to the rules then obtaining of the American Arbitration Association. Any award rendered shall be final and conclusive upon the parties and a judgment thereon may be entered in the highest court of the forum, State or Federal, having jurisdiction. The provisions of this Paragraph shall not affect the rights of the Limited Partners under the Federal Securities Law.

TWENTY-SEVENTH: This Agreement may be executed in counterparts, all of which taken together shall be deemed one original.

TWENTY-EIGHTH: Each of the Partners agrees that one original of this Agreement (or set of original counterparts) shall be held at the office of the Partnership, that a Certificate of Limited Partnership shall be filed in the office of the County Clerk of the County of New York, and that a duplicate original (or set of duplicate original counterparts) shall be held at the office of the Attorney for the Partnership, and that there shall be distributed to each partner a conformed copy thereof.

TWENTY-NINTH: Each of the Partners does hereby make, constitute and appoint the General Partner or any one of the General Partners, his true and lawful Attorney, and in his name, place, and stead to make, execute, sign, acknowledge and file (i) the Certificate of Limited Partnership of the Partnership, and to include therein all information required by the laws of the State of New York, (ii) such amended certificates of Limited Partnership as may be required hereunder and (iii) all papers which may be required to effectuate the dissolution of the Partnership after its termination.

THIRTIETH: In the event the General Partners shall desire the Partnership to organize a Company or Companies in addition to the original one to present the Play in the United States, Canada, or Great Britain (if the rights to Produce the Play in Great Britain accrue to the Partnership), then the General Partners shall have the right so to do and in such event no Net Profits shall be distributed until there is further accumulated in the Bank Account, in addition to the reserve (sinking fund) provided for in Paragraph SECOND hereof, a sum which, in the opinion of the General Partners will be sufficient to pay the Production Expenses of each such additional Company. In the event there is more than one Company being presented at the same time, the reserve fund provided for in Paragraph SECOND shall be maintained for each separate Company before the repayment of contributions or distribution of Net Profits.

The Partnership may also enter into an Agreement with respect to the disposition of British Production and subsidiary rights of the Play, with any Partnership, Corporation, or other firm in which the General Partners may be, in any way interested, provided that such Agreement shall be on fair and reasonable terms.

In addition, any of the General Partners may be associated in any way with any person, firm or corporation which may produce or co-produce a second company of the Play, and may receive compensation therefore without any obligation whatsoever to account to the Partnership or the Partners hereof; provided, however, that the Partnership shall receive from any entity producing such a second company the customary fees and royalties payable to it, as Producer of the original Company, in connection with such second company.

The General Partners shall have the right in their discretion to make arrangements to license the road rights to any other party or parties they may designate, provided the Partnership receives reasonable royalties or other reasonable compensation therefor, and provided further that the Partnership shall not be involved in any loss or expenses by reason thereof. In the event of any such license of rights, none of the Limited or General Partners shall be disqualified from participating in such proposed action by investment of their funds or otherwise as a separate enterprise, but in such event the reasonableness of the royalties or other compensation payable to the Partnership for such license shall be passed upon by the then President of the League of New York Theatres. In the event of any such license of rights any General Partner may render services to the licensee in connection with the exploitation by the licensee of the rights so licensed.

THIRTY-FIRST: In the event that the General Partners at any time after the first public performance of the Play shall determine in good faith that continuation of the run of the Play is not in the best interests of the Partnership and should be abandoned, they shall have the right to make arrangements with any person to continue the run of the Play on such terms as they may feel is to the best interests of the Partnership.

THIRTY-SECOND: If, upon the termination of the Partnership, the first or second class production rights of the Play for the United States and Canada, with or without the physical production of the Play and with or without the Partnership's interest in the proceeds of the subsidiary rights of the Play, are purchased by a General Partner (as distinguished from a Limited Partner or Partners), then, and in that event, the amount paid by said party shall be the fair and reasonable market value thereof, or an amount equal to the best offer obtainable, whichever is the higher.

THIRTY-THIRD: It is recognized and agreed that one or more of the Limited Partners may be a Motion Picture Company or a person nominated or otherwise controlled by a Motion Picture Company; that such Motion Picture Company may acquire the Motion Picture rights in and to the Play; and that the Partnership shall be free to deal with such Motion Picture Company without liability on the part of said Motion Picture Company to account therefor to the Partnership or to the General Partners or any Limited Partner for any profits it may derive from or in connection with the rights acquired by it.

THIRTY-FOURTH: The management of the affairs of the Partnership shall not be centralized in one or more persons acting in a representative capacity.

SPECIAL ARRANGEMENTS

A. The contract entered into with the Author is a Minimum Basic Production Contract of the Dramatists Guild, Inc. with certain changes incorporated therein. The Producer paid the sum of Two Thousand ($2,000.00) Dollars for the right to produce the Play for a period of one (1) year from

September 15, 1968. If the Producer has hired a Star for the show who is unavailable until the extended option period, the option may be extended for the play to open on or before March 15, 1970, upon the payment of an additional One Thousand Two Hundred Fifty ($1,250.00) Dollars. The Contract further provides that the Author is to be paid a royalty of ten (10%) percent of the gross box office receipts.

B. There is no overcall and hence no additional contribution will be required of the Limited Partners above the original contribution.

C. All monies raised shall be held in trust by Donald Pro, one of the Partners of Pro and Pro, the Attorneys for the Production, in a special account with the Tenth National City Bank until the aggregate Limited Contributions have been raised, and will thereafter be held by the Producers in a Special bank account or accounts in trust until actually employed for preproduction or production purposes or returned to the investors.

D. The Producers will be paid in the aggregate, in addition to the cash office charge, compensation for their services in an amount equal to one (1%) percent of the gross weekly box office receipts.

E. If the aggregate Limited contributions have not been contributed on or before September 15, 1969 (or prior to such later date provided that the option agreement with the Author to produce the Play has been extended), then all contributions received shall be immediately returned to the Investors and the Partnership will not be formed. In no event will the aggregate Limited contributions, that is the original capital, be less than One Hundred Thirty Thousand ($130,000.00) Dollars nor will the Partnership be formed until at least One Hundred Thirty Thousand ($130,000.00) Dollars has been invested.

F. In the event that a Producer finds it necessary to perform any services of a third person, the Producer may, if he so desires, receive reasonable compensation in the amount that the third person would have received for said services.

IN WITNESS WHEREOF the parties hereto have hereunto set their hands and seals to the Limited Partnership Agreement of The Blossom Out Company the day and year first above written.

AS GENERAL PARTNERS

	00 Central Park South, New York, N.Y.
.... Henry Harrison	
	000 Central Park West, New York, N.Y.
.... Robert Roberts	
D & F Productions, Inc.	0 Somewhere Road, Someplace, N.Y.
By......................................	

AS LIMITED PARTNERS

Name	Soc. Sec. Number	Residence Address	Cash Amount Agreed to Be Contributed	Percentage of Profits to Be Received
....			....	....
	....			

The following sign the foregoing Agreement as Limited Partners and agree that their contribution may be used forthwith by the General Partners for the business of the Partnership. Persons so signing do not waive refund in the event of insufficiency of funds or abandonment prior to formation of the Partnership, unless such waiver is contained in writing in a separate agreement.

....

....

The following sign the foregoing Agreement as Limited Partners, but in lieu of a cash contribution, agree to make their contribution not in cash, but (pursuant to the Provisions of Paragraph EIGHT (a) of the Within Agreement) by giving or causing to be given the following described obligation of the following face amount:

	Organization	Face Amount and Percentage of Profits
....	....	....

....

ESTIMATED PRODUCTION BUDGET
FOR MUSICAL
"OH GEE!"

SCENERY		
Design	$ 7,500.	
Building & Painting	70,000.	
Misc. Purchases	5,000.	$ 82,500.
PROPS		
Purchases & Rentals		12,000.
COSTUMES		
Design	5,000.	
Execution	60,000.	65,000.
REHEARSAL EXPENSES		
SALARIES		
Company	7,500.	
Crew	10,000.	
Stagehands	20,000.	
Wardrobe & Dressers	2,000.	
Chorus	20,000.	
Musicians	5,000.	
Conductor	3,000.	
Dance Arranger	2,500.	

Stage Managers	4,000.	
REHEARSAL SPACE	6,000.	
SCRIPTS & PARTS	1,000.	
AUDITIONS	2,000.	
MISCELLANEOUS	1,000.	84,000.
PRELIMINARY ADVERTISING		
Press Agent	2,500.	
Newspapers	16,000.	
Photos & Signs	5,000.	
Printing	2,000.	25,500.
ELECTRICAL & SOUND		10,000.
DIRECTORS		
Stage	5,000.	
Choreographer	5,000.	10,000.
OTHER EXPENSES		
General & Company Managers	4,000.	
Office	3,500.	
Welfare Fund	4,000.	
Legal	8,000.	
Audit	1,500.	
Transportation	5,000.	
Payroll Taxes	3,500.	
Charting	3,500.	
Orchestrations	42,000.	
Insurance	1,500.	76,000.
PRODUCTION COST		365,000.
PRE-PRODUCTION EXPENSES		40,000.
BONDS & DEPOSITS		25,000.
CONTINGENCY		70,000.
CAPITAL		$500,000.

PLUS 20% OVERCALL

ESTIMATED WEEKLY OPERATING COSTS FOR MUSICAL "OH GEE!"

SALARIES		
Cast	$ 6,000.	
Chorus	4,500.	
Musicians & Conductor	4,000.	
Crew	2,500.	
Stage Manager	900.	
Gen. & Company Managers	750.	
Press Agent	350.	
Wardrobe & Dressers	1,500.	
Extra Stagehands	1,500.	$ 22,000.
ROYALTIES (13½% @ 52,000.)		7,020.
DEPARTMENTAL		
Four Departments	750.	
Rentals	1,000.	1,750.
PUBLICITY		
Share of Advertising	2,500.	
Photos & Signs	300.	
Printing & Promotion	450.	
Press Expense	100.	3,350.
MISCELLANEOUS		
Office	500.	
Legal	150.	
Audit	150.	
Payroll Taxes	1,000.	
Insurance	300.	
NYC Excise Tax	250.	
League Dues	50.	
Share of Box Office Staff	400.	
Miscellaneous	100.	2,900.
TOTAL	37,020.	

@ 52,000.

Show Share	38,000.
Theatre Share	14,000.

	@ 60,000.	@ 70,000.	@ 80,000.	@ 90,000.
BEFORE PAYOFF				
Show	44,000.	51,500.	59,000.	66,500.
Theatre	16,000.	18,500.	21,000.	23.500.
Profit	4,800.	10,800.	16,800.	22,800.
AFTER PAYOFF				
Profit	4,000.	9,000.	14,000.	19,000.

OFFERING CIRCULAR FOR SEC REGISTRATION
50 UNITS
$500,000 Total Selling Price*
ANYTHING COMPANY
(A New York Limited Partnership to Be Formed)

PRE-FORMATION LIMITED PARTNERSHIP INTERESTS (hereinafter referred to as "Limited Partnership Interests") being offered for subscription by Doe, Roe and Hoe, Inc. as General Partner of ANYTHING COMPANY, a New York Limited Partnership to be formed for the purpose of producing the dramatico-musical play presently entitled ANYTHING (hereinafter sometimes referred to as the "Musical").

For information as to the Speculative Nature of the Offering, see "GENERAL INFORMATION REGARDING THIS OFFERING."

* Subject to a fifteen per cent (15%) involuntary overcall. If the entire overcall is exercised, the aggregate dollar amount will be $75,000 and the total selling price will be $575,000.

PROSPECTUS

THESE SECURITIES HAVE NOT BEEN APPROVED OR DISAPPROVED BY THE SECURITIES AND EXCHANGE COMMISSION, NOR HAS THE COMMISSION PASSED UPON THE ACCURACY OR ADEQUACY OF THIS PROSPECTUS. ANY REPRESENTATION TO THE CONTRARY IS A CRIMINAL OFFENSE.

UNTIL 90 days after the effective date, ALL DEALERS EFFECTING TRANSACTIONS IN THE REGIS-

TERED SECURITIES, WHETHER OR NOT PARTICIPATING IN THIS DISTRIBUTION, MAY BE REQUIRED TO DELIVER A PROSPECTUS. THIS IS IN ADDITION TO THE OBLIGATION OF DEALERS TO DELIVER A PROSPECTUS WHEN ACTING AS UNDERWRITERS AND WITH RESPECT TO THEIR UNSOLD ALLOTMENTS OR SUBSCRIPTIONS.

Limited Partnership Interests Offered for Subscription

	Price to Public[2]	Underwriting Discounts and Commissions[2]	Proceeds to Limited Partnership[3,4]
Per Unit[1]	$ 10,000.00	None [3]	$ 10,000.00
Total	$500,000.00	None	$500,000.00

As of April 1, 1969, $300.000.00 in Limited Partnership interests have been sold, including the commitment of ANYTIME Records (see "Record Album Income").

[1] Aggregate limited contributions are not actually divided into a specified number of units and amounts; but for the purpose of illustration they may be considered as consisting of 50 units of $10,000.00 per unit (with the right reserved to issue fractional units). This is subject to a 15% involuntary overcall. A contribution of $10,000.00 ($11,500.00 in the event the entire overcall is made) will entitle a limited partner to receive 1% of the Net Profits. No contribution of less than $500.00 will be accepted except with the consent of the General Partner. (See caption entitled "ESTIMATED COST OF PRODUCITON AND AGGREGATE CONTRIBUTIONS BEING OFFERED.")

[2] Doe, Roe and Hoe, Inc. and John Doe, Richard Roe and Harold Hoe, who are in control thereof, may be deemed to be underwriters within the meaning of Section 2(11) of the Securities Act of 1933. The offering is being made by them as an incident to their services as the Producers of the Musical. For its services as Producer, Doe, Roe and Hoe, Inc., will receive fifty percent (50%) of the Net Profits of the Partnership. (See caption entitled "NET PROFITS.") There is no assurance that sufficient proceeds will be received to form the

Partnership. If $500,000 shall not have been contributed to the capital of the Partnership by September 15, 1969, each Limited Partner shall promptly thereafter receive the return of his contribution (without interest) except to the extent that said contribution has been expended pursuant to his written consent. (See captions entitled "RETURN OF CONTRIBUTIONS IF PARTNERSHIP NOT FORMED" and "GENERAL PARTNER'S REMUNERATION.")

[3] The General Partner has entered into an agreement with Anytime Records, a division of Anytime Television Studios, Inc. whereby this record company acquired the original cast album recording rights in the Musical. For such rights, Anytime Records will pay a basic royalty of 25% of the wholesale price of 90% of the albums sold. Anytime Records has also agreed to purchase, through its nominee, Jack Jones, $200.000 in Limited Partnership interests. Anytime Records may be deemed to be an underwriter within the meaning of Section 2(11) of the Securities Act of 1933.

[4] It is anticipated that the expenses of the offering, including legal fees, disbursements, mimeo costs, filing fees and publication costs will not exceed $5,000. Accordingly, the total net proceeds to ANYTHING COMPANY will amount to approximately $495,000, or if the entire overcall is exercised, approximately $575,000.

TABLE OF CONTENTS

CAPTION PAGE

Limited Partnership Interests Offered for Subscription
Introductory
The Producer
Acquisition of Property
Estimated Cost of Producing and Aggregate
  Contributions Being Offered
Return of Contributions If Partnership Not Formed
General Nature of Offering
  Plan of Offering Interests to Public
  Subscription to Limited Partnership
Restrictions on Limited Partners
  Right of Limited Partner to Withdraw from
  the Partnership
  Right of Assignee of a Limited Partner

Use of Proceeds
Purpose of Partnership
Commencement of Partnership
Contracts and Assignment Thereof
Sources of Partnership Income
    Record Album Income
Expenses of Conducting Business
Disposition of Partnership Income
    Return of Contributions: Profits and Losses
    Net Profits
    Effect of Federal Income Taxes
    Additional Funds
Additional Companies
Theatre Tickets
Control by General Partner
Remuneration of General Partner
Reimbursement of General Partner
Interests of General Partner in Certain Transactions
Abandonment of Production
The Creative Elements
Termination of Partnership
Other Information
Underwriting

INTRODUCTORY
GENERAL INFORMATION REGARDING THIS OFFERING

I. The General Partner of ANYTHING COMPANY wishes to emphasize that no one should consider the purchase of the interests being offered without recognizing the speculative nature of and the risks of loss involved in the purchase of an interest in an enterprise devoted to a particular theatrical production. There can be no assurance as to income or as to return of the investment. An investor purchasing a limited partnership interest should understand that he may lose his entire investment or may not receive any return thereon. Additional risk factors are discussed in this prospectus which should be studied carefully prior to purchasing the limited partnership interests offered hereunder.

While no accurate industry statistics are available, it has been claimed that approximately 80% of the plays produced for the New York stage in the 1967/68 season resulted in loss to investors.

On the basis of estimated expense, the Musical will have to run for a minimum of 35 weeks (approximately 280 performances) on Broadway to a full capacity house to return to limited partners their initial contribution. Approximately 80% of the plays produced for the New York stage in the 1967/68 season failed to run this long. Of those which did, most did not play continuously to full capacity audiences.

II. It should be borne in mind that there probably will not be a ready market for the limited partnership interests offered hereunder; that no assignee of a Limited Partner shall have the right to become a substituted Limited Partner in the place of his assignor, and the Partnership shall not be bound by any assignment of any Limited Partner's interest unless the General Partner consents thereto; that there is no right to withdrawal from the Partnership except as described under the caption "RETURN OF CONTRIBUTIONS IF PARTNERSHIP IS NOT FORMED."

III. The Musical will be financed by the organization of a New York limited partnership which will be formed for the purpose of producing, presenting and turning to account the rights held by it in the Musical. The Limited Partners (the public investors) will furnish all of the capital initially required and will bear any losses incurred by the Partnership, up to the aggregate amount of their contributions. In return they will receive 50% of any of the Net Profits remaining after the payments discussed below.

The General and Limited Partners' share in Net Profits, if any, will be computed only after payment to others of approximately 45% of gross weekly box office receipts and 4% of the net profits (which percentage figures may be increased at the sole discretion of the General Partner by contracting for talent or services on a basis which includes a percentage of gross receipts or net profits) and deduction of all other expenses from the balance of the gross receipts.

Each Limited Partner may be required to contribute an amount equal to 15% of his original investment in satisfaction of an overcal." Each Limited Partner will be required to contribute his pro rata share of the overcall if made, or else be liable for breach of contract.

The General and Limited Partners will be responsible for the return of any net profits and, in the case of Limited Partners, any capital, distributed to them if the Partnership does not after such distribuion maintain sufficient assets to meet its obligations.

The General Partner, which will make no cash contribution, will receive (a) 50% of any Net Profits; (b) 1% of the gross receipts as a management fee; (c) $400 per week office expense charge for each company presenting the Musical. It should be noted that the General Partner may abandon the production at any time prior to its New York opening, for any reason whatsoever and, at the same time, may enter into a production agreement for its own account with the Authors. Reference is made to the captions "REMUNERATION OF GENERAL PARTNER" and "INTERESTS OF GENERAL PARTNER IN CERTAIN TRANSACTIONS" for additional details with respect to other disadvantages and compensation which may enure to the benefit of the General Partner.

The General Partner is not prohibited from furnishing risk capital and from participating as a Limited Partner, but the proposed General Partner of ANYTHING COMPANY does not intend to participate as a Limited Partner therein. If it should participate as a Limited Partner, however, its liability as the General Partner would in no way be affected. The Limited Partners may take no part in the conduct or control of the business or affairs of ANYTHING COMPANY, such participation in and control of the business and affairs thereof vesting exclusively in the General Partner. Except with respect to certain liabilities under the Securities Act of 1933, as amended, no Limited Partner of ANYTHING COMPANY may hold the General Partner, its officers, directors and/or employees, liable for any action they may take in good faith within the scope of their authority.

IV. Considerable competition exists among producers in the acquisition of theatrical properties for production and in acquiring suitable talent and theatres in connection with the production. To an extent, the success or failure of the theatrical venture is dependent upon the ability of the producers thereof to select not only suitable talent but also to secure a literary property that will appeal to the theatre-going public. There can be no assurance that such talent, including the cast and scenic and costume designers will be available or will be engaged at a remuneration acceptable to the Producer. Although the conduct and control of the business and affairs of a theatrical limited partnership vests exclusively in the general partner thereof, ultimately it is for the professional drama critics and the audience to determine whether the production will be a commercial success or failure.

V. The Partnership will acquire from Doe, Roe and Hoe, Inc. the rights in the Musical it has acquired pursuant to the Minimum Basic Production Contract in respect of production rights in the Musical, certain agreements with Billy Bore in respect of his contributions to the Musical, Cal Coe for him to direct the Musical, Mary Moe for her to choreograph the Musical and Sally Star for her to star in the Musical.

VI. The general partner or general partners, as the case may be, of a theatrical limited partnership usually, and, in the case of ANYTHING COMPANY shall make all decisions relating to the conduct of the Partnership business. The General Partner of ANYTHING COMPANY will have all the rights and powers given to general partners under the provisions of the Partnership Law of the State of New York. All decisions relating to the production of the Musical will be made by the General Partner. It should be noted that the

Limited Partners will be deprived of the use of their money from the date of their initial investment until such time, if ever, as distributions are made, which cannot be until some time after the Partnership is formed.

THE PRODUCER

The General Partner of the proposed Limited Partnership (herein sometimes referred to as the "Partnership") will be Doe, Roe and Hoe, Inc., having its principal place of business at 000 Park Avenue, New York City, New York, and such other firms or persons as it may designate, provided that if any other firms or persons are so designated, this Prospectus will be amended accordingly. Pursuant to the Partnership Law of the State of New York, after the Partnership has been formed, the Producer may not designate other firms or persons as general partners without the written consent or ratification of said act by all of the Limited Partners. The Producer is also the promoter. John Doe, Richard Roe and Harold Hoe, by virtue of the fact that they are the persons in control of Doe, Roe and Hoe, Inc., may also be considered promotors.

Doe, Roe and Hoe, Inc., have produced the following plays. (*Note*: The Plays are then listen together with a graph showing the name of the play, New York City opening and closing dates, number of Broadway performances and approximate gain or loss per dollar invested).

ACQUISITION OF PROPERTY

The Musical is based upon the novel, ANYTHING, by Terrence Toe, and the dramatic play of the same name by Peter Poe. The story is based upon episodes in the life of the author.

It is presently anticipated that the show will have a cast of approximately thirty five people, at least eleven of which will be major roles. However, it should be pointed out that substantial revisions are frequently made in the plot and the cast prior to the Broadway opening and there is therefore no assurance that the cast and/or Musical will not be changed substantially prior to opening night.

The Partnership will acquire from Doe, Roe and Hoe, Inc. the rights it has acquired under the following contracts:

1) Minimum Basic Production Contract of the Dramatists Guild, Inc. with Terrence Toe, author, Peter Poe, bookwriter, Robert Brown, composer and Jack Johnson, lyricist, which contracts are dated September 15, 1968. In consideration for the rights granted, the Partnership will pay a royalty of 9% of the gross weekly box office receipts of each company presenting the Musical; provided, however, that until production costs (excluding bonds and other recoverables) of the original company shall have been recouped, the aforesaid collective royalty shall be 8%.

2) Agreement dated October 1, 1968, with Billy Bore pursuant to which Mr. Bore will receive $5,000 plus ½% of the gross weekly box office receipts of each company presenting the Musical, in consideration of the termination of his rights under agreement dated October 19, 1965.

3) Agreement with Cal Coe pursuant to which he will direct the Musical for which his compensation will be $5,000 plus 2½% of the gross weekly box office receipts of each company presenting the Musical (provided, however, that until production costs (excluding bonds and other recoverables) of the original company shall have been recouped, or until 26 weeks after the New York City opening of the Musical, whichever is sooner, the aforesaid royalty shall be 2%), plus 4% of the net profits of the Partnership (computed prior to the deduction of net profits payable to anyone else).

4) Agreement with Mary Moe for her to choreograph the Musical for which her compensation will be $4,000 plus 1% of the gross weekly box office receipts of the original company and each additional company choreographed by her.

5) Agreement with Sally Star pursuant to which she

will star in the Musical for which her compensation will be $2,000 per week for the first 26 weeks starting with the first paid public performance of the Musical, $2,250 per week for the next 26 weeks, $2,500 per week for the next 26 weeks, and $2,750 per week thereafter.

The motion picture rights in the novel and the play upon which the Musical is based are owned by Henry Brothers Pictures, Inc. An oral agreement with Henry Bros. provides that Henry Bros. will grant the right to the authors to license the making of a musical motion picture based on the Musical and the exhibition thereof for a limited number of years. As consideration for the rights granted, Henry Bros. will receive 1% of the gross weekly box office receipts and a pro rata share as an "author" of subsidiary rights (other than motion picture rights). In addition, Henry Bros. will receive one-third of the price paid by any motion picture company which may purchase such motion picture rights (or will have the right to match any offer therefor and acquire such rights itself at a reduction of one-third of the price offered).

In addition to granting the Producer the right to produce the Musical, the Production Contract provides, in part, that if the Musical shall be produced pursuant to the terms thereof, the Producer will be entitled to share for the period therein specified in the proceeds derived from the disposition of certain so-called "subsidiary" rights in the Musical, which rights include television, stock and amateur rights and, if certain underlying rights are obtained from Henry Brothers Pictures, Inc. as described below, motion picture rights. See caption "SOURCES OF PARTNERSHIP INCOME – Record Album Income" with respect to "show album" rights.

No representation is made that the oral agreement referred to above is binding upon the parties.

If the world-wide motion picture rights or, with respect to the United States and Canada, such other subsidiary rights are disposed of within ten (10) years after the last public performance of the last first-class run of the Musical the Partnership will be entitled to receive 40% of the net receipts derived therefrom. Thereafter, the Partnership will share in the net receipts derived from the disposition of any rights as follows:

if within the next succeeding two years, 35%;
if within the next succeeding two years, 30%;
if within the next succeeding two years, 25%;
if within the next succeeding two years, 20%.

If any of such subsidiary rights are disposed of more than eighteen (18) years after the last public performance of the last first-class run of the Musical, the Partnership will not be entitled to receive any part to the net receipts derived therefrom. The first-class run of the Musical includes the company presenting the Musical on Broadway and on tour thereafter.

The Production Contract further provides that if the Producer becomes entitled to share in subsidiary rights, it likewise shall have the right to produce the Musical in the British Isles; in addition, it becomes entitled to receive 40% of the net proceeds derived by the Authors from all contracts executed within seven (7) years after the New York City opening with respect to performances and other subsidiary uses of the Musical outside the continental United States, Canada and the British Isles.

All of the foregoing contracts are on file and available for inspection at the office of Counsel and Counsel, 000 Park Avenue, New York City, New York 10022, the attorneys for the Partnership. Copies of said contracts have been included as Exhibits to the Registration Statement filed with the Securities and Exchange Commission in Washington, D. C., and are available for public inspection, and photo copies of them may be obtained from the Commission by payment of the fee as required by the Commission.

Upon the formation of the Partnership, the Producer will assign the foregoing contracts to the Partnership (see captions "CONTRACTS AND ASSIGNMENT THEREOF" and "REIMBURSEMENT OF GENERAL PARTNER"), and the Partnership, as such, rather than the Producer, will thereupon be entitled to share in the said additional and subsidiary rights.

ESTIMATED COST OF PRODUCTION AND AGGREGATE CONTRIBUTIONS BEING OFFERED

The General Partner believes that the total cost of offering a first-class production of the Musical in the United States, including all production expenses, will not exceed $500,000. If, after formation of the Partnership, the General Partner believes that additional money is necessary to carry on the business of the Partnership or pay debts thereof, it shall have the right to call upon each Limited Partner to make an additional contribution of up to 15% of his original contribution, and each Limited Partner agrees in the Partnership Agreement to make such contribution if called upon in writing by the General Partner to do so. [If, prior to or after making said 15% overcall, the General Partner believes that additional money is necessary to carry on the business of the Partnership or pay unpaid debts thereof, it shall have the right to loan to the Partnership such sums as it may deem advisable, which loans shall be repaid in full prior to the return to any of the Limited Partners of their respective contributions to the capital of the Partnership.] No charge for interest may be made by the General Partner for any such loan.

The aggregate limited contributions being offered hereunder are $500,000, at an aggregate offering price of $500,000, subject to 15% involuntary overcall, which, if made, will raise the aggregate offering price to $575,000. As indicated above, the aggregate limited contributions are not actually divided into a specific number of units. No contribution of less than $500 will be accepted except with the consent of the General Partner. The aggregate limited contributions entitle those so contributing to 50% of the Net Profits; thus the Limited Partners will be entitled to share in the Net Profits of the Partnership at the rate of 1% of such Net Profits for every $10,000 contributed if the overcall is not made, or for every $11,500 if the full overcall is made. If an overcall is made it must be met within 48 hours, exclusive of Saturday, Sunday and Holidays (plus such additional time, if any, to which the General Partner may, in its sole discretion, consent) after written demand is made for such additional contribution. If a limited partner does not contribute his pro rata share of an overcall he will be liable for breach of contract. The term "Net Profits" means the excess of Gross Receipts over all Production Expenses, Running Expenses and Other Expenses as same are understood in the theatrical industry and as are expressly defined in the Partnership Agreement. If the cost of production exceeds $575,000., the General Partner has the right, in its sole discretion, to advance or cause to be advanced or to borrow in the Partnership's name, any additional amount which it deems necessary therefor. The General Partner has no obligation to personally advance said monies and, therefore, the entire $575,000 could be expended without the Musical actually being publicly presented.

RETURN OF CONTRIBUTIONS IF PARTNERSHIP NOT FORMED

All contributions shall be payable at the time of the execution of the Partnership Agreement. All such contributions will be held in a special bank account in trust by the General Partner, as trustee, until employed for production or preproduction purposes or until returned to the investors. It is anticipated that the aforesaid account will be at the Trusty Trust Company. If $500,000 shall not have been contributed to the capital of the Partnership by Sept. 15, 1969, each Limited Partner shall promptly receive the return of his contribution (without interest), except to the extent that said contribution has been expended pursuant to his written consent. Any monies expended by the General Partner prior to the formation of the Limited Partnership for items which, if incurred by the Partnership, would constitute Production Expenses, Running Expenses or Other Expenses, shall, for the purpose thereof, be deemed to be equivalent of a cash contribution to the capital of the Partnership if the General Partner elects not to have such monies reimbursed to it.

GENERAL NATURE OF OFFERING

Plan of Offering Interests to Public

The registrant is ANYTHING COMPANY, a Limited Partnership which will be formed pursuant to the laws of the State of New York when the aggregate contributions amounting to $500,000 have been raised as a result of the efforts of the General Partner on behalf of the Partnership. (See caption entitled "COMMENCEMENT OF PARTNERSHIP"). The contributions will be offered to the public through use of the mails, by telephone and personal solicitation by the Producer as an incident to its services as the Producer of the Musical. In addition, the Producer intends to solicit Motion Picture record and companies for substantial contributions to the capital of the Partnership.

Subscription to Limited Partnership

Offers to subscribe to Limited Partnership interests may be made only by signing copies of the Limited Partnership Agreement of the Partnership (hereinafter sometimes referred to as the "Partnership Agreement") and delivering same together with the full amount being subscribed to the Producer at its office. Offers to subscribe are subject to acceptance by the Producer.

The form of Limited Partnership Agreement of the Proposed Partnership setting forth the rights and participation of the General and Limited Partners will be furnished upon request made to the Producer. See the following captions: "RETURN OF CONTRIBUTIONS IF PARTNERSHIP NOT FORMED," "DISPOSITION OF PARTNERSHIP INCOME" and "TERMINATION OF PARTNERSHIP."

RESTRICTIONS ON LIMITED PARTNERS

Right of Limited Partner to Withdraw from the Partnership

The Prospective Limited Partner, upon execution of the Partnership Agreement, shall be obligated to become a Limited Partner of the Partnership, when formed, and shall have no right to withdraw from the Partnership or reduce his contribution thereto, except as described under caption above, "RETURN OF CONTRIBUTIONS IF PARTNERSHIP NOT FORMED."

Right of Assignee of a Limited Partner

No Assignee of a Limited Partner shall have the right to become a substituted Limited Partner in the place of his assignor, and the Partnership shall not be bound by any assignment of less than the entire interest of a Limited Partner unless the General Partner consents thereto.

USE OF PROCEEDS

The Limited Partnership interests are not to be offered for the account of any person other than for ANYTHING COMPANY. There is no priority in the use of the proceeds.

The present estimate as to the allocation of proceeds for the purpose hereinabove set forth is as follows:

SCENERY EXPENSE		
Designing & Lighting	$ 9,000.00	
Building & Painting	79,500.00	88,500.00
PROPERTY PURCHASE & RENTALS		15,000.00
COSTUME EXPENSE		
Designer & Designing Expense	5,000.00	
Purchases	60,000.00	
Wigs & Hairpieces	1,500.00	
Shoes and Accessories	3,500.00	70,000.00
ELECTRIC & SOUND		
Rentals & Purchases		8,500.00

REHEARSAL EXPENSE		
Salaries:		
Cast (34 x $115 x 6 wks.)	$23,460.00	
Stage Managers (3)	5,500.00	
Company Crew	5,000.00	
Dance Assistant	1,750.00	
Wardrobe & Dressers	1,000.00	
Audition & Reh. Pianist	4,000.00	
Musicians	5,000.00	
Production Secretary	650.00	
Hairdresser	200.00	
General & Company Manager	5,500.00	
Theatre & Reh. Hall Rentals	5,000.00	
Script Expense	1,000.00	
Administrative Expense	500.00	$ 58,560.00
FEES		
Director	$5,000.00	
Choreographer	3,500.00	
Dance Music Arranger	1,000.00	
Musical Director	1,500.00	
Hair Stylist	1,000.00	$ 12,000.00
PRELIMINARY ADVERTISING		
Press Agent Salary & Expense	$ 1,750.00	
Newspaper Advertising	17,500.00	
Outdoor & Billposting	2,500.00	
Photos, Signs, Printing, etc.	2,000.00	
Subscription & Box Office	2,000.00	$ 25,750.00
ORCHESTRATION & COPYING		30,000.00
OFFICE EXPENSE		4,000.00
AUDITING		1,000.00
LEGAL FEE & DISBURSEMENTS		9,000.00
PAYROLL TAXES		3,500.00
INSURANCE		11,000.00
HEALTH & WELFARE		2,500.00
CAST PER DIEM		1,500.00
OUT-OF-TOWN LIVING EXPENSE		10,000.00
TRANSPORTATION		8,000.00

HAULING		14,000.00
CASTING		2,000.00
TAKE IN & HANG PRODUCTION		
1st Tryout	$14,000.00	
New York City	10,000.00	$ 24,000.00
NEW YORK OPENING NIGHT EXPENSE		1,000.00
TELEPHONE, TELEGRAPH & MISC.		1,000.00
TOTAL EXPENDITURES		$400,810.00
*BONDS		40,000.00
RESERVE		59,190.00
TOTAL ESTIMATED PRODUCTION COST		$500,000.00

* The item "BONDS" covers performance bonds that are or may be required by various unions or theatres with which contracts are to be entered into.

The above estimate is not based upon any bids of third parties and nothing herein contained shall limit the right of the General Partner of ANYTHING COMPANY to make such changes in the above allocation as may be deemed necessary or advisable. Except for such changes in said allocations as may be occasioned by increased or decreased costs of necessary services and materials, it is not presently intended that any other changes shall be made. However, the above estimate includes expenditures already made and expenditures which have heretofore been committed. For a discription of such expenditures see caption "REIMBURSEMENT OF GENERAL PARTNER."

PURPOSE OF PARTNERSHIP

The Partnership shall be formed for the purpose of managing and producing the Musical, and for the purpose of exploiting and turning to account the rights at any time held by the Partnership in connection therewith and for no other purpose.

COMMENCEMENT OF PARTNERSHIP

Until the Partnership shall be formed, all monies contributed shall be held in a special account in trust as described under caption "RETURN OF CONTRIBUTIONS IF PARTNERSHIP NOT FORMED." As soon as all of the capital has been contributed, the General Partner shall take the steps required by the Partnership Law of the State of New York to form the Partnership and the Partnership shall thereupon commence. The Producer agrees that upon said commencement it will, in the name of the Partnership, open and thereafter maintain, a special bank account or accounts, in which shall be deposited all the capital of the Partnership and all of the Partnership receipts, and no other funds. These monies shall be used solely for the business of the Partnership.

CONTRACTS AND ASSIGNMENT THEREOF

As stated under caption "ACQUISITION OF PROPERTY," Doe, Roe and Hoe, Inc. has entered into written agreements with Terrence Toe, Peter Poe, Robert Brown and Jack Johnson, and has made an agreement with Henry Bros. Pictures. Inc. It is anticipated that, prior to the commencement of the Partnership, the Producer will enter into contracts with members of the cast, designers and other persons who will render services to the Partnership. After the formation of the Partnership (as provided for under caption "COMMENCEMENT OF PARTNERSHIP"), the Producer shall assign to the Partnership all of the foregoing contracts, as well as the record album contract with Anytime Records.

SOURCES OF PARTNERSHIP INCOME

The Partnership shall receive its income from the turning to account of all rights held by the Partnership in the Musical presently entitled ANYTHING including income from additional subsidiary rights. See captions "ACQUISITION OF PROPERTY" and "INTERESTS OF GENERAL PARTNER IN CERTAIN TRANSACTIONS."

Record Album Income

The General Partner has entered into an agreement with Anytime Records, a division of Anytime Television Studios, Inc., whereby Anytime Records acquired the original cast album recording rights in the Musical. For such rights, Anytime Records will pay (other than with respect to albums sold through the Anytime Record Club) a basic royalty of 25% of the wholesale price of 90% of the albums sold. Of such royalties the Authors will receive 12%, Sally Star will receive 1% and the Partnership will receive 12%. In addition, Anytime Records has agreed to purchase $200,000 in Limited Partnership interests.

EXPENSES OF CONDUCTING BUSINESS

"Production Expenses" refer to the total expenses, charges and disbursements of all kinds incurred by the Partnership in connection with the production of the Musical preliminary to the New York City opening. See caption entitled "USE OF PROCEEDS."

The principal items of "Running Expense" which will be incurred by the Partnership are, without limitation, the following: authors', directors', designers', choreographers', arrangers', and conductor's royalties and other compensation of the cast, musicians, general manager, company manager, business manager, theatre party representative, production associates, production assistants, production secretaries and stagehands, theatre rentals and other charges, transportation charges, office facilities, insurance, legal and auditing expenses, advertising, publicity and promotion expenses (including the right to engage an advertising agency at the usual commission and to contract for additional payments for merchandising, exploitation, sales promotion and publicity) and rentals of equipment and props.

The term "Running Expenses" shall also include any percentage of the net profits (however computed or defined) of the Partnership or of the Net Profits or of the Gross Receipts of the Partnership payable to any author, member of the cast, scenic designer, costume designer, director, choreographer, or to any other person or firm rendering or furnishing services or materials or granting rights to be used by the Partnership in connection with the production or presentation of the Play or the exploitation of any of the rights therein. In this connection see caption "ACQUISITION OF PROPERTY" and the contracts listed thereunder.

The term "Running Expenses" shall also include the 1% management fee and the weekly office charge payments. See captions "GENERAL PARTNER'S REMUNERATION" and "INTERESTS OF GENERAL PARTNER IN CERTAIN TRANSACTIONS."

DISPOSITION OF PARTNERSHIP INCOME

Return of Contributions; Profits and Losses

The contributions of the Limited Partners will be repaid pro-rata before any Net Profits, as said term is defined in the Limited Partnership Agreement, are distributed and will be repaid pro-rata in monthly installments after the New York City opening if any when there shall be a cash reserve of $30,000.00, which reserve may be increased at the discretion of the General Partner in respect of additional companies, in addition to providing for all liabilities. Until Net Profits have been earned, losses incurred by the Partnership, up to the aggregate contributions shall be borne entirely by the Limited Partners in proportion to their respective contributions.

After Net Profits have been earned, then, to the extent of such Net Profits, the General Partner and Limited Partners shall share losses in the same proportion as they are entitled to share in the Net Profits. If any repayment of contributions or distribution of Net Profits shall have been made at any time, and at any time subsequent thereto there shall be any unpaid debts, taxes, liabilities or obligations of the Partnership, and the Partnership shall not have sufficient assets to meet them, then the Limited Partners and the General Partner shall be obligated to repay to the Partnership such an amount, not in excess of the capital so returned and Net Profits so distributed, with interest thereon as required by law, that the General Partner may need for such purposes and may demand. In such event, the Limited Partners and General Partner shall first repay any Net Profits theretofore distributed to them, such repayments by them to be made in proportion to the amounts of such Net Profits theretofore distributed to them respectively, and if such distributed Net Profits shall be insufficient, the Limited Partners shall return contributions of capital which may have been repaid to them, such return to be made in proportion to the amounts of contributions of capital which may have been so repaid to each Limited Partner. All such repayments by Limited Partners are to be made promptly after receipt by each Limited Partner from the General Partner of a written notice requesting a payment. If any Limited Partner does not return his share of Net Profits distributed to him or contribution of capital repaid to him, or if other persons who receive a share of Net Profits do not return their share thereof, the remaining Limited Partners may be liable to creditors of the Partnership for any deficiency. However, the total liability of each Limited Partner, as aforesaid, is limited to the total amount of Net Profits received by such Limited Partner plus the total amount of contributions returned to such Limited Partner plus interest thereon.

Net Profits

The Net Profits in which the General Partner and the Limited Partners share are the net profits remaining after there shall have been deducted therefrom such share of the net profits which may be payable to persons who shall render services or grant rights in respect of the Musical. The General Partner may enter into contracts providing for payment of shares of the net profits to persons rendering services to the Partnership, such as the star or stars. The remaining net profits shall be divided between the Limited Partners and the General Partner. Distributions of Net Profits to both the General and Limited Partners will be made monthly. As indicated on Page 1 of this PROSPECTUS, Limited Partnership interests aggregating $500,000 are being offered hereunder, and are subject to a 15% involuntary overcall. (See caption entitled "ESTIMATED COST OF PRODUCTION AND AGGREGATE CONTRIBUTIONS BEING OFFERED.")

Each Limited Partner contributing part of the original capital of the Partnership shall receive that proportion of 50% of the Net Profits as the amount of his contribution bears to the aggregate contributions. By way of example, a contribution of $10,000 ($11,500 if the full overcall is made) will entitle a Limited Partner to receive 1% of the Net Profits of the Partnership. The General Partner will be entitled to receive the remaining 50% of the Net Profits for which it will make no cash contribution.

As of the date of this Prospectus, as amended, projected Running Expenses include payments to the authors, the owner of certain underlying rights in the Musical, the star, the director and choreographer, and the producer, amounting to 15% of the gross weekly box office receipts, plus 4% of the net profits computed prior to the payment of any net profits to anyone else. In addition, it is presently anticipated that it will be necessary to pay a theatre rental of approximately 30% of the gross weekly box office receipts. The effect of the foregoing is to reduce the Limited Partners' share to 48% of the net profits attributable to 55% of the gross weekly box office receipts of the Musical. It is possible that additional payments out of gross weekly box office receipts and/or net profits will be made to members of the cast and others who contribute services to the Partnership.

Effect of Federal Income Taxes

In the opinion of Counsel and Counsel, 000 Park Avenue, New York, New York, counsel to the Issuers and to the Partnership, under the present Federal income tax laws, the Net

Profits, if any, of the Partnership will be treated by the Partners as ordinary income and any losses deductible from ordinary income. The individual limited partners will be taxable in any year in their individual capacities upon their pro rata in any year in their individual capacities upon their pro-rata them or not. Any distributions by the Partnership will not be taxable to a partner if not in excess of such partner's adjusted basis for his Partnership interest at the time. In general, a partner's basis for his Partnership interest includes his initial investment with adjustments for, among others, net profits, losses and distributions.

Additional Funds

If the General Partner believes that additional funds are necessary for the carrying on of the Partnership affairs, it shall have the right, in its sole discretion, to advance or to cause to be advanced or to borrow in the Partnership's name, the amount which it deems necessary. In such event, the money so advanced or borrowed shall be repaid before any of the contributions are repaid to any of the Limited Partners. In addition, the General Partner may, at its discretion, furnish or cause to be furnished, union and theatre bonds and guarantees in lieu of using Partnership Funds for this purpose, in which case the amount of such bonds and guarantees shall be repaid to the persons so furnishing them before any of the contributions are repaid to any of the Limited Partners.

ADDITIONAL COMPANIES

After the original company of the Musical shall have been produced by the Partnership, it shall have the right, if the General Partner deems it advisable, to produce or co-produce with any other party a second company or companies, or a British company (either as a first-class production or a second-class production) and to invest Partnership funds in any such production. The General Partner may accumulate funds without limitation to defray production expenses of additional companies before return of capital or distribution of Net Profits.

THEATRE TICKETS

Certain people connected with the production and presentation of the Musical will be entitled to purchase choice orchestra seats for each performance of the Musical at the regular box office prices thereof. Such seats are known as "house seats." Terrence Toe, Peter Poe, Robert Brown and Jack Johnson, as authors of the Musical, are each contractually entitled to purchase two pair of house seats for each performance of the Musical in New York City. Billy Bore will be entitled to purchase two pair of house seats for each performance of the Musical in New York City. It is presently anticipated that the director, the stars and possibly the featured players will also be entitled to purchase one or two pair of such house seats. It is also presently anticipated that when a theater contract is entered into in respect to the presentation of the Musical in New York City that both the producer and the owner of the theater will each be entitled to purchase up to fifty pair of such house seats for each performance of the Musical in New York City. Anytime Records will also be entitled to 2 pair of such seats.

CONTROL BY GENERAL PARTNER

The General Partner shall have the complete control of the production of the Musical including choice of cast, directors and designers, properties, sets, prices of tickets, time of opening and closing of the New York City company and all other companies, and organizing and arranging for additional companies.

The General Partner agrees to render in connection with the Musical, services customarily and usually rendered by theatrical producers and to devote as much time thereto as may be necessary. However, subject to the faithful performance by the General Partner of its obligation, it may engage in other business, including other theatrical productions.

REMUNERATION OF GENERAL PARTNER

The General Partner shall receive a management fee of 1% of the gross weekly box office receipts of each company presenting the Musical. Said 1% payment shall be deemed to be a Running Expense for the purpose of computing Net Profits. Except as otherwise stated herein, the General Partner may not receive compensation for services customarily rendered by a general partner of a theatrical venture in his status as a general partner, but if the General Partner performs other services for the Partnership, it may receive a fair compensation for said services.

The General Partner may engage in other theatrical ventures, including productions thereof, without restriction, while receiving remuneration from the Partnership.

REIMBURSEMENT OF GENERAL PARTNER

The General Partner, as of February 15, 1969, has advanced approximately $10,000 to the authors, owner, choreographer, scenic designer and lighting designer, as advances against royalties payable to them and has advanced other sums for scripts, auditions, recordings, transportation, long-distance telephone calls, mimeographing and other expenses totaling approximately $4,500 in connection with the Musical. It is contemplated that the General Partner will advance further sums as needed for pre-production expenses. All of the foregoing expenditures by the General Partner will be reimbursed by the Partnership upon its formation, unless the General Partner elects not to have said expenditures reimbursed to it but elects instead to have said expenditures treated as a cash contribution to the capital of the Partnership. (See caption "RETURN OF CONTRIBUTIONS IF PARTNERSHIP NOT FORMED.")

INTERESTS OF GENERAL PARTNERS IN CERTAIN TRANSACTIONS

The General Partner has agreed to furnish office facilities

Partner shall liquidate the affairs thereof. Pursuant to the Partnership Agreement the General Partner will have a power of attorney from the Limited Partners to prepare and file all documents necessary to form and dissolve the Partnership. If the Partnership is terminated prior to the time that the Partnership's interest in the additional or subsidiary rights expires, the Limited Partners would nonetheless be entitled to their share thereof, but there is no specific provision in the Partnership Agreement in respect thereof.

OTHER INFORMATION

Legal matters in connection with the issuance of securities hereby will be passed upon by the firm of Counsel and Counsel, 000 Park Avenue, New York, New York. Legal matters for the Underwriter will be passed upon by the firm of Henry Hertense, Inc., 00 Wall Street, New York, New York 10000.

Since ANYTHING COMPANY is not yet formed, there are no appropriate financial statements available for the Partnership, or any statement of income, expense or charges prior to the formation thereof. Upon the formation of the Partnership, the General Partner will furnish the Limited Partners with financial statements as required by law, including certified annual statements of operations.

DOE, ROE AND HOE, INC.

MOTION PICTURE RIGHTS AGREEMENT

NOTE: (The following is an agreement in which the owner of the motion picture rights grants to an author, composer and lyricist the rights to produce or cause to be produced a motion picture based on a musical stage adaptation of a play which was originally a movie and in which the moving picture company still retains the motion picture rights.

This kind of an agreement is very often made by a Producer (if he owns the play production rights) to acquire such rights so that when he puts together a musical and engages an author, composer and lyricist, he may grant to the author, composer and lyricist the rights to deal with the motion picture rights based on their musical play, if it is successful.

There are many variations in the terms of these agreements. The following is an example applicable only to a particular property and upon specifically negotiated terms, which are not unusual.)

AGREEMENT made this 21st day of February, 1969, by and between John Green, Robert Blue and Henry White (hereinafter collectively referred to as the "Adapters") and Movies, Inc. (hereinafter referred to as the "Owner").

WHEREAS, The Owner represents and warrants that it has acquired by *mesne* assignment from Everywhere Pictures, Inc., all the motion picture and allied rights in that certain play entitled "NOW OR NEVER" by Ralph Smith (hereinafter called the "original play") which rights were granted to Everywhere Pictures, Inc., pursuant to the agreement set forth in Schedule A annexed hereto and made a part hereof, that it has not disposed of or encumbered any of the foregoing rights and that it has the right to make this agreement, and

WHEREAS, The Adapters represent and warrant that they have entered into an agreement with the duly authorized representatives of the Estate of Ralph Smith, dated December 20, 1968, a true copy of which agreement is annexed hereto as "Exhibit B" and made a part hereof, pursuant to which the Adapters have acquired the right to write a dramatico-musical version (hereinafter called the "Musical Play") of the original play and to produce, or cause to be produced, the Musical Play pursuant to the terms of the Minimum Basic Production Contract of the Dramatists Guild, Inc.

WHEREAS, The Adapters, each for himself, represent and warrant that he has full warrant and authority to enter into this agreement.

NOW, THEREFORE, in consideration of the respective covenants herein contained, and for other good and valuable consideration, the parties hereto agree as follows:

1. The Adapters shall have the right to select the person or persons to produce the Musical Play (such person or persons selected being hereinafter referred to as the "Producer"). The Adapters agree to cause the Producer to sign a counterpart of this agreement upon which happening this agreement shall constitute an agreement between the Owner and the Producer and all references herein to the Adapters shall be deemed to refer to the Adapters and the Producer, as their interests may appear, it being understood however that the obligations and liabilities of the Adapters and Producer hereunder shall be joint and several.

2. In consideration of the payment of $1,000 paid to the Owner simultaneously with the execution of this agreement, the Adaptors have the right to write and produce, or cause to be produced, a musical play based on the original play, which musical play must open in a first-class theatre not later than two (2) years from the date of this agreement. If the musical play is not written and so produced within two (2) years from the date hereof, this agreement shall automatically terminate and the Owner shall be fully released from all of its obligations hereunder and none of the provisions of this agreement shall be of any further force or effect. The Adapters shall have the right to extend this Agreement for one (1) additional year, upon the payment of $1,000 (One Thousand Dollars) to Owner Thirty (30) days prior to the expiration of the two (2) year period above.

3. In consideration of the rights herein granted by Owner

to Adapters, the following payments shall also be made to Owner:

(a) The Adapters agree that they will pay, or cause to be paid, to the Owner an amount equal to one (1%) per cent of the gross weekly box office receipts realized from every first-class stage presentation of the Musical Play produced by the Producer alone or in association with or under lease to another producer, in the United States, Canada and the British Isles. Such gross box office receipts shall be computed in the manner provided for in the Minimum Basic Production Contract of the Dramatists Guild, Inc. and shall be paid to the Owner at the same time and accompanied by the same statements as are provided for therein in the case of authors.

The payments hereinabove provided for in paragraph "2" of this agreement shall be deemed to be non-returnable advances against the Owner's share of the gross weekly box office receipts as herein provided in this paragraph [3 (a)].

(b) In addition, the Owner shall be entitled to receive that proportion of the "author's share" (as such share is defined in the aforesaid Minimum Basic Production Contract) realized from the sale, lease or license or other disposition of the rights specified in FOURTH (e), SEVENTH and EIGHTH of said Minimum Basic Production Contract (after deducting, in the case of motion picture and allied rights, the one-third (1/3) share payable to the Owner pursuant to subparagraph " (d) " of this Paragraph "2" if such rights are sold to a third party) as the one (1%) per cent royalty payable to the Owner hereunder bears to the aggregate percentage of box office receipts from first-class speaking stage presentations of the Musical Play payable to the Owner, the Adapters and the Estate of Ralph Smith.

(c) In addition the Owner will be paid an amount equal to five (5%) per cent of the net profits of the limited partnership or other producing entity formed to produce the Musical Play, which said net profits shall be payable from the Producer's share of the profits and shall be payable at the same time and subject to the same terms and conditions that profits are payable to the Producer.

(d) In respect of motion picture and allied rights in the Musical Play, if the Owner shall fail to exercise the option granted to it pursuant to Paragraph "5" hereof, the Owner shall be entitled to receive one-third of the gross proceeds received in respect of the disposition of motion picture and allied rights in the Musical Play, subject only to the deduction of one-third of the Dramatists Guild Negotiator Fee payable in connection therewith. It is understood and agreed that the monies payable in respect of the disposition of the motion picture and allied rights in the Play shall be payable to the Negotiator, who shall remit directly to the Owner its share of such proceeds.

4. If the Musical Play shall be written and produced pursuant to the terms hereof, then, subject to the terms and conditions hereof, the Adapters shall have the right to sell, lease or license the motion picture and allied rights in the Musical Play and, at the request of the Adapters, the Owner will grant, assign and transfer to the Adapters, or to the persons, firms or corporations designated by them, the rights acquired by Everywhere Pictures pursuant to the agreement set forth in Schedule A annexed hereto, but subject to all rights which Owner may have in the existing motion pictures based upon the underlying literary property. Anything to the contrary herein contained, it is expressly understood that, in the event the motion picture and allied rights in the Musical Play shall not have been sold or otherwise disposed of on or before the expiration of four (4) years from the permanent close of the first-class stage production of the Musical Play in New York City, the right of the Adapters to sell, lease, or license the motion picture and related rights in the Musical Play shall terminate, and this agreement shall be of no further force and effect.

5. It is agreed that at such time as the Adapters determine to dispose of motion picture and allied rights in the Musical

Play, they will give the Owner written notice thereof by registered mail, setting forth all the terms and conditions, including the price, that they desire to obtain. The Owner shall have a period of fourteen (14) days, exclusive of Saturdays, Sundays and Holidays, after receipt of such notice to notify the Adapters by registered mail that Owner elects to acquire such rights so offered upon the terms and conditions so offered, and in the event Owner shall give such notice then the Adapters shall grant such rights to the Owner upon such terms and conditions, except that the price therefor shall be two-thirds of that which the notice stated that the Adapters would be willing to accept. If, within said period of fourteen (14) days, the Owner shall fail to notify the Adapters that it elects to acquire such rights so offered or it notifies the Adapters that it does not elect to acquire such rights, then and in either of such events the Adapters shall be free to offer such rights to any other party upon terms and conditions, including price, no less favorable to the Adapters than was offered to the Owner. In the event the Adapters shall not have disposed of such rights within a period of six (6) months from the expiration of said fourteen day period and thereafter the Adapters desire to dispose of such rights, they shall give the Owner written notice thereof by registered mail and the aforesaid procedure shall be followed as though such notice were the first notice given to the Owner with respect to such rights, and this same procedure shall be followed until there shall have been a disposition of such rights.

6. The Producer agrees to keep or cause to be kept full and faithful books of account in which shall be entered fully and accurately each transaction relating to the production and presentation of the Musical Play and the excercise of the Producers' rights of any kind with respect thereto. All of said books of account shall be open to the inspection and examination of the Owner or its representatives, at all times during regular business hours. The Producer shall have available for examination and inspection at any time during regular business hours box-office statements received from the theatre (or

theatres) at which the Musical Play shall be shown. The Producer agrees to deliver to the Owner all statements required by the Laws of the State of New York for filing with the Attorney General of the State of New York and all other statements required to be furnished to the Author by the Minimum Basic Production Contract of the Dramatist Guild, Inc. All such statements shall be prepared by certified public accountants experienced in the theatrical business. The Owner shall have the right to audit the Producer's books and records at any time upon giving not less than ten (10) days notice of the Owner's intention to do so; provided, however, the Owner shall have no rights hereunder to so audit the Producer's books and accounts except at reasonable hours of business days and not more than semi-annually. In addition to the foregoing rights of inspection, examination and audit given the Owner in this paragraph, the Owner shall also have the same rights of inspection, examination and audit and be entitled to the same statements as the investors shall have and be entitled to pursuant to their financing agreements with the Producer.

7. The Producer shall hold two (2) pairs of house seats for the Owner, or its designee, for all performances of the Musical Play in New York City. Said house seats shall be held until 6:00 P.M. of the day prior in respect of all performances. All such house seats, if purchased by or on behalf of the Owner, shall be paid for at the regularly established box-office prices.

8. Nothing contained in this agreement shall in anyway be construed to constitute or evidence any intention of the parties hereto to be partners or engaged in a joint venture.

9. The Adaptors and/or the Producer may assign this agreement to a limited partnership in which the Producer is a general partner thereof or to a corporation in which the Producer shall be one of those in control thereof or to a joint venture in which the Producer or a limited partnership, of which the Producer shall be a general partner thereof, or a

corporation in which the Producer shall be one of those in control thereof shall be one of the joint venturers. This agreement and all rights hereunder shall be fully assignable by the Owner and shall be binding on its successors and assigns. After the production of the Musical Play, but not before, this agreement and all rights hereunder shall be fully assignable by each of the Adapters and shall be binding on the personal representatives and assigns of each of them.

10. Unless otherwise notified by registered mail, the addresses of the parties hereto are as follows:

Owner: Movies, Inc.
1000 Sun Street
New York, N.Y.

Adapters: John Green, Robert Blue and Henry White
2000 Moon Drive
New York, N.Y.

11. Any and all disputes, differences and controversies between the Producer and the Owner, and/or the Owner and the Adapters, arising out of, under or in connection with this agreement or the breach or alleged breach thereof (other than disputes, differences and controversies which are to be settled by arbitration under the arbitration provisions of the Minimum Basic Production Contract) shall be submitted to arbitration to be held in New York City under the rules and regulations of the American Arbitration Association, and the parties hereto agree to be bound by the determination of the majority of the arbitrators.

12. This instrument constitutes the entire agreement between the parties hereto and shall inure to the benfit of and shall be binding upon the parties, their respective heirs, administrators, executors, successors and assigns. Wherever executed, it shall be deemed made in and governed by the laws of the State of New York and may not be modified orally.

IN WITNESS WHEREOF, the parties hereto have hereunto set their hands and seals the day and year first above written.

....
John Green

....
Robert Blue

....
Henry White

Movies, Inc.
By: ....

Each of the undersigned agree to be bound by the provisions thereof insofar as they are concerned:

Estate of Ralph Smith

By: ....
Mary Smith

AGREEMENT FOR ACQUISITION OF BASIC RIGHTS

NOTE: (The following is an example of an agreement between a Producer and the widow of an author, wherein the Producer acquires the rights to do a musical stage adaptation of a novel written by the author, which novel had previously been adapted for a motion picture.

These agreements vary in many respects. Sometimes rights are acquired by an author, composer and lyricist, or any combination of them. Sometimes the rights are sold by the author, if he be then living, or by someone who has acquired the rights from the author other than as a result of his death. Sometimes there has not been a movie previously made and sometimes there have even been previous stage adaptations. Then too, the nature of the basic work may vary as it may consist of a motion picture screenplay, a short story, an autobiography, or even a comic strip.

The differences in each of these and other items would be reflected in the agreement as finally prepared.)

AGREEMENT made as of this 3rd day of February, 1969, by and between Jack Jack, residing at 100 West 1000th Street, New York, N.Y. (hereinafter sometimes referred to as the "Purchaser") and Mary Writer, residing at 2000 Main Drive, Los Angeles, California (hereinafter sometimes referred to as the "Owner").

In consideration of the covenants and conditions herein contained and other good and valuable considerations, it is agreed:

1. The Owner does hereby warrant and represent that:

(a) Henry Writer was the sole author of an original literary work entitled "THIS IS IT" (hereinafter referred to as the "Work"); that the Work was registered for copyright in the United States Copyright Office on the 20th day of January, 1933, under Entry No. A 12345 in the name of Henry Writer.

(b) The aforesaid copyright was renewed in the United States Copyright Office in the name of Henry Writer on the 1st day of March, 1960 under Entry No. R 54321.

(c) Pursuant to a series of copyright assignments, motion picture rights in the novel have been conveyed to Motion Pictures International, Inc., and the last assignments of said copyright recorded in the Copyright Office are an assignment from All Pictures, Inc., to Motion Pictures International, Inc., executed January 28, 1968, and recorded February 4, 1968, in copyright volume 1294, pages 00-000, and an assignment Our Productions, Inc., to Motion Pictures International, Inc., recorded on February 4, 1968, in copyright volume 1294, pages xx-xxx.

(d) Henry Writer died on October 22, 1963, survived by his wife, Mary Writer, and a son, John. Mary Writer, widow of the deceased, was duly appointed Executrix of said Last Will and Testament of Henry Writer. The estate of Henry Writer has been closed, all bills paid and distribution of the assets of the Estate made to the persons entitled thereto.

(e) The Owner has full right and authority and is free

to enter into this Agreement and to grant, upon the terms and conditions hereof, the rights herein granted and that, except as set forth and described in Exhibit A, annexed hereto and made a part hereof, no right, title and interest now valid or outstanding for or to the work or the rights herein granted by which such rights or the full enjoyment and exercise thereof might be encumbered or impaired heretofore has been conveyed or granted to any other person, firm or corporation by the Owner or her predecessor in interest.

(f) No adverse claim has been made on her in respect to the rights herein granted in the Work, and that she knows of no claim that has been made that the Work infringes upon the copyright in any other work or that violates any other rights of any person, firm or corporation, and that the Work was not copied in whole or in part from any other work.

(g) The Owner, as the surviving widow of Henry Writer, deceased, has acquired all rights held by the deceased at the time of his death in and to the Work and the copyright renewal therein, and that the Owner owns the rights hereinafter conveyed and has authority to enter into this Agreement.

(h) That the Owner has the sole unencumbered, unrestricted and lawful right to enter into this Agreement and to make the grant hereinafter provided for and has the full right, power and authority to make, enter into and to fully perform this Agreement in each and every respect; that no consent or permission of any authors' society, performing rights society, firm or corporation whatsoever is required in connection with the grant in this Agreement made, or in connection with any of the subject matter of this Agreement.

(i) At the present time there are no outstanding rights to present a stage adaptation or a television or radio production based on the Work and the only rights heretofore granted which are still in effect are the motion picture rights as set forth in Exhibit A, annexed hereto and made a part hereof.

(j) There are no claims or litigations concerning or purporting to affect the Owner's rights or title in or to the Work as herein represented or conveyed.

2. The Owner does hereby convey, grant and assign to the Purchaser the sole and exclusive rights to use, adapt, translate, subtract from, add to and change the Work and the title thereof in the production of a legitimate musical stage presentation, and to use the Work or any part or parts thereof and the title and any similar title and any or all of the characters and characterizations of the Work in connection with such legitimate musical stage presentation (hereinafter sometimes referred to as the "Play"), based upon the Work; together with the further sole and exclusive rights, by mechanical or electrical means, to record, reproduce and transmit sound, including the spoken words, dialogue, music and songs, whether extracted from the Work or otherwise, and to change such spoken words, dialogue, music and songs if extracted from the Work, and to interpolate other spoken words, dialogue, music and songs in or in connection with or as part of the production, performance and presentation of such Play; the sole and exclusive right to make, use, license and vend any and all records required and desired for such purpose; to produce or cause the musical play to be produced upon the regular speaking stage throughout the world, and to use, sell, lease or otherwise dispose of the musical play and all rights of every kind and nature therein now or hereafter ascertained and to authorize others so to do for any and all purposes and by any and all means throughout the world subject, further however, to the rights in the Work previously granted as hereinabove set forth; and, subject to the reservations of rights or reverter to the Owner hereunder, the exclusive right to copyright the Play in the name of the Purchaser or his nominee, and to obtain extensions and renewals of such copyright. The right to use the title "THIS IS IT" is granted exclusively only for and in connection with the Play, based in whole or in part upon the Work, and the Owner makes no warranty with respect to the rights of the Purchaser so to use such title, except insofar as same is affected by Owner's acts or omissions.

3. The Purchaser will cause a completed musical play to

be written and composed and upon completion of the Play, any and all rights therein, whether presently known or hereafter ascertained of any kind, nature and description, including but not limited to television, radio, motion picture, foreign, commercial, second-class touring, stock, amateur, tabloid, sequel, remake, shall become the sole and exclusive property of the author (s), composer (s) and lyricist (s) [the author (s), composer (s) and lyricist (s) are sometimes hereinafter jointly referred to as the "Authors"] throughout the world. The Purchaser is acquiring the right, to be assigned by the Purchaser to the Authors, to copyright the Play in their names and to hold the said copyright as their respective interests may appear.

The Owner understands that the Purchaser proposes to cause a play to be written based on the Work and to enter into Dramatists Guild Contracts and to convey certain rights to the Authors thereunder. The Owner specifically authorizes the entering into of Dramatists Guild Contracts with such Authors and agrees to be bound by the terms and provisions thereof, and that the terms and provisions thereof shall be applicable to this Agreement, except as may be herein otherwise expressly set forth.

There was, as is hereinabove set forth, a previous grant of the motion picture rights. The grant of the rights herein conveyed is in all ways subject to the said grant previously more specifically set forth in Exhibit A annexed hereto.

4. The Purchaser has paid to the Owner, upon the execution hereof, the sum of One Thousand ($1,000.) Dollars as an advance payment on account of the following royalties, also to be paid the Owner:

(a) One percent (1%) of the gross box office receipts from all first-class stage presentations of the musical in the United States of America, the Dominion of Canada and Great Britain, authorized or licensed hereunder as provided in the Dramatists Guild, Inc. Minimum Basic Production Contract for a musical.

(b) That proportion of the Authors' share of all proceeds, emoluments and other things of value received from the sale, lease and disposition of any and all other rights in the musical, including, but not limited to, motion picture, radio, television, stock, amateur, foreign, commercial, operetta, grand opera, second-class touring, "remake," "sequel" and condensed tabloid versions and all other rights now known or hereafter to be known in the proportion that one (1%) percent shall bear to the total percentages of the gross box office receipts payable as royalties to the Authors including the royalties payable to the Owner.

(c) The advance referred to in this Article 4 and the further advance referred to in Article 6 of this Agreement shall be charged only against royalties due from first-class stage productions and not otherwise. Under no circumstances shall such advances be required to be repaid by the Owner.

5. The rights herein granted shall cease and terminate and shall automatically revert to the Owner without any obligation of any kind to the Purchaser:

(a) Unless on or before the 15th day of May, 1970, the Purchaser shall have caused a completed play (a minimum of 80 pages, double-spaced, plus a score consisting of music and lyrics for at least 12 songs) to have been written based on the Work, pursuant to the provisions of a Minimum Basic Production Contract or Contracts with a member or members of the Dramatists Guild, Inc. (which Agreement is hereinafter sometimes referred to as the "Dramatists Guild Contract"), and a copy of which completed Play, as well as such Dramatists Guild Contract (s) shall have been furnished to the Owner, and;

(b) Unless the Play be presented on the stage, in a first-class theatre in a first-class manner, with a first-class cast and a first-class director, on or before the 15th day of May, 1971.

Nothing herein contained shall be deemed to obligate the Purchaser to produce the Play. The time period herein provided may be extended as hereinafter provided for in Article 6 of this Agreement.

6. The Purchaser shall have the option of extending the

time which to cause the completed Play to be written and/or produced, as hereinabove provided, for an additional period of one year, upon serving written notice upon the Owner, of the exercise of such option on or before the 15th day of March, 1970, and by paying to the Owner the additional sum of $1,000, together with the exercise of such option. In the event that the Purchaser exercises the option to extend the time to cause the completed Play to be written and/or produced, then upon said notice and the payment to the Owner, the option to produce the Play shall automatically be extended for an additional period of one year, that is, until May 15, 1972.

7. It is mutually agreed that:

(a) The Authors shall be deemed to be the sole Authors of the musical for all purposes hereof, and shall have full and exclusive rights and privileges as Authors with respect to all matters relating to the production of the musical (such as, but not limited to, choice of cast, director and sale of motion picture (if not in conflict with any existing contracts concerning the motion picture rights) and other subsidiary rights, etc.). No signature of the Owner shall be necessary in connection with any of the foregoing, provided, however, that the Authors will furnish to the Owner fully conformed copies of each Agreement made regarding any sale or other disposition of additional or subsidiary rights, immediately upon the execution of any such Agreement.

(b) Commencing with the date hereof and continuing until the termination of all the Purchaser's rights hereunder, the Owner will not grant the right to adapt or redramatize the Work or any part thereof in any form and will not sell, lease, license, assign or otherwise dispose of any performing rights in or to said story.

(c) Upon the presentation of the musical on Broadway for the minimum number of performances required for the Producer to acquire an interest in the motion picture and subsidiary rights to the musical, pursuant to the provisions of the Dramatists Guild, Inc. Minimum Basic Production

Contract above provided for, the musical and the Work shall be deemed merged forever and in perpetuity in the sense that the Owner shall not convey or dispose of any rights in or to the Work, including the copyrights therein and thereto, without the prior written consent of the Authors. Notwithstanding any such merger, however, the Owner and her assignees and licensees may continue exclusively to exercise their respective rights of publishing and selling copies of the novel "THIS IS IT" (as distinguished from the musical) in any and all territories of the world and to derive and retain for their account all royalties and proceeds therefrom, and in this connection, the Owner's right in the United States copyrights of the Work or any part thereof shall continue to be vested in the Owner, subject, however, in all respects, to the terms and conditions of this Agreement. If the Work shall merge in the Play as herein provided, then the Authors [i.e., bookwriter (s), composer (s) and lyricist (s)] shall have the sole right to sell, lease, license or otherwise dispose of the motion picture and subsidiary rights therein. In extension and not in limitation of the foregoing, it is specifically understood and agreed that the Authors' rights in motion picture, subsidiary rights, British Isle production rights and other related rights, as set forth in the Dramatists Guild, Inc. Minimum Basic Production Contract, shall be effective upon a merger of the Work and the Play as herein provided. If the original run of the musical shall terminate prior to the aforementioned minimum period, the Owner shall thenceforth be completely free to exploit any and all of her respective rights in such story for the sole and exclusive benefit of herself, her successors, licensees and assigns.

(d) The Owner shall promptly execute, acknowledge and deliver, or procure the execution and delivery to the Purchaser, at his own cost and expense, any and all agreements, assignments or instruments which from time to time reasonably may be required by the Producer, the Dramatists Guild, Inc. or Authors to evidence, confirm and secure the rights of the Producer or Authors hereunder, but nothing herein in this paragraph contained shall require the Owner to grant to Purchaser any greater or additional property than elsewhere in this Agreement provided for, or to assume any other or greater liability than elsewhere in this Agreement imposed on her.

(e) All leases, licenses or other disposition of any right or interest in or in connection with the musical and/or the subsidiary and/or the motion picture rights thereof shall be in writing and made in good faith on the basis of the best efforts and interests of all concerned.

(f) All contracts executed by the Purchaser and Authors of the musical in connection with any of the rights in the musical or pertaining thereto, which are the subject of this Agreement, or the rights of the Owner therein or herein, shall acknowledge the interest of the Owner pursuant to the terms of this Agreement. In instances where the Owner is entitled to any of the proceeds, express provision shall be made for payments directly to the Owner through her agent as hereinafter provided and copies of all such contracts relating to the rights herein, confirming, affecting or relating to any of the Owner's rights hereunder shall be furnished to the Owner through her agent, as hereinafter provided, promptly upon the execution thereof.

(g) The Owner shall not be entitled to receive any share from, nor to receive any accounting for, any and all royalties and other compensation from publication of the libretto (except where the libretto was published and is sold in conjunction with the exercising and/or licensing of subsidiary rights hereunder), original lyrics and music in and of the musical, mechanical reproductions and recordings including statutory and copyright royalties (as distinguished from show album royalties), and so-called small rights arising out of the music publication and recording contracts by the Authors or anyone else for their original music and lyrics, and all royalties and dividends, etc. that may be derived by the Authors or anyone else, as lyricists and composers, from such organizations as the American Society of Composers, Authors and Publishers, Broadcast Music, Incorporated, and other similar organizations. It is understood, however, that any sale or disposition of synchronization rights for use in connection with the making of a motion picture and/or of a television program shall be deemed a disposition of motion picture and/or television rights, as the case may be, and the Owner shall share in the proceeds therefrom in accordance with her rights to share in the disposition of motion picture and television rights as herein provided for. As to original cast album royalties and the proceeds from the sale of copies of the libretto published and sold in conjunction with the exercising and/or licensing of subsidiary rights hereunder in the musical, Owner shall share in such royalties and/or proceeds in the same manner as she is entitled to share hereunder in the proceeds from any disposition of subsidiary rights in the musical.

8. If the musical shall not be completed or produced on the legitimate speaking stage, pursuant to the terms hereof on or before the date herein provided for, as the same may be extended pursuant hereto, then,

(a) All rights in the Work granted to or acquired by the Purchaser hereunder shall forthwith revert to the Owner with the same force and effect as if this Agreement had never been entered into.

(b) All rights in such portion of the musical as shall not be contained in or taken from or incidental to the Work shall forthwith revert to the Purchaser and/or Authors as their respective interests may appear.

(c) The Authors shall be free to make such use and disposition of their original music and lyrics of the musical as they see fit, but it is expressly understood and agreed that neither the Purchaser nor the Authors shall have any right to retain or use the name of the Play which together make up the Work (or any title of which such name or title is a part) as the title of any works or rights which may revert to them hereunder, or in any way have the right to capitalize on the fact that such rights and/or their music and/or lyrics were once a part of the musical and/or associated with any version of such Play.

9. The Purchaser agrees that the name of Henry Writer shall appear in all advertising and publicity issued by or with the consent or under the control of the Purchaser wherever the Authors' names shall appear, with the same size and prominence as Authors' names. If the title, "THIS IS IT" is not used as the title of the Play, then that title will appear in the credits as the story on which the Play is based.

10. The Purchaser agrees to hold in the name of the Owner, two (2) pairs of house seats for each performance of the Play in New York City (except theatre parties and benefit performances), which seats shall be held until noon of the day preceding the performance with respect to a matinee performance and until 6 P.M. of the day preceding with respect to evening performances, which seats shall be paid for at the regularly established box office prices therefor. The Owner shall also have the right to purchase four (4) pairs of house seats for the New York opening.

11. Subject to the terms and conditions hereof, the term of this Agreement shall be for the period of the original copyright of the musical and the renewal thereof.

12. Purchaser will advise or cause the Owner to be advised in writing, in full and complete detail, of all offers for the purchase of the motion picture and/or television rights to the musical as soon as possible after the receipts of such offers but not later than forty-eight (48) hours prior to the acceptance of any such offer.

13. Purchaser will keep and maintain, or by contract cause to be kept and maintained, full and correct books and records relating to the presentation of the musical hereunder and all transactions in which the Owner may have an interest hereunder and the proceeds derived therefrom. Such books and records will be kept in New York, N.Y. The Owner and/or her agent and/or representatives shall have access to such books and records during all regular business hours and may take or cause to be taken excerpts and/or extracts therefrom. Payments herein required to be made to the Owner shall be

made at the same time and in the same manner as payments to Authors are made pursuant to the terms and conditions of the Dramatists Guild, Inc. Minimum Basic Production Contract and the rules and regulations of the Dramatists Guild, Inc. Payments to the Owner shall be accompanied by copies of all such statements as are required to be furnished to Authors by such Dramatists Guild, Inc. Minimum Basic Production Contract and such rules and regulations.

14. The Owner warrants and represents that she will not, prior to the opening of the musical play or prior to the period covered by this option as extended (whichever date first occurs) grant the right to adapt or redramatize any writings of Henry Writer controlled by the Owner, nor will she sell, lease, license or otherwise dispose of any such dramatic or performing rights in any media. After the opening of the musical play or the expiration of the option period hereunder as extended (if the play does not open), then the Owner will not sell, lease, license or otherwise dispose of any of the dramatic or performing rights of any Henry Writer writings controlled by her without first giving the Purchaser hereunder the opportunity to acquire said rights upon the same terms and conditions.

If the Owner wishes to dispose of any of said rights, she must first give the Purchaser 30 days notice in writing which sets forth the terms of a bona fide offer. The Purchaser may accept said offer in writing within said 30 days or if he rejects said offer (failure to respond in writing shall constitute a rejection of said offer), the Owner may dispose of said rights, but only upon the terms set forth in the notice. If said rights are not disposed of, then each and every proposed disposition must first be offered to the Purchaser in the manner hereinabove set forth.

15. The addresses of the parties herein shall be for all purposes as follows:

Mary Writer	Jack Jack
2000 Main Drive	100 West 1000th Street
Los Angeles, California	New York, N.Y.

Copies of all notices to both parties shall also be mailed to Mr. Sam Agent, 1000 Sunny Boulevard, New York, N.Y., and to Richard Lawyes, Esq., Lawyer & Lawyer, Esqs., 2000 75th Avenue, New York, N. Y. All notices required to be given hereunder shall be in writing and sent by registered mail addressed as above provided, except as may, from time to time, be otherwise directed in writing by the respective parties.

16. Any claim, dispute, misunderstanding or controversy, or charge of unfair dealing arising under, or in connection with, or out of this Agreement, or the breach thereof, shall be submitted to arbitration to be held under the rules and regulations of the American Arbitration Association. Failure by the Producer to pay any amount claimed to be due by the Owner is evidence of a dispute entitling the claimant to an arbitration. Judgment upon the award rendered may be entered in the highest court of the forum, state or federal, having jurisdiction. The arbitrators are empowered to award damages against any party to the controversy in such sums as they shall deem fair and reasonable under the circumstances. The arbitrators are also empowered to require specific performance of a contract, or in the alternative award money damages, and have power to grant any other remedy or relief, injunctive or otherwise, which they deem just and equitable.

The arbitrators are also empowered to render a partial award before making a final award and grant such relief, injunctive or otherwise, in such partial award as they deem just and equitable. The arbitrators may determine and indicate in their written award by whom and in what proportion the cost of arbitration shall be borne.

17. The Owner hereby acknowledges that Sam Agent (hereinafter referred to as "Sam") has acted for the Owner in the negotiation and consummation of this Agreement, and the Owner therefore agrees that so long as the Owner or her assignees shall have any rights under this Agreement or any extensions or renewals hereof or under any agreements amendatory hereof or in substitution hereof or under any

first-class dramatic production agreement which may proceed from this Agreement, Sam shall be the sole exclusive and irrevocable agent of the Owner with respect to the Owner's interest in this Agreement and in the rights and privileges granted herein, with the sole and exclusive rights and power to deal therewith for the Owner and, further, that as such agent, Sam shall be entitled to receive any and all monies due to the Owner pursuant to the terms hereof and to deduct and retain for itself ten percent (10%) thereof, except where such monies are applicable to an excercise of the amateur rights of the musical, in which case it may deduct and retain for itself twenty percent (20%) of such monies. This designation of Sam as sole and exclusive agent for the Owner shall be irrevocable and Purchaser hereby is directed by the Owner to make payment to Sam of any and all sums payable to the Owner hereunder. The Owner acknowledges that all such payments by the Purchaser to Sam when made, shall be deemed to be payments by the Purchaser to the Owner hereunder.

18. This Agreement, irrespective of its place of execution, shall be construed and interpreted in accordance with the laws of the State of New York as though, and with the same effect, as if it had been actually executed and delivered within such State.

19. This Agreement shall be binding upon and shall inure to the benefit of the parties hereto and their respective heirs, executors, administrators, personal representatives, successors and assigns.

20. Purchaser shall have the right to assign this Agreement, provided, however, that the assignee shall in all respects be subject to, and assume in writing directly to the Owner, each and every term, provision, condition and obligation herein contained, and provided further, that the Purchaser is one of the principals of the assignee.

21. This Agreement constitutes the entire understanding

between the parties hereto and no warranty, representation, inducement or agreement not contained herein shall be binding on the parties. This Agreement can be modified only by a written instrument duly authorized by the parties hereto or the authorized representatives of each of the parties.

IN WITNESS WHEREOF, the parties hereto have executed this Agreement as of the day and year first above written.

....
Mary Writer

....
Jack Jack

APPROVED:

....
John Writer

ACCEPTED AND AGREED TO:

....
Sam Agent